Collins

CAMBRIDGE
IGCSE® ENGLISH
REVISED EDITION

SERIES EDITOR:

Julia Burchell

AUTHORS:

Mike Gould, Geraldine Dunn,
Keith Brindle and Steve Eddy

Complete coverage of
the Cambridge First Language English syllabuses 0500 and 0522

Contents

Introduction

The Collins *Cambridge IGCSE English Student Book* offers a skills-building, progress-focused approach to the Cambridge IGCSE First Language English syllabuses. The Cambridge IGCSE prepares you for everyday and workplace communication in the English-speaking world, with its focus on being able to adapt what you say and write for a wide range of audiences and purposes. It is also a solid foundation from which to launch into further study of English Language or Literature. The course encourages you to read a wide range of literary and non-literary texts and to explore the way that language works in them to create meaning and influence readers.

How the book is structured

Section 1 is a preparation section where the fundamental skills that you will use in Sections 2 to 5 are taught.

We have called Section 1 'Building Key Skills' because this is exactly what it does: it teaches you all of the skills that will enable you to tackle a range of different tasks in your IGCSE course. We have split this preparatory section into three chapters – Key Reading Skills, Key Technical Skills and Key Writing Skills – so that you can clearly see where these fundamental skills are taught.

Many of the IGCSE tasks require you to deploy a range of different skills together. For instance, the ability to summarise is impossible to achieve unless you have three basic skills: the ability to skim, scan and select. These fundamental reading skills are all introduced in Section 1, Chapter 1 and then the task of writing a summary is covered in Section 2, Chapter 4.

The approach is used throughout the book. This means that the key task of writing about writer's effects, which is taught in Section 2, Chapter 5, is prepared for through the study of selecting information, understanding explicit and implicit meanings and being able to recognise emotive and sensory language in Section 1, Chapter 1.

Your writing skills are also developed in the same way.

Accuracy is fundamental to any English course and we have included a specific chapter in the first section of this book, to help you improve your technical skills.

The ability to write in a range of forms and for a range of purposes and audiences is a central feature of the Cambridge IGCSE syllabus and a vital part of success when attempting the extended response, directed writing and composition tasks covered in Section 2, Chapters 6 and 7 and the coursework tasks in Section 3, Chapter 8. Section 1, Chapter 3 therefore provides a whole chapter of preparation on these key writing conventions.

Each chapter of **Section 2** covers one type of question or task that you may encounter in your examinations, showing you how to apply the key reading, writing and technical skills developed in Section 1.

In **Section 3**, students opting for coursework will find out how the key reading, writing and technical skills developed in Section 1 can be used to best effect in their coursework assignments.

Section 4 provides a dedicated chapter on Speaking and Listening to guide you in preparing for the presentation and discussion tasks you are likely to meet in your exam or in-class assessment.

Finally, **Section 5** offers extended exam practice to help you hone your examination technique under timed conditions.

Checking your progress

It is important to know how you are progressing, and we have therefore included activities throughout the book which could be used as assessment opportunities. They are supported by sample responses at different mark bands to exemplify how you can improve your work. These sample tasks and responses are written by teachers, not the examination board, but should help to provide a useful indicator of how you are doing. In examinations the way marks are awarded to questions like these may be different.

Most students aiming to use their English in the workplace would wish to be achieving at least a Band 1 (Core) or Band 3 (Extended). A highly effective and skilled communicator would aim for Band 1 (Extended).

Throughout the book, there are regular 'Check your progress' features.

Sound progress	Excellent progress
• You use clear, easy-to-follow sentences and make some attempt to engage the ~~reader.~~	• You use a full range of sentence types fluently to create a range of effects th~~at~~ sustain the reader's inter~~est~~

Core and Extended content is clearly signalled by these icons:

 Core   Extended.

We hope our skills-building approach helps you to unlock the fundamentals of your Cambridge IGCSE First Language English course.

Julia Burchell
Series Editor

Section 1 Building Key Skills

Section 1 introduces you to the key skills and concepts you will need during your IGCSE course.

- You will be shown examples of the different writing **forms** and **purposes** you might be asked to produce in your IGCSE assessment, and given the opportunity to practise their conventions.

- You will learn how to adapt your writing for different **audiences** and how to write in role by creating a convincing '**voice**'.

- You will learn how to **skim**, **scan** and **select** relevant points, where appropriate putting them in your own words.

- You will be taught how to analyse the **effects** of individual words and phrases, and how to write about **emotive** and **sensory language**.

- You will be reminded of how to write correct **sentences** of different lengths and types for effect, how to use **paragraphs** and make coherent links between them, and how to choose **vocabulary** that will interest your reader and suit your **audience** and **purpose**.

Having explored these ideas and practised these skills in isolation in Section 1, you should feel more confident about applying them together in the later exam-focused Section 2 and coursework-focused Section 3 chapters.

Key reading skills

In this chapter you are going to develop a range of fundamental reading skills, which you will use throughout your IGCSE course.

You will learn how to:

- skim and scan to locate information
- select information
- understand explicit meanings
- infer and deduce implicit meanings
- synthesise information.

On their own, some of the skills may seem simple, but remember that they are building blocks to completing larger and more complex tasks later on.

- Tasks that ask you to find a word or phrase require you to skim, scan and understand how to select information.

- Questions that ask you to explain or put something into your own words draw on your ability to comprehend at explicit or implicit levels.

- Tasks that ask you to retell or reuse a text in a more succinct way require you to synthesise.

Sections 2 and 3 will show you how to apply these key skills to specific question types and coursework tasks.

1 Locating information: skimming

Learning objectives

- To learn how to skim texts to locate information.

Exploring skills

There are two ways to find information in a text. The first is to **skim** and the second is to **scan**.

We use these skills in everyday life as well as study. We skim and scan to find information from a train timetable or from websites, for example.

Skimming means reading the whole text, quickly, to get an overall picture of what it is about and to see if it is worth reading more closely. Even a very quick skim-read (skim) will tell you a great deal about a text.

1. Skim the following extract from the opening chapter of *The No.1 Ladies Detective Agency* by Alexander McCall Smith and answer the questions in the table opposite.

Mma Ramotswe had a detective agency in Africa, at the foot of Kgale Hill. These were its assets: a tiny white van, two desks, two chairs, a telephone, and an old typewriter. Then there was a teapot, in which Mma Ramotswe – the only lady private detective in Botswana – brewed redbush tea. And three mugs – one for herself, one for her secretary, and one for the client.

What else does a detective agency really need? Detective agencies rely on human **intuition** and intelligence, both of which Mma Ramotswe had in abundance. No inventory would ever include those, of course.

But there was also the view, which again could appear on no inventory. How could any such list describe what one saw when one looked out from Mma Ramotswe's door? To the front, an acacia tree, the thorn tree which dots the wide edges of the Kalahari; the great white thorns, a warning; the olive-grey leaves, by contrast, so delicate. In its branches, in the late afternoon, or in the cool of the early morning, one might see a Go-Away Bird, or hear it, rather. And beyond the acacia, over the dusty road, the roofs of the town under a cover of trees and scrub bush; on the horizon, in a blue shimmer of heat, like improbable, overgrown termite mounds.

What type of text is this?	Does the passage feature a character?
Where is it set?	Is strong attitude or message being presented by the text?
Is this passage full of action?	What is the purpose of this text?
Is this passage very descriptive?	Do you get a sense of what might happen next/later?

Building skills

In a school or exam situation, we usually skim in order to become familiar with a text when it comes to answering questions.

2 Would you now know where in the passage to look if you had to answer the following more specific questions?

(a) Describe the kind of vegetation near Mma Ramotswe's office.

(b) Does Mma Ramotswe employ any staff?

(c) What sort of woman is Mma Ramotswe?

Developing skills

Sometimes a text may be too long or complex to skim in one go. In this case it helps to give each paragraph a heading.

3 Look back at the passage opposite. What headings would you give to its two paragraphs? Does this make it easier or harder to answer questions 2(a), (b) and (c)?

4 In the passage, both paragraphs could be annotated to show that they contain two sets of information. What would you write and where?

Applying skills

5 Answer questions 2 (a), (b) and (c) in full sentences as if approaching part of a comprehension question.

Checklist for success

✔ Quickly skim-read the text to understand what it is about.
✔ Use annotations and headings to identify the content of each paragraph.
✔ Use these annotations to locate the information you need to answer the questions.

2 Locating information: scanning

Learning objectives

- To learn how to scan texts to locate information.
- To use the key words in the question to sift information.
- To develop the skills to understand the precise meaning and context of information.

Scanning is the reading skill that we use after we have **skimmed** the text. It means looking for particular details or information. You dip in and out, reading certain words or phrases closely to check whether they are useful or not.

Exploring skills

In real life we scan when we are looking for something particular, for instance the cost of an item or the closing date for an application.

We do it by first deciding what we are looking for and then finding something which fits that requirement.

Top tip

In everyday life scanning is like fishing around in your sock drawer looking for the other half of a matching pair!

1 Complete the table below by matching each numbered box with a lettered box.

Text	Information you need	What you would scan for
Cinema home page	1 Show times	A The words *donate*, *giving*; or types of information: how you can help, an address, telephone number, text number
Take-away menu	2 Their email address	B For example, their name, adjectives near their name, pieces of dialogue that they are in
Advert for a Zumba class	3 The name of the instructor	C The words *boots*, *shoes*, *footwear*
A charity leaflet	4 How to donate	D The @ symbol
A novel	5 Quotes about a character	E The phrase *pleased to inform you* or the word *regret*
A receipt	6 The price of a pair of boots to get a refund	F A word beginning with a capital or the words *instructor*, *teacher*, *led by*
A letter	7 Did I get the job?	G Numbers in time format

Building skills

In your exams you may need to select points for a summary, analyse the effects a writer has created or extract information to use in a piece of directed writing. You would not have time to read the whole text again. To find the information, you would need to **scan**.

The clue is always in the key words of the question.

(2) Look at the following question.

> ***Select four unpleasant aspects of the narrator's house.***

Here *unpleasant* and *the narrator's house* are the key words. First, you need to 'unpick' the word *unpleasant*.

> unpleasant = not nice, would be uncomfortable to live with, would make daily life hard

Top tip

Remember scanning is the reading version of matching socks, so you need to look carefully at the one in your hand before you can find its pair.

Secondly, make a mental checklist of what you are looking for:
- I am looking for details about a building.
- I am going to be scanning mainly for comments about it that do not sound nice.
- I should look out for descriptive details (adjectives/adverbs) with negative meanings.

As you scan, your brain will ask itself whether the words you are reading fit the checklist.

Here is the extract that goes with the question. It is from *Q & A* by Vikas Swarup.

I live in a corner of [the city ...], in a cramped hundred-square-foot shack which has (a) no natural light or (b) no ventilation, with a corrugated metal sheet serving as a roof over my head. It vibrates violently whenever a train passes overhead. There is no running water and no sanitation. This is all I can afford. But I am not alone [...]. There are a million people like me, packed in a two-hundred-hectare triangle of swampy urban wasteland, where we live like animals and die like insects. Destitute migrants from all over the country jostle with each other for their own handful of sky in [the world's] biggest slum. There are daily squabbles – over inches of space, over a bucket of water – which at times turn deadly.

3 Complete this table which helps you to sift the words and phrases from the first few sentences of the *Q & A* extract on page 11 to decide what is and is not relevant.

Words read	Is this about a house?	Are the words used unpleasant?	Other thoughts
I live in a corner of [the city]	No, about an area		Corner sounds like a trap – not nice
in a	Yes, 'in' suggests we are going to get a description of a house next		
cramped		Yes, means too small for comfort	
hundred-square-foot	Yes, about its size		I am used to a bigger room so I would not like this
shack	Another word for a house	This word means not well made or temporary, so yes	
which has (a) no natural light			
or (b) ventilation			
with a corrugated metal sheet serving as a roof over my head			
It vibrates violently			
whenever a train passes overhead			
There is no running water			
and no sanitation			

Developing skills

Usually scanning the rest of the sentence around the key words is useful in helping you to find the correct information. This is called using the context. It is particularly important in a selective summary.

Use the whole sentence to clarify factual information such as the specific person or place being described.

(4) How could you use the whole sentence below to work out the specific meaning of the word *migrants*?

> *Destitute migrants from all over the country jostle with each other for their own handful of sky in [the world's] biggest slum.*

Applying skills

Sometimes you will need to skim a whole sentence or paragraph in order to identify the gist or a general feeling. You will then go back to scan for the words that are key to creating this effect. This is particularly useful when approaching questions that look at how writers achieve effects.

(5) Use the strategies that you have learned to scan for relevant information to answer the following question about the extract on page 11.

> *How does the writer suggest that life is not easy for the narrator?*

Checklist for success

✔ Use the key words in the question to help you sift what is relevant from what is not relevant in the text.

✔ Find relevant, short words, phrases or details that answer the question.

✔ Make sure you understand the precise meaning of each word, phrase or detail by looking at the context of the whole sentence around it.

3 Selecting information

Learning objectives

● To develop the skills to identify, and select precisely, what is relevant for an answer.

Once you have got the gist of a text (**skimmed**) and identified where the information that you need is (**scanned**), you will have to select exactly what you need to use in an answer.

Top tip

Simply copying out whole sentences will often mean that you lose marks in a **summary** response where being concise and using your own words are important, or in a **directed writing** response where you need to adapt material to a new purpose.

Exploring skills

You need to make sure that you are **selecting** only the **most relevant information** to include in your answer.

1 Read the following question and extract. Then identify the unnecessary material in the two sample answers below.

> *Name two aspects of Portugal that Jack Petchey wanted others to experience.*

> In 1970 45-year-old Jack Petchey stood on a hilltop overlooking one of the most beautiful bays on Portugal's Algarve and envisaged a time when people would come and marvel at the same view, walk on those white-gold sands and swim in that perfect sea – and they would do it all from the comfort of a luxury holiday resort complex.
> *Leisure Magazine*

> Petchey wanted people to have his experience of the white-gold sands and to swim in the perfect sea. He wanted them to 'marvel at the view'.

> Petchey liked the hill above a lovely bay and the amazing view that he was enjoying so he wanted to share it.

Building skills

Look at the two sample answers to this question.

> *What made Jack Petchey decide to build Club Praia da Oura?*

> Jack Petchey decided to build the club because he enjoyed that part of the Algarve coast and he wanted other people to be able to enjoy it too.

> Jack Petchey decided to build the club because one day he was out for a walk and the view reminded him how lovely it was on the beach and in the sea and he wanted other people to be able to do it too so they needed somewhere to stay.

2 Using the headings below, find examples of what makes one answer more effective than the other.

- It removes specific examples.
- It removes descriptive detail.
- It ignores irrelevant additional details.
- It combines different examples into larger points.

> **Top tip**
>
> Never include descriptive detail, examples, anecdotes or quotations in a short answer or a response to a **summary** question.

Developing skills

Writers will often develop their ideas by adding anecdotes. An anecdote is a short story to exemplify or back up the writer's point. For instance:

> I really don't like cats; they scare me. If I see one coming I run. Well okay, I step hesitantly backwards and wait for them to pass, never losing eye contact with their slinky panther-like frames. They're mysterious, aloof creatures. Give me a soppy canine anytime. One look at its face and you know it all: 'keep away, I'm not in the mood' or 'yes, yes, yes, let's play now!' It all started when I was a small child and I was left in the garden on my own. Next door's cat came walking up to me. It looked harmless enough; in fact it looked cuddly and kind, so I put my arms out and pulled it towards me. Yowl! It made a terrible noise, and swiped me across the cheek with its paw. I began to wail even louder than it had! So there you have it: the reason I hate our furry friends, in a nutshell.

3 What is the main point being made here? Where does the anecdote start and finish?

Sometimes you will need to use your own words, rather than the writer's, to answer a question concisely.

4 Write the following phrase into your own words. In particular think about using alternative verbs and adjectives (synonyms).

> It looked harmless enough; in fact it looked cuddly and kind.

Applying skills

5 Answer the following question on the passage above. Remember to summarise concisely, using your own words, and to group ideas together in longer complex sentences.

> *How does the writer feel about cats and why?*

Sound progress

- You usually select the precise information needed to answer a question.
- You mostly use synonyms and your own words to achieve a concise answer.

Excellent progress

- You always select the precise information needed to answer a question.
- You always use synonyms and your own words to achieve a concise answer.

4 Explicit meaning

Learning objectives

● To understand that some information in a text is obvious (compared with some that is more subtle or open to interpretation).
● To develop the skills to find this type of information.

Exploring skills

Sometimes the information that you are scanning for is very obvious or **explicit**. For example:

● you might be looking for a precise piece of information, such as a name or even a number

● the narrator may tell us something about a character, a place or feelings in a direct way.

Summary tasks and low-scoring 'closed' exam questions often test this type of understanding. You also need to be able to find and adapt explicit information in directed writing tasks.

To do this, use the following four steps of basic scanning skills (explained on pages 10–11).

1 Look carefully at the question.

2 Decide exactly what you are looking for.

3 Jump to the rough location of that information.

4 Cross-examine what is there to see if it matches your checklist.

> **Top tip**
>
> Understanding explicit meaning is also vital for **extended response** and **directed writing** tasks when you will have to gather and select information from the texts provided and adapt it for a different purpose. (**For more on this see pages 159–190.**)

(1) Read the following extract from *The Salt Road* by Jane Johnson. Then use the four steps to select explicit information from it to answer the following questions.

(a) Where did the writer, Izzy, escape to when her parents argued?

(b) Name **two** things in paragraph 2 that the house was 'stuffed with'.

(c) Give **four** examples of things about Izzy in paragraph 2 that annoyed her parents.

(d) Choose **three** words that summed up Izzy's parents' interests.

(e) What kind of things did Izzy like doing?

When I was a child, I had a wigwam in our back garden: a circle of thin yellow cotton draped over a bamboo pole and pegged to the lawn. Every time my parents argued, that was where I went. I would lie on my stomach with my fingers in my ears and stare so hard at the red animals printed on its bright decorative border that after a while they began to dance and run, until I wasn't in the garden any more but out on the plains, wearing a fringed deerskin tunic and feathers in my hair, just like the brave in the films I watched every Saturday morning in the cinema down the road.

Even at an early age I found it preferable to be outside in my little tent rather than inside the house. The tent was my space. It was as large as my imagination, which was infinite. But the house, for all its **grandeur** and **Georgian** spaciousness, felt small and suffocating. It was stuffed with things, as well as with my mother and father's bitterness. They were both **archaeologists**, my parents: lovers of the past, they had surrounded themselves with boxes of yellowed papers, ancient artefacts, dusty objects; the fragile husks of lost civilisations. I never knew why they decided to have me: even the quietest baby, the most house-trained toddler, the most studious child, would have disrupted the artificial, museum-like calm they had wrapped around themselves. In that house they lived separated from the rest of the world, in a bubble in which dust motes floated silently like the fake snow in a snow-globe. I was not the child to complement such a life, being a wild little creature, loud and messy and **unbiddable**.

[...] I had dolls, but more often than not I beheaded them or scalped them, or buried them in the garden and forgot where they were. I had no interest in making fashionable outfits for the **oddly attenuated** pink plastic **mannequins** with their insectile torsos and brassy hair that the other girls so worshipped and adorned.

from Jane Johnson's *The Salt Road*

4 Explicit meaning

Building skills

Writers choose words very carefully for their precise meanings.

As you read a passage, you need to think about the precise meaning of individual words and ask yourself why the author has chosen them. What effect does he or she want to create?

2 Look back at the extract on page 17. A range of words has been highlighted. Look them up in a dictionary and then complete a table like the one below.

Word	Precise meaning	How this affects me	What the writer wanted to convey
infinite	Endless, not possible to calculate	Makes it clear how vast her imagination is	Understanding of girl's character
stuffed	Very full	Large number of objects in house is made clear	Understanding of girl's home environment
yellowed			
dusty			

Developing skills

Some questions will ask you to explain the meanings of words and phrases and their effects.

Try using a range of sentence stems to start this kind of explanation, for example:

> The writer chooses the word ... which in everyday language means...

> When ... is written, the writer wants us to understand that...

> The writer uses the phrase... which suggests... and makes the reader...

3 Use each of these sentence starters to write about three of the highlighted words in the extract.

Applying skills

There is a range of exam questions that test your understanding of explicit meanings. (All of the following questions relate to *The Salt Road* extract on page 17.)

The most common are the simple 'closed' questions that appear in comprehension questions.

For example:

> *Give two reasons why the girl likes to go outside.*

> *How did the girl treat her toys?*

Another comprehension question type requires you to explain the explicit meaning of the writer's words.

For example:

> *Explain how the girl liked to enjoy herself.*

> *Explain, using your own words, what the writer means by 'In that house they lived separated from the rest of the world, in a bubble in which dust motes floated silently like the fake snow in a snow-globe'.*

There will also be a summary question. For example:

> *By using details that you have learned from the passage, sum up what you now know about the girl's childhood.*

4 Answer the first four of the questions above in full sentences using the extract from *The Salt Road* on page 17.

Sound progress	Excellent progress
• You almost always locate suitable words or phrases to answer a question. • You usually consider the meanings of words and show you understand their effects on the reader.	• You always locate a wide range of the correct words or phrases needed to answer a question. • You always consider the precise meanings of words and demonstrate you fully understand the writer's intended meaning and purpose, and their effects on the reader.

5 Implicit meaning: character

- To understand that ideas about people or characters in a text can be implied by subtle clues.
- To 'read between the lines' to find these implied meanings and consider their effects.

Exploring skills

Sometimes the meaning that you are looking for is not immediately obvious from the explicit meaning of words alone. You might be:

- looking for subtle aspects of a character
- trying to work out how a character feels about something or someone
- trying to define the relationship between two or more people
- exploring the writer's feelings or attitudes
- looking for a particular effect that the writer wants to create (for example, sympathy with a particular character).

This is called **implicit meaning**.

Most of us are actually very good at finding implicit information in everyday situations. This is particularly true when we meet a new person. The process is called **inferring**.

> **Key terms**
>
> **inferring**: reading between the lines and drawing conclusions from subtle clues

(1) Ask yourself the following question and complete the spider diagram to record the clues that you use to reach your decisions.

> *How do you know whether or not your teacher is in a good mood?*

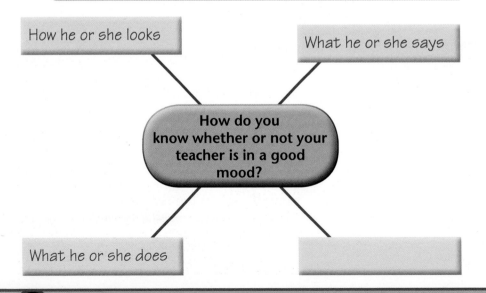

How he or she looks

What he or she says

How do you know whether or not your teacher is in a good mood?

What he or she does

Building skills

Writers give us very similar clues to guide our responses to characters. We look for these clues and draw our own inferences from them.

2 Answer these questions about the passage below.
- What is implied about the daughter in paragraph 1?
- What inferences can you draw from paragraph 2 about the mother and the daughter?

> 'It's no good!' she groaned. 'I don't want her at my birthday party and that's the end of this discussion!'
>
> Sasha's mother smiled, but her eyes were troubled as she scooped up the invitations from the table and began sliding them swiftly into the beautifully addressed envelopes. 'Well it doesn't seem kind to me to leave out just one girl in your class, sweetheart. I think you'll just have to accept that you can't have absolutely everything your own way…'. She looked up and tried to catch Sasha's eyes, which had already moved on to the photographs of elaborate cakes she had downloaded from the computer months ago.

5 | Implicit meaning: character

Developing skills

3 Read this extract from the opening chapter of *Great Expectations* by Charles Dickens. As you read, note down what each character looks like, says and does and how others react to him. Then think about the **effect** of what we are shown: what it tells us about the two characters, Pip and the convict, Magwitch.

Record your ideas in a separate table like the one below, for each character.

Pip: What is said/done/how others react/words used to describe him	Effect: What it tells us about him	Effect: What it suggests about his relationships

'Hold your noise' cried a terrible voice, as a man started up from among the graves at the side of the church porch. 'Keep still, you little devil, or I'll cut your throat!'

A fearful man, all in coarse grey, with a great iron on his leg. A man with no hat, and with broken shoes, and with an old rag tied round his head. A man who had been soaked in water, and smothered in mud, and lamed by stones, and cut by flints, and stung by nettles, and torn by briars; who limped, and shivered, and glared and growled; and whose teeth chattered in his head as he seized me by the chin.

'O! Don't cut my throat, sir,' I pleaded in terror. 'Pray don't do it, sir.'

'Tell us your name,' said the man. 'Quickly.'

'Pip, sir.'

'Once more,' said the man, staring at me. 'Give it mouth!'

'Pip. Pip, sir.'

'Show us where you live,' said the man. 'Point out the place!'

I pointed to where our village lay, on the flat in-shore among the alder-trees and pollards, a mile or more from the church.

The man, after looking at me for a moment, turned me upside down, and emptied my pockets. There was nothing in them but a piece of bread. When the church came to itself – for he was so sudden and strong that he made it go head over heels before me, and I saw the steeple under my feet – when the church came to itself, I say, I was seated on a high tombstone, trembling, while he ate the bread ravenously.

'You young dog,' said the man, licking his lips, 'what fat cheeks you ha' got.'

I believe they were fat, though I was at that time undersized for my years, and not strong.

'Darn me if I couldn't eat em,' said the man, with a threatening shake of his head, 'and if I han't half a mind to 't.'

I earnestly expressed my hope that he wouldn't, and held tighter to the tombstone on which he had put me; partly, to keep myself upon it; partly, to keep myself from crying.

 4 Use your notes to write a paragraph about each character.

Applying skills

A range of exam questions will test your understanding of implicit meanings.

Usually the implicit information will be identified and you will be asked to find the words that create it.

> *Reread the description of Pip's first meeting with the convict, Magwitch. Choose two words or phrases that suggest he is scared and explain how the writer helps us to imagine this.*

At a higher level, you will be asked to select words or phrases that have an effect on you and to identify what this effect is.

> *Reread the descriptions of Magwitch in the extract. Selecting words and phrases from the extract, explain the effects that the writer creates for you.*

 5 Answer the two questions above in complete sentences.

Sound progress

- You locate some of the words or phrases that carry implicit meaning in the text.
- You can begin to explain the effects that these words or phrases create.

Excellent progress

- You locate a wide range of the words or phrases that carry implicit meaning in the text.
- You explain the effects that these words or phrases create clearly and link this to the writer's purpose.

6 Implicit meaning: setting

● To understand that some information in texts is not obvious and needs to be worked out by careful reading.

Exploring skills

Most of us are actually very good at finding out implicit information in everyday situations. This is true particularly when we go to a new place. The process is called **inferring**.

Key terms

inferring: reading between the lines and drawing conclusions from subtle clues

1 Ask yourself the following question. Copy and complete the spider diagram to record the clues that you use to reach your decisions.

> *When you first visit a new place what affects your attitude towards it?*

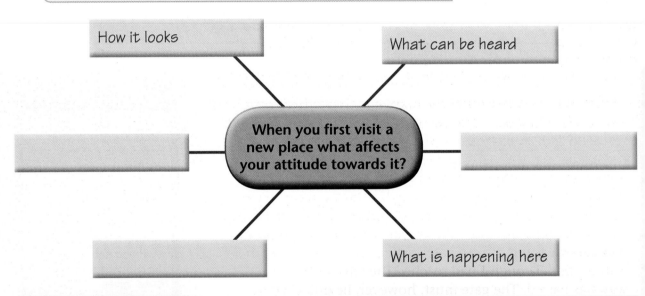

How it looks

What can be heard

When you first visit a new place what affects your attitude towards it?

What is happening here

Building skills

Writers give us similar clues to guide our responses to places. They imply meanings through the details they give us about settings to create a mood or atmosphere.

2 Read the paragraph at the top of page 25. Then think of three words you could use to sum up the atmosphere in the room.
   ● How does the writer want you to feel about the event being described?
   ● Why might the writer have this intention?

The room buzzed with energy and everything appeared to be moving slightly as if to echo the **frenetic** hum of cheerful voices. Balloons gently swayed in the breeze, bunting swished above heads as couples danced or chatted with animation. Even the edges of the brightly patterned table cloths lifted as dresses swept by.

Sometimes a writer will use **pathetic fallacy** in describing a place.

3 Try to add two more examples of this technique by making small changes to the passage.

Developing skills

Read this extract from *Set in Stone* by Linda Newbery. A young man has arrived late at night and is searching for 'Fourwinds', a house deep in the countryside.

Darkness swallowed me; the branches arched high overhead; I saw only glimpses of the paler sky through their tracery. My feet crunched beech mast. I smelled the coolness of the mossy earth, and heard the trickle of water close by. As my eyes accustomed themselves to dimmer light, I saw that here, on the lower ground, a faint mist hung in the air, trapped perhaps beneath the trees. I must be careful not to stray from the path, which I could only dimly discern; but before many minutes had passed, wrought-iron gates reared ahead of me, set in a wall of flint. Though I had reached the edge of the wood, my way was barred. The gate must, however, be unlocked, as my arrival was expected.

I peered through the scrollwork of the gates. The track, pale and broad, wound between specimen trees and smooth lawns; I had some distance still to walk, it seemed. The mist clung to the ground, and the trees seemed rooted in …

… a vaporous swamp. I tried the fastening; the left-hand gate swung open with a loud grating squeal that echoed into the night.

At the same moment another sound arose, competing for shrillness with the gate's protest: a sound to make my heart pound and my nerves stretch taut. It was a wailing shriek that filled my head and thrummed in my ears; close enough to make me shrink against the gate, which I pushed open to its fullest extent against the shadows of the wall. Whether the cry was animal or human, I could not tell. If human, it was a sound of terrible distress, of unbearable grief. I felt the hairs prickle on the back of my neck, my eyes trying to stare in all directions at once. Instinct told me to hunch low till the danger passed. Dropped into such strangeness, I had acquired, it seemed, the impulse of a wild creature to hide myself and survive whatever perils were near. The metal bit into my hands as I clung into the gate. Attempting to retain a clear head, I reminded myself that I was unfamiliar with the sounds of the countryside at night. It must be a fox, a badger, some creature yowling in hunger or pain.

The passage creates an atmosphere of foreboding without the writer saying so directly. She does not say, 'I arrived at the house after a long journey and was really scared when I heard something screaming.' Instead we work this out from the details she includes.

(4) Copy and complete the table below to help you analyse the different ingredients the writer uses to create the mood. Add any further words or phrases from the extract that help to create this effect.

> **Top tip**
>
> Remember in your own creative writing to **show** rather than **tell**. This technique will help you imply subtle meanings of your own.

Words/phrases	Time of year	Time of day	Weather	Landscape	Objects	Actions	Sounds
darkness	✔						
branches							
mossy earth							
trickle of water							
faint mist							
wrought-iron gates							
a loud grating squeal							

5 The mood could be completely altered by changing the words and phrases in the table. Add another column to the table with words and phrases that would make the approach to the house exciting and optimistic.

> **Top tip**
>
> Many writers use the ingredients in the top row of the table to create atmosphere. Try them out when you are writing your own descriptions.

Applying skills

A range of exam questions will test your understanding of implicit meanings.

Usually the implicit meaning will be identified and you will be asked to find the words that create it.

> *Reread the description of the narrator's arrival at Fourwinds. Choose two words or phrases that suggest he is afraid and explain how the writer helps us to imagine this.*

At a more sophisticated level you will be asked to select words or phrases and identify and explain their effects on you.

> *Reread the description of the gate opening. Selecting words and phrases from the extract, explain the effects that the writer creates for you.*

6 Answer the two questions above in complete sentences.

Sound progress	Excellent progress
• You locate some of the words or phrases that carry implicit meaning in the text. • You can begin to explain the effects that these words or phrases create.	• You locate a wide range of the words or phrases that carry implicit meaning in the text. • You explain clearly the effects that these words or phrases create and link this to the writer's purpose.

7 Emotive language

Learning objectives

- To understand that words or phrases can create an emotional reaction.
- To develop the skills to analyse the effects of emotive language.

Exploring skills

Emotive language is the term we use to describe words or phrases that make us feel a particular emotion.

Some words are very obviously emotive because of their explicit meaning. For example, the word 'afraid' clearly tells us how someone feels.

Sometimes the emotional effect is less obvious. For example, the word 'graveyard' has negative emotional associations or **connotations** for most people. You might consider graveyards to be sad or even frightening places. The word might evoke your own memories or make you feel unhappy or uneasy.

Key terms

connotations: the associations of a word or thing. For example, a flag can immediately make someone think 'my country'.

Top tip

In cases where your personal interpretation is different to the usual one, it is safest to assume that the writer meant the word to be interpreted in the more popular way.

1 What are the emotional effects of the following words? Is the effect created by the explicit meaning of the word or phrase, or by its connotations?

- sullen
- sunset
- red rose
- irritable

Building skills

Different words have different connotations and levels of intensity. For instance, there are many words that mean someone does not have very much body fat, but they all carry different connotations.

2 Consider the emotional effects of the following adjectives. Which have a positive effect and which have a negative one? Are any neutral?

- thin
- slim
- slender
- skeletal
- scrawny

It is also important to consider **how** strong or weak the emotional intensity of a word is. For instance, there are many words to describe whether or not we feel affection for something:

- keen on
- like
- adore
- love.

If we place these words on a scale of intensity, it becomes clear that some suggest a stronger feeling than others.

1 like   **4** adore

3 Where would you place the rest of the words in the list?

4 Now make your own intensity line for words related to 'dislike'.

Developing skills

It is also important to consider **why** a writer chooses to use a word with a particular emotional connotation or intensity. It might be to express their own feelings or to provoke a reaction in the reader. This will depend on the overall **aim** of the piece of writing.

Emotive language

5 Copy and complete the following table to show how the purpose and type of writing can determine the use of emotive language.

Type of writing	Purpose of writing	Express own feelings	Use words to evoke emotions	Why?
Diary entry	To record personal feelings/ events			
Charity campaign leaflet	To persuade/ enlist			
Advertisement	To promote		✓	To sell the product the reader needs to feel its benefits
Report	To inform	✗	✗	

6 Read the text on page 31. It is taken from a campaign leaflet for schools by Animal Aid, the UK's largest animal rights group. Copy and complete a table like the one below.
   - Identify the emotive words used in the text.
   - Alongside each word, make a note explaining how the word would affect the reader.
   - Next consider why the writer wanted to create that effect.

Word/phrase	Effect on reader	Reason why writer wants to create that effect
collapse	We think of something losing all power, strength and natural order.	They want us to understand that the cod population is very severely affected by the over-fishing – it is not just a minor change.
stripped bare		

Is this the greatest animal welfare scandal of our time?

The forgotten victims

Oceans on the brink of collapse

Over-fishing is causing populations such as cod to collapse. Fish are being caught before they have time to breed, giving numbers no time to recover. The seas are being stripped bare and the oceans are dying. Farming fish increases the problem because three to five tons of ocean-caught fish are needed to produce feed for one ton of farmed fish.

Wildlife at risk

Hundreds of thousands of marine animals die every year as a result of being accidentally caught in fishing nets. They include whales, dolphins, porpoises, sharks and endangered turtles. Long-line tuna fishing kills approximately 100 000 albatrosses every year. The birds dive for the bait planted on the end of the lines, swallow it, hook and all, and are pulled underwater and drowned. Animals also suffer horrific injuries when they become tangled in discarded nets.

Environmental damage

Deep-water trawling nets plough through fragile coral reefs, devastating ocean floors. Fish farms also damage their surrounding environment. The pollution from fish farming in Scotland is comparable to sewage produced by 9.4 million people. In some places, the water surrounding the farm becomes so heavily contaminated that no life can survive.

Applying skills

 7 Write up your notes as an answer to the following exam-style question.

> *Reread the Animal Aid leaflet. How does the writer make the reader feel concern for the sea and the creatures that depend on it?*

You could use the following prompts to organise your answer:
- how the writer uses emotive language
- how the writer makes the scale of the problem clear
- how the writer uses facts and examples
- how the writer uses comparisons.

Sound progress

- You select some words and phrases that create an emotional effect.
- You can consider the words and phrases and begin to explain their implications.
- You consider the possible reasons why the writer has created those effects and begin to explain them.

Excellent progress

- You select a wide range of words and phrases that create an emotional effect.
- You consider the words and phrases and explain clearly the inferences you draw from them.
- You evaluate the possible reasons why the writer has created those effects and explain them clearly with reference to the reader and the writer's intention.

8 Sensory language

Learning objectives

- To understand how words or phrases can appeal to our five senses.
- To develop the skills to write about the effects of sensory language.

Exploring skills

Sensory language stimulates our imagination so that we almost feel as if we are there. We can imagine exactly what we would be able to see, hear, touch, taste or smell at the scene.

It can help to analyse sensory language in the form of a flow chart.

You need to think not just about what a word means literally (its **denotation**) but what associated ideas it brings to mind (its **connotations**).

Top tip

Being able to spot words with a sensory appeal and explain their effects is a skill that is tested in the examinations. Sensory language is also a powerful technique to use in your own descriptive and narrative writing.

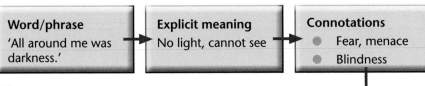

Word/phrase	Explicit meaning	Connotations
'All around me was darkness.'	No light, cannot see	● Fear, menace ● Blindness

Effect
- Character feels scared
- Place is frightening
- Something bad is going to happen

1. Make a flow chart for the following phrases:
   - 'a wailing shriek'
   - 'I could smell the coolness of the mossy earth'.

2. Consider this description of a summer's day at the beach. Make a list of any words or phrases that stimulate the senses. You could use a table like the one started below.

> Slush-grey and ice-white gulls scream and sticky toddlers wrestle over plastic spades, giggling carelessly. Their voices and the sweet smell of candyfloss wafts along the pebbled beach towards me. Striped deckchair canvases billow in the breeze and the commanding flags advertising ice-cream companies arch like stretching beauties as the warm wind catches them.
>
> The waves race towards us and their white crest curves up and over, scooping sand and stray flip-flops in its grasp. I lurch as the water sucks at my feet pulling me towards its grey-green depths and grimace as the salt spray lingers on my stinging lips and tongue. There is no laughter in my mouth, just the harsh taste of loneliness.

See	Hear	Touch	Taste	Smell
Slush-grey and ice-white gulls toddlers wrestle	scream	sticky	salt spray lingers	candyfloss wafts

Building skills

(3) Write a description of a person who is in the beach scene above. Try to include at least three words or phrases to stimulate each of the senses. Swap your description with a partner and see if they can pick out your sensory details.

Developing skills

Writers choose words very carefully to create precise pictures in our minds.

Think about the difference between saying that the gulls were 'grey' and saying that they were 'slush-grey'. Which description helps you to picture them most clearly?

Writers will use adjectives, adverbs and even carefully selected nouns and verbs to create particular effects.

(4) Look again at the description of the beach. Copy and complete the table by picking out examples of each type of word and considering their impact on the reader.

Word/phrase	Noun	Adjective	Verb	Adverb	Effect
Slush-grey		✔			Precise colour, makes us picture dirty snow. This does not sound positive and adds to the feeling of unease or unhappiness.

Applying skills

(5) Answer the question below.

> *Reread the description of the beach. Selecting words and phrases from the extract, explain the effects that the writer creates by using these descriptions.*

Checklist for success

✔ Identify particular words and phrases relating to the senses.
✔ Consider the intended effects of this language and how it helps the writer to create a mood or convey the narrator's feelings.

Sound progress

- You can find several examples of sensory language.
- You identify the effect of sensory language and begin to explain how it is achieved.

Excellent progress

- You can find a broad range of examples of sensory language.
- You analyse the different possible effects of sensory language and explain clearly how it is achieved.

9 Synthesis

Learning objectives

- To develop the skills to locate and combine information from different parts of a text.
- To develop the skills to draw information together in an organised way.

Exploring skills

Synthesis is the skill of bringing information together from a range of sources and making sure that it is clearly organised for purpose.

Synthesis is useful in everyday life, when we often need to consider a wide range of written information on a topic. For instance:

- if you were planning to purchase a new mobile phone, you would probably check the details of several phones in store or on the internet
- if you were planning a holiday, you might gather information about a country from holiday brochures, the internet and a guidebook.

However, synthesis is not simply about collecting information from different locations. It is also about sifting and sorting relevant information into a clear and concise order.

Your exams may require you to gather information from several places and use it in one piece of writing. Directed writing tasks ask you to draw your answers from all parts of one text or even from two texts. Summary questions only ask you to look at one text at a time but it is very important to use information from across the whole text.

Top tip

Synthesis is a little bit like cooking a meal. It would be very inefficient, when you wanted to start cooking, if the ingredients were still jumbled up in your shopping bag. Good cooks unpack their ingredients and organise them according to when they are needed and which items will be combined with each other.

1 Look at the ingredients below. Some are used to make tortillas (simple pancakes made of flour and water) and others to make the fillings of chilli, salad, sour cream, cheese and salsa. Sort the ingredients into two lists: one for the tortillas and one for the fillings.

red onion, finely sliced	
cheddar cheese, grated	two hot green or red chillies
fresh tomatoes	
fresh coriander, chopped	sour cream
	lettuce cucumber
juice of one lime	1 cup of water
plain flour	
tinned tomatoes	minced lamb
sour cream	

Building skills

If the question is a simple one, you may only be looking for one type of information from the text or texts. For example:

> *Summarise the problems caused by extreme weather conditions as shown in the passage.*

It is tempting in these circumstances to simply start reading and to write out your answer as you go along. However, this can lead you to waste time and lose marks if similar points are repeated in several places in the text.

This is even more of a problem if you need to use two or more texts to answer a directed writing task. For example:

> *Imagine that you are a journalist putting together a radio broadcast about the kinds of aid that are needed after a natural disaster. You have read the extract below and you have also made the following notes taken from an interview with an aid worker from an international charity. Explain:*
> * *what kinds of problems arise from natural disasters*
> * *what can be done in advance to make recovery easier*
> * *what needs to be done after the disaster has occurred.*

Extreme winds, such as those found in hurricanes, tornadoes and some thunderstorms, can overturn caravans, tear off roofs and topple trees causing extreme distress to many people and financial hardship to whole communities. Some of the strongest tornadoes can demolish houses completely, leaving people homeless and vulnerable to disease and criminal harm. People may be knocked down or struck by debris and many places may lose electricity. Flooding and storm surges can destroy buildings and roads, contaminate water supplies, halt other essential services and drown people. Large hail stones can damage cars and roofs, and destroy crops, but rarely kill people. Heat waves can lead to drought, which causes crop loss as well as health issues and death from dehydration.

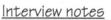

Interview notes

Need supplies, fresh water, medicines, tents

Disease spreads fast when pipes are broken

People should not rely on the state, they can get private insurance

Rapid response teams need to be formed to remove debris and search for/treat survivors

Rough terrain vehicles needed

Extra police presence helps to reduce looting

After you have digested the question, first scan the text to locate information. Then go back over the text and categorise the information into the different types requested in the question.

9 Synthesis

You could use colour coding to group similar pieces of information together so that when you write your answer you only make each point once.

2 Reread the passage on page 35 and list all the different statements about problems caused by extreme weather conditions.

Developing skills

It is important to group ideas together, as you are reading, to save time.

3 Look back at your list of problems caused by extreme weather conditions. Group the information into five to nine different categories. Each time you come across a new piece of information, decide whether it would go under an existing heading or whether you need to create a new heading.

You can go through the same process with two or even more texts. You simply add to the categories you have created or add details to existing ones.

> **Top tip**
>
> Making notes can also help to keep your answers balanced. In **directed writing** tasks, students sometimes focus too much on one text and forget to use points from the other. By making notes you can ensure that both texts are fully covered.

Applying skills

When making notes for a directed writing task, you should use the bullet points given in the question to help you decide on the category headings.

4 Now consider the whole directed writing task on page 35. Make a complete set of notes for the task, using the interview notes as well as the passage that appears with the question.

Checklist for success

✔ Use the question to decide on your categories for making notes or annotations.

✔ Decide on the best method of recording information from a text so that it is most useful for summary questions or directed writing tasks.

Sound progress

- You locate a fair amount of information from across a whole text or texts.
- You record the information using straightforward headings.
- You are able to use the information, including some supporting detail, in an orderly and effective way.

Excellent progress

- You locate a broad range of information from across a whole text or texts.
- You record the information using category headings that show perceptive reading of the task.
- You are able to use the information in an extremely orderly and effective way, always including supporting detail and adding your own relevant ideas.

Key technical skills

In this chapter you are going to develop a range of fundamental technical skills that you will use throughout your IGCSE course.

You will learn how to:

- use a range of sentence types for effect
- punctuate accurately and effectively
- use paragraphs to organise ideas effectively and to create cohesion
- use a wide range of vocabulary to interest and engage the reader
- use formal and informal language effectively
- cater for the needs of different audiences
- write in a variety of voices and roles.

On their own, some of the skills may seem simple, but remember that they are building blocks to completing larger and more complex tasks later on.

- Tasks that ask you to write for specific audiences will require you to understand and cater for the needs of different audiences in your writing.

- Questions that ask you to write in role draw on your ability to create distinctive voices.

- Tasks that require you to structure pieces of work to present information, arguments, narratives or descriptions will draw on your ability to use paragraphs effectively.

- All writing tasks will require you to pay close attention to your word choice, drawing on a wide range of vocabulary.

Sections 2 and 3 will show you how to apply these key skills to specific question types and coursework tasks.

1 Sentence types, functions and varieties

● To understand and use the different types of sentences and their functions.

Exploring skills

Sentences are the backbone of most forms of writing. The best writing:
- uses a **range of sentences** for **effect and impact**
- uses sentences **accurately** so that the **meaning is clear**.

At the most basic level, remember that sentences begin with a capital letter and end with a **full stop** (.), **question mark** (?) or **exclamation mark** (!). These punctuation marks point towards the different **functions** that sentences have, as follows:

Declarative (for suggestions or statements)	Interrogative (for questions, requests or queries)
Maybe we could go for a swim later.	*How does this work?*
The crowd clapped enthusiastically.	*Is someone following us?*
	Do you honestly expect us to believe that?
Exclamatory (for stressing a point or showing strength of feeling)	**Imperative** (for instructions, orders or commands)
How beautiful that dress is.	*Press the button now!*
What a shame!	*Turn left by the mosque.*

Different meanings and effects are created by the different functions.

1 Copy and complete the table. Write at least one sentence for each function that is appropriate to the given text.

Text	Sentence function	My sentence
A report of a visit to a sports or music show	Declarative	*The show took place at the Beach Hotel.*
A story with a mysterious event	Interrogative	
Instructions about how to get from home to the nearest shop	Imperative	
An email to a friend after you have met a favourite celebrity	Exclamatory	

Building skills

2 With a partner, take turns to describe how to get from your home to your school. Try to use all the sentence functions between you. First, read the examples on page 39.

3 Write a continuation of the paragraph as the man is followed up the tower by his pursuers. Use a mix of simple sentences and complex ones.

Developing skills

Compound sentences could also be used in the tower story, like this:

His pursuers were determined and they knew the terrain perfectly.

This would explain the two equal threats the narrator faces.

All these sentence types can help you build paragraphs. Note how the example below uses different sentence types to:

- introduce the topic of the paragraph
- develop what happens
- end with a significant moment or change.

The old man watched me from his crate every morning as I struggled to capture the stray goats and herd them into the rickety pen my father had built. He said nothing and betrayed no emotions as I stumbled here and there, trying to round them up. Then, one morning, he stood up.

4 What does the use of the short sentence suggest about what is about to happen?

A similar effect can be created by using a single-word sentence:

He walked towards me, and I realised he had something to tell or show me. He held out his hand and in it was a small wooden whistle. I took it from him and waited for him to explain how to use it. I continued to wait, staring at him. Nothing. He simply turned and walked away. Some help!

5 What do the one-word and two-word **minor sentences** suggest about how the writer feels?

Applying skills

6 Now write the opening 125–150 words of a descriptive piece called 'The secret lake'. Include detailed description of what can be seen and heard as dawn breaks. Build logically towards a significant description or moment and use sentences for specific effects.

Sound progress

- You use clear, easy-to-follow sentences and make some attempt to engage the reader.

Excellent progress

- You use a full range of sentence types fluently to create a range of effects that sustain the reader's interest.

3 Punctuation

- To understand the main forms of punctuation.
- To use the full range of punctuation accurately and effectively.

You learned on pages 38–39 how sentences always start with a capital letter and end with a full stop, exclamation mark or a question mark. However, you must use the full range of punctuation to gain top marks.

Exploring skills

Using commas and apostrophes correctly is a basic punctuation skill, which you must get right in your exams and coursework.

Commas

Use them to separate items in a list.

- *I bought fajitas, tomato sauce, onions and fried chicken to prepare for the party.*

Use them to separate adverbs, clauses or phrases (often as a way of adding detail or organising your ideas).

- *Although I was angry, I didn't say anything.*
- *First of all, I'd like to deal with the problem of traffic in the city centre.*
- *Jose, on the other hand, believes the biggest problem is pedestrians.*

Apostrophes

Use them to indicate possession.

- If the owner is singular, the apostrophe goes **before** the 's'.
  For example: *Japan's government* and *my uncle's bald head*.
  Watch out for names already ending in 's' as in *Dickens's novels*.
- If the owner is plural, then the apostrophe comes **after** the 's'.
  For example: *managers' problems with their teams and footballers' wives*.
- There are exceptions for special plural words: for example, *children's, men's, women's*.

Also use apostrophes to show omission. The apostrophe goes where a letter, or series of letters, has been removed. For example:

- *There isn't (is not) much you can do.*
- *You'll (you will) be lucky!*

1 Read this text and then rewrite it, adding commas and apostrophes as appropriate. If you need to change or add any words, then do so.

> Even though it was raining we all went to the park. Shamira brought bread cheese salad and iced tea. Alina however brought nothing which made us all mad. Id brought a snack and so had Shan. Alinas excuse was that shed not had time to go the shop. However it didnt matter. Tourists hats were getting blown off so we knew a storm was coming and left after ten minutes.

Building skills

The following example sets out the main conventions of using speech marks.

speech marks around actual words spoken, including any punctuation

a new line for each new speaker

a comma after the speaker and the speech inside speech marks, if the speaker comes first

a comma goes before the closing speech mark when the speech is not a question or exclamation

the speaker can be mentioned mid-sentence; if the speech continues, the first word doesn't have a capital letter

'How are you feeling?' asked my father.

'He looks pale,' said my mother.

I replied, 'I don't want to do it, but I guess I'll have to.'

'In that case,' said my father, 'you need to hurry, or you'll miss the bus.'

'I wish my mathematics exam was over,' I said. 'Can't I just pretend I'm ill?'

where the speaker is mentioned between two separate sentences, use a full stop and then a capital letter to start the next part

sentences containing speech begin with a capital letter and end with a full stop

Top tip

For effective storytelling, do not mention the speaker's name every time they speak as this can be repetitive and interrupt the flow. The new line for each speaker should make it clear who is talking for a few lines of dialogue. For example:

'The bus is here!' called my mum.
'I'm coming.'
'Hurry up – or you'll miss it.'
'Alright – just getting my bag,' I replied.

2 Continue the following dialogue between a boy who is late for school and his teacher, using the conventions you have learned. Be sure to express the teacher's irritation at being kept waiting.

> I ran up the corridor towards the exam room. Out of breath, I turned the handle and burst in.
> 'You're late!' hissed my teacher.

Developing skills

Other forms of punctuation can be used more subtly for different effects and are especially useful in certain forms of writing.

Colons and semi-colons

A **colon** can introduce a list, following a general statement, like this:

We can be proud of last year: increased sales, more customers and higher profits.

It can also introduce a clause that explains the first clause:

She was overjoyed: the bag was exactly what she wanted.

Semi-colons are useful for contrasts and comparisons, to link two clauses of equal importance. For example:

Rajesh likes table tennis; Irina prefers hockey.

> **Top tip**
>
> Make use of colons in analytical or report writing to help provide clear explanations.
> Be careful not to overuse semi-colons. Use them sparingly and only when you are sure it is correct to do so.

3 Read this short article from a school website. Rewrite it, adding colons or semi-colons as appropriate.

```
The new library is wonderful more shelf space an
internet zone and comfy chairs for relaxing with
a favourite book. The internet zone is already
popular the computers are booked up every day.
Some students come in early to do homework on
them others use them once lessons have ended.
```

Brackets and dashes

These can be used to provide additional information or to make details stand out: for example, when describing a situation or event, or adding a humorous comment.

We didn't mind hanging around at the beach in the winter (despite the cold) as it was where all our friends went.

Florent told us he'd bought a secondhand car – not too expensive – to replace his battered old Ford. It was secondhand – a Ferrari!

4 Rewrite the following paragraph, using dashes (or brackets) as appropriate for additional information or for any text that needs to stand out.

> It was peaceful at night except for the occasional buzzing moth and I slept like a baby. When our guide woke me at 5:30 a.m. I felt refreshed despite the time. Outside our driver a huge man in khaki shorts waited while we climbed into the jeep.

Applying skills

Your main goal is to ensure that your use of punctuation is accurate.

Checklist for success

✔ **Before you write**, plan to use a variety of sentences and punctuation, as you are more likely to pay attention to accuracy when thinking about the effects you can create.

✔ **As you write**, check punctuation carefully at regular intervals (for example, after each paragraph).

✔ **When you have finished**, look over your completed work for any errors.

Top tip

Avoid comma splicing. This is a common error where two clauses, which should have been split into separate sentences or organised using a linking word/ phrase, are mistakenly separated by a comma. For example, *I went to see the film, it was fantastic.* is not a grammatical sentence. This could be rewritten in several ways:
I went to see a film, which was fantastic.
I went to see a film. It was fantastic.
I went to see a film: it was fantastic.

The best way of testing your punctuation skills is by doing a real task rather than lots of exercises (although they can help).

5 Write the opening two paragraphs of an article in which you argue that exams are bad for your health. Try to use the full range of punctuation (though perhaps not speech-marks, unless you include an interview). Check your work as you go along – and afterwards. You could:

- start with a question (for example, *Do you remember the first time that…?*)
- contrast two ideas with a semi-colon
- make a point and use bracketed text or dashes to give extra information or a humorous aside
- use a colon to introduce a list.

Sound progress

- You take care to write in clear sentences using a reasonably accurate range of punctuation.

Excellent progress

- You use a wide range of punctuation accurately for deliberate effects.

4 Paragraph cohesion

- To understand how to use paragraphs and a range of linking connectives to organise ideas.
- To decide on the best order for a set of paragraphs.

Exploring skills

Paragraphs help us introduce a new point or topic, or a different time, place or person, and to develop and expand on previous ideas.

Read how this student describes the build-up to a holiday.

> I had been looking forward to our holiday for weeks. Each day I crossed off a date on the calendar. I mooched around the kitchen getting under mum's feet. I sat and stared out of the window at our street. The hours dragged by, but eventually it was time for us to go. I crossed off the last day on the calendar and went to bed even though I couldn't sleep.
>
> The next morning, the bus ride to the airport was dreadful: we had roadworks, a demonstration and even a herd of cattle that wouldn't move! I thought we weren't going to make it.
>
> Finally, we made it to Check-in. As we queued up I could see the look of relief on dad's face.
>
> At the desk, the assistant looked at us blankly when we handed over our passports and ticket printout. 'Your flight is tomorrow, not today,' she said, pointing to the date on our tickets.

topic sentence introduces idea that this is about holidays and writer's feelings

details within the paragraph develop the topic

linking phrase (connective) relating to time

topic sentence introduces terrible bus ride

sequence word (connective) relating to feelings and time

topic sentence introduces where this part of narrative takes place

(1) Note down how this text is held together by **cohesion**. Consider:
   - the different topics or information in each paragraph
   - how time or sequence phrases help
   - how the content is organised. For example, why is 'airport' not mentioned again once 'Check-in' appears in paragraph 3?

Key terms

cohesion: how a paragraph is knitted together and linked to other paragraphs around it. Topic sentences, connectives and linking phrases all help to make a text cohesive.

Building skills

(2) Add a further paragraph to the text above. Use one of the following situations and a topic sentence to make the situation clear:
   - the ride back in the bus
   - Mum and Dad arguing back at the flat
   - the next morning.

Developing skills

Different types of connective can help you link your ideas both within and between paragraphs. These include:

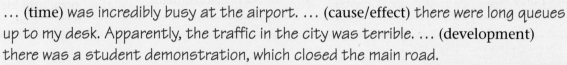

- **chronological/time sequence ordering**: *at first, next, later that day*
- **simple ordering of events or actions**: *first, second, finally*
- **logical ordering (often related to cause and effect)**: *therefore, consequently, as a result*
- **contrasting**: *on the other hand, in contrast, however, although*
- **developing ideas**: *what is more, in addition, moreover, furthermore.*

(3) Add appropriate connectives to the following email written by the check-in assistant to her boss, who was ill and away from the airport for the day.

> … (time) was incredibly busy at the airport. … (cause/effect) there were long queues up to my desk. Apparently, the traffic in the city was terrible. … (development) there was a student demonstration, which closed the main road.
>
> … (contrast) most passengers made it on time, … (contrast) one family, poor things, had a nasty shock when they handed me their tickets. They'd got the wrong day!

Applying skills

Deciding on the order of paragraphs in your writing and how you link them is a key skill.

(4) Here is student's plan for a descriptive piece of writing called 'My perfect holiday'. The points are not yet in a logical order.

Decide which paragraph to begin with, then reorder the others into a logical sequence.

Finally, write the paragraphs.

- Things I would like to do on my perfect holiday
- Terrible holidays I have had in the past
- The sort of place/country/location I would like to go
- My worst ever holiday
- Who, if anyone, I would take with me

Checklist for success

- ✔ Use a topic sentence to state the main idea of the paragraph.
- ✔ Link paragraphs with connectives.
- ✔ Use connectives within paragraphs to link sentences.

Sound progress

- You use paragraphs, if not always with sufficient thought or attention to effect.

Excellent progress

- Your paragraphs are well constructed and logically ordered with a clear sense of the task's purpose and effect.

5 Vocabulary

Checklist for success

✔ Use appropriate words for the purpose and audience.
✔ Do not repeat words unnecessarily; find alternatives.
✔ Be precise in your choice of words and phrases to convey an accurate picture.
✔ Use imagery to make ideas vivid.

Exploring skills

Choosing the appropriate words for the purpose is vital. For example, you might use:

● **emotive words** to convey or produce powerful feelings:
  desperation, incredible, joyous, golden, shadowy, abandoned
● **technical terms** or **phrases** for information writing: *species,
  habitat, migration, plumage.*

(1) Read this short text, which combines both emotive and technical
vocabulary. Identify examples of both.

> Playing my first concert was a fantastic experience. As
> soon as I sat down at the pure, ivory keys of the piano,
> I felt a shiver of expectation run through me. My heart
> raced wildly as I began the first bars of the concerto, and I
> faltered momentarily as the adagio sequence started.

Building skills

If you are writing about a particular topic, try to avoid repeating the same words or phrases.
For example, a police officer might warn people about the *serious situation following the fire*,
but they could also say *grave, important, worrying* or *drastic*.

(2) In pairs, discuss how strong each of these choices is and how they differ in meaning.

You might also choose longer, more powerful words or phrases to replace commonplace ones.
For example: *It was a **really bad** game* could become *It was an **absolutely atrocious** game.*

(3) Copy the following text, replacing the highlighted words to use
more powerful vocabulary.

> The storm in the desert was very bad. The sand was thrown up in the air and got
> into our ears, eyes and mouths. The wind made a loud noise and it was very hard
> to walk. It really was so bad.

Consider all parts of speech when improving vocabulary. For example:

- **nouns**: objects/things (*mango*, *table*), proper nouns (*Aisha*), emotions/ideas (*love*), places (*Santiago*)
- **adjectives**: qualify or add more information to a noun (telling us things such as its quality, size, colour: **tiny green** *kiwi fruit*, **wonderful** *film*)
- **verbs**: express actions or states (*leave*, *think*, *run*)
- **adverbs**: usually describe or modify verbs and adjectives (*leave* **quickly**, *Fernando is* **extremely** *fast*).

Developing skills

You can also use vocabulary to be more precise and to add further information. For example, 'The wind uprooted the trees in the park.' could become:

specific type of wind ——— *The tornado uprooted the tall, slender*
precise type of tree ——— *cedars around the battered sports ground.*

adjectives add visual detail
adjective and precise noun provide even more detail
preposition adds location

(4) Rewrite this sentence about the storm, adding your own details in the same way.

> The … (adjective) *waves crashed down on the* … (adjective), … (adjective) … (noun) … (preposition) *the* … (adjective) beach.

Imagery

You can use imagery to help readers visualise a scene or understand how a character feels. Often imagery works by describing one thing in terms of another.

Similes make comparisons using *like* or *as*. For example: *My brother paced the room like a wolf in a cage.*

Metaphors are comparisons that don't use *like* or *as*. For instance: *The tornado* **danced furiously** *in the sky above, a* **hyena howling** *at the* **trembling earth** *below.*

Personification is when non-human things are given human characteristics. Can you identify two examples of this in the sentences above?

> **Top tip**
>
> Any images you use need to fit the overall atmosphere or tone of your writing.

Applying skills

(5) Write 100–125 words describing a deep cave in the side of a mountain as night falls. Try to convey the atmosphere – what can be seen and heard as the sun goes down – using precise, powerful vocabulary and imagery.

Sound progress	Excellent progress
• You use appropriate vocabulary, but it adds little to the tone or atmosphere.	• Your vocabulary is varied and used confidently for a range of effects and purposes that enhance the tone, style and content of what you write.

6 Audience: formality and informality

Learning objectives

- To understand the difference between formal and informal language.
- To use appropriate formal and informal conventions and structures.

Exploring skills

What is the difference between **formal** and **informal** language? Consider the way you might speak or write to your close friends about everyday things. Then contrast this with how you might communicate with an adult in authority about a more serious subject.

Formal

more impersonal (less friendly, a sort of studied politeness) with 'distance' between the writer and recipient

Excuse me, Mr Bosingwa, what would be the best time to attend the job interview?

uses few if any, abbreviations, slang or exclamation marks

formal vocabulary or conventions to match the context or audience: *attend* rather than *turn up for*

Informal

generally adopts a close and personal tone

Hey, Frankie, what's the best time for me to turn up for this chat, then?

uses the sentence tag 'then'

informal vocabulary and abbreviations to match the context or audience

(1) Look carefully at examples A and B below. Make notes to identify the formal and informal elements in each.

A

Well, you wouldn't believe it, Carlos, but there's me, kicking a ball around in our backyard when the Real Madrid boss trots by!

B

Dear Mr Mourinho,

Thank you for your kind invitation to attend a training session with the first team on Monday, 23 March. I would be delighted to come and would like to thank you for noticing my skills when you passed by our house last week.

Yours sincerely,
Didier Brillianti

Structure

Formality in a letter, for example, means beginning and ending in specific ways that you would not use in an email to a friend.

Imagine your head teacher has written a letter inviting you to give a speech to new students about your positive experiences at the school. A formal reply would look something like this:

Dear Mrs De Witt, ——— standard opening for a formal letter

I am writing in reply to your letter of the 17 May, inviting me ——— refers back to Mrs De Witt's letter

to speak to new students at the school. I am extremely honoured ——— reminds reader of the subject

to be asked and would like to thank you for offering me this opportunity. ——— polite tone

I would be delighted to accept the invitation and will arrange ——— response to the request

to meet with you at a mutually ——— next action

convenient time, as requested.

Yours sincerely, ——— standard closing when a name is used in the opening

Sinitta Long

——— full name

The order of information is a natural and logical one: subject, thanks for the invitation, acceptance, further action, close of letter.

(2) Write a comic, informal reply to replace the formal letter. Think about what you would need to change in the order and content. You could start like this:

> Hi Tanya!
>
> How ya doin? Ta for the invite...

Top tip

Be careful that your **informal** letters do not come across as rude. Make sure you are confident about how the recipient will react to this style and tone. **Formal** language can also seem comic or rude if exaggerated or used in the wrong situation. For example, you would not ask someone to move on a bus by saying, *Excuse me, my good man, could I trouble you to shift your position so that my bodily form can be located alongside yours?*

6 Audience: formality and informality

Developing skills

Some formal texts require an **impersonal tone**, especially when an authoritative or factual account is needed.

3 Read the text below. In pairs, discuss how the objective, impersonal tone is achieved. Look carefully at:
- the way the verbs are used
- who is speaking or writing.

> The shark was observed at 7 a.m. breaking the surface of the water approximately half a mile from the shore. Local coastguards were alerted and the shark was guided out to sea to safer areas before any harm was done to tourists.

4 Now read this eye-witness account of the same event. What differences do you notice?

> *I saw the shark at around seven this morning in the sea, I guess about half a mile or so out. I called the coastguards and they guided it out to sea before it could do any damage.*

If you are still not sure how the different tone is achieved, consider the verbs in the following examples and then go back to the task above.

Active form

> *I noticed the fire starting in the factory and called the police.*

subject of the sentence ('I') is present and 'does' the action (noticing the fire/calling police)

Passive form

> The start of the fire was noticed and the police were called.

the subject (person who noticed the fire) is missing, so the text seems more objective and 'distant'

The passive, impersonal style is especially useful for news reports or accounts by someone who wishes the text to have authority.

5 Turn this short account into a formal news report by changing the active forms, where you can, to the passive.

> I discovered the shipwreck yesterday as our fishing boat returned in the evening. I saw the hull shining deep down, then dived in. While underwater, I took photographs with my waterproof camera and returned to the surface where I passed them to the captain who sent them using a mobile phone to a local newspaper.

You will need to change the *I* of the text to *he* or *she*. Begin with:

The shipwreck was discovered yesterday by a local fisherman as his...

Applying skills

Correctly handled, informality can be useful when establishing a convincing voice in a dialogue or in conversation in a narrative.

> *So, Olga, you're saying* Avatar *is the best film ever, right? Because it's not in my book. No way.*

Other distinctive features of informal dialogue are **contractions**, **tags** and **idiom**. Here are examples from the speech above:

- **contraction**: *you're = you are; it's = it is*
- **tag**: *right?*
- **idiom**: *not in my book* doesn't mean the speaker has a book of favourite films; it's a turn of phrase meaning 'in my view'.

Idioms appear in both formal and informal language but are more likely to be used conversationally. They can make the voice of your speakers sound convincing, but they do need to be used carefully and only when appropriate: for example, in informal speech between two close friends.

6 Draft a dialogue between a police officer and the boy he is interviewing, who is suspected of stealing a toy from a shop. Use informal usages like contractions and tags for the boy to establish his voice and a more formal style for the officer.

> *So, Mr Ferrer, we observed you leaving the shop with the toy. How do you explain that?*

> *Well, it's not how it looks, honest! You see, when you **clocked** me leaving …*

Key terms

idiom: typical phrase common to a language: for example, *dead funny* meaning 'really funny'; *a right laugh* meaning 'a lot of fun'.

AVATAR

Glossary

clocked: London English, local dialect usage meaning 'saw' or 'noticed'

Sound progress

- You generally use language and conventions accurately and appropriately but do not adjust them to create voice or tone.

Excellent progress

- Your choice of language and conventions is very fit for purpose, well matched to the audience and creates convincing voice or personality.

---

7 Choosing the right style for your audience

Learning objectives

- To understand how different audiences affect content, structure and language.
- To develop the skills to write for a particular audience, sustaining an appropriate style.

Exploring skills

Getting the style right for the audience is not just about choosing the right level of formality. You also need to think about:

- **content** – the information and ideas included
- **structure and presentation** – how the information is organised and displayed
- **language** – the choice and difficulty of vocabulary as well as the length and complexity of sentences.

1 Read this short newspaper report. With a partner, note down:
- the key facts or information presented which might appeal to a five- or six-year-old child
- the words or phrases which would not be suitable for the child
- from the language and presentation, who the target audience might be.

Birth of Asian elephant is trumpeted by zoo

WHIPSNADE THE FIRST ASIAN elephant to be born at Whipsnade Zoo in Bedfordshire makes her public debut at the age of six days under the watchful trunk of her mother, Kaylee, 27. The 3ft-tall female calf, yet to be given a name by keepers at the zoo, weighs 126 kg (278 lb). The zoo's elephant population has declined this year after two of its animals died from a herpes virus. David Field, Whipsnade's director, said that the calf's birth was important for its endangered species programme. The calf's sire, Emmett, is the only male in the zoo's herd of eight elephants.   *The Times*

Building skills

This is how the text might have started if it had been written for a five- or six-year-old child:

> Look at this baby elephant.

> She is only six days old!

> She was born at Whipsnade Zoo.

> Her mother's name is Kaylee.

Note the simple, short sentences and how some information has not been included.

2 Rewrite the second sentence of the article as three simple sentences suitable for a young child to read.

Developing skills

(3) Now imagine that you are going to write a letter to David Field, the zoo director, expressing your support for the zoo's endangered species programme and your concern about the decline in its elephant population. Think about the conventions of letters, and about the style needed for the recipient. Then copy and complete the table below.

Text features	Newspaper article	Letter
Presentation	Headline and photo	Address and opening greeting – 'Dear …'
Purpose	To inform	
Style and key features	No reference to first person Lots of facts and stats	Written from 'I' point of view (in the 'first person') Tone still quite formal but personal as letter is to one named individual

(4) Now look at how one writer has begun this letter.

> Dear Mr Field,
> There was a newspaper article about the birth of the elephant at the zoo. It was pleasing to see the work done by the staff …

Top tip

Remember to match the tone of your writing to your audience as well as your style. Mr Field is not a long-lost friend, so keep you style and tone friendly but also quite formal.

This doesn't sound very personal! Discuss with a partner how this first paragraph could be improved.

(5) Now draft the next two paragraphs of the letter. You need to express the following points.
- **Paragraph 1:** your sadness about the death of the other baby elephants (think of strong, emotional words that will strike a chord with Mr Field).
- **Paragraph 2:** your concern about the declining elephant population (using any evidence from the article you can).

Applying skills

(6) Swap your draft with a partner. Does your partner's draft use:
- the first person
- the right style and tone for a letter to Mr Field
- the correct form of presentation for a letter?

Sound progress	Excellent progress
• You use some of the information from the original text in your letter.	• You select the most relevant information from the original text.
• The style of your writing is largely appropriate to your audience.	• You write in a highly appropriate style for the chosen audience.
• You use most of the conventions for the chosen form of writing.	• You demonstrate the conventions of the text well in your writing.

Voice and role

Learning objectives

- To understand that the voice or role adopted for a task affects language and content.
- To write in different voices or roles.

Exploring skills

As individuals we all have different views of the same situation and therefore express things in different ways.

Voice is the particular, personal expression and language that an individual uses (for example, chatty or serious, anxious or optimistic).

Role is the particular part, profession or identity someone has (for example, a ten-year-old child, schoolteacher or angry neighbour) and will affect the **voice**, among other things.

1 Match these different voices (A–D) to their roles (1–4). They are all responding to the same situation.

Voice A

> So, Sunil – this is your first major stage role and it looks like you nailed it, according to the reviews. Does this mean you'll be looking for parts in films soon?

Role 1: actor, Sunil

Voice B

> Sunil Vaswani's landmark performance in the central role was a revelation. He combined a certain vulnerability and power at the same time and spoke Shakespeare's verse with clarity and control.

Role 2: Sunil's mum

I felt so nervous. Of course, we'd rehearsed for weeks but nothing prepares you for curtain up. Waiting in the wings felt like an eternity. I didn't think it went that well, to tell the truth.

Role 3: interviewer

Voice D

Naturally, we were very proud to see our lad up on stage. To think it was only two years ago that he left home and started his career. We took so many photos!

Role 4: theatre reviewer

The clues come, of course, from:

- what is said (it is unlikely a reviewer would talk about being 'proud')
- how it is said (an informal phrase like 'you nailed it' is likely to be conversational)
- conventions: an interview contains questions; a review might use typical phrases such as *landmark performance*.

Top tip

Punctuation can also help to convey 'voice'. For example, an exclamation mark might suggest excitement, and perhaps a less formal response, or a semi-colon used to weigh up two ideas might suggest a more objective response.

Building skills

To capture the voice or role, you also need to have a good understanding of:

- the **context** or **situation** and the **reason** for writing
- the **character** or **background** of the person whose voice you are writing in.

For example, imagine you are a student called Poppy. You have just taken part in a spelling tournament against other students from around the country, which took place over a weekend. Here is your diary entry for the morning of the competition:

Day 1: preparing for the competition

Got up at 8 a.m. and went down to join all the other students for breakfast. I'd made a sort of friend with a girl called Sonya last night – at least I thought I had, but this morning she ignored me and spent all breakfast with her nose in a dictionary. This made me laugh. If you don't know the spellings by now, then you never will. Mind you, I was so nervous I couldn't eat anyway. Breakfast just made me think of cooking-related spellings: 'restaurant' (remember the 'au'!), 'lasagne', 'cucumber' (not 'queue cumber'!!) and 'temperature' all kept on going through my head. Am I going mad? Is it all worth it? I was about to text Mum and Dad, but then in came the organiser – a thin, severe looking man in a grey suit – and told us Round 1 was going to start in 10 minutes in the Main Hall.

(2) With a partner, discuss:
- What impression do you get of Poppy as a person from this diary extract?
- What do we learn about her feelings towards other people?

(3) Join up with two or three other people in your class. Between you, take on the roles of Poppy, Sonya, and one or two other competitors (Raj is a very confident competitor who was runner-up the year before; Jed is a student who is not very good at spelling and was entered by mistake by his school!). Role-play the conversation you have before Round 1 begins.

Developing skills

Creating a successful voice means conveying a character's personality and emotions through the language and vocabulary used. For example, we could say Poppy is:

- nervous (about the competition)
- quite witty
- close to her mum and dad
- friendly, but competitive
- observant.

(4) How could Poppy's characteristics be shown in a follow-up piece of writing? Write her next diary entry. Use what you know about her already, including:

- questions that show her doubting her abilities
- references to her parents
- possibly comical observations about other competitors or the organisers.

Maintain Poppy's voice in the diary. For example, she mixes present-tense observations and past-tense recollections. You could start:

> Day 2: late morning – Round 1
>
> After breakfast we all made our way to the Main Hall. My tum was rumbling and suddenly I felt hungry. Typical! ('al' or 'le'...?) Anyway, that Sonya was just in front of me, looking like...

Top tip

To help maintain the voice of a character, try imagining what they would say and do in different situations. Do they have a favourite phrase or two, for example?

(See pages 70–71 for more on the conventions of diary entries.)

Of course, if the type of text you are writing changes, then your voice will need to adapt. For example, imagine Poppy's teacher has asked her to give a speech to her year group entitled, 'Why taking part in competitions is good for you!'

(5) Make some brief notes on the following questions.

- How is the **purpose** of this task different from the diary entry?
- How will the **form and style** of the text be different from the diary form?
- In what way will you need to be selective about the details you include and leave out in your speech?
- What elements of Poppy's **voice** will you continue using in the speech?

Applying skills

6 Read these two sample speeches written in Poppy's voice and decide how well each:
- makes use of information about Poppy and what happens to her (for example, which one provides more detail about the events?)
- shows Poppy's feelings through the style and tone (for example, which uses variety of sentences and punctuation?)
- focuses on the purpose of the speech, rather than the diary (for example, which one shows the positive aspects of taking part?)
- uses the right style for a speech. **(See pages 62–65 for more on the conventions of speeches.)**

Lucy's response

> Well, it all started when we got there. I wanted to win the competition really badly and made friends with this girl. But she wasn't very nice and just wanted to revise for the test. I was nervous so I tried to call my mum and dad. The competition was really scary and the organiser wasn't exactly friendly. I don't know why I did it, really.

Theo's response

> This weekend I have been at a spelling competition. You may think I'm an idiot (no, don't answer that!) after all, who actually likes spelling? But from the moment I arrived, representing our school, I knew it was good for me. Yes, I was nervous. Yes, I had to face people who smiled to my face one evening, then ignored me at breakfast, but I had to grow up fast. I didn't care if I beat the snooty girl from breakfast (well, ok – I did a bit) – it was more about competing with myself, my nerves and being on my own away from home. And – I did it!

7 Now write two entries from the diary of the other girl, Sonya. In fact, she is shy and nervous and thinks Poppy and the others are really confident. She does not have many friends at school, but English is her favourite subject.
- Use the diary conventions from Poppy's entry.
- Convey Sonya's character, feelings and observations through her voice.

Sound progress	Excellent progress
• You include appropriate basic content in your response based on the ideas and details provided.	• You include appropriate content and draw on it to develop your own ideas, but using the appropriate voice.
• You make some attempt to create a voice or role but not always convincingly.	• Your voice or role remains convincing throughout, using language fluently and assuredly.

Key writing skills

In this chapter you are going to develop a range of fundamental writing skills that you will use throughout your IGCSE course.

You will learn how to write a number of forms:

- speeches
- dialogue and interviews
- diary and journal entries
- reports
- news reports
- feature articles
- letters.

You will also learn how to write for a range of purposes:

- to persuade
- to argue
- to analyse
- to explore and discuss
- to inform
- to review
- to describe
- narrative writing.

On their own, some of the skills may seem simple, but remember that they are building blocks to completing larger and more complex tasks later on.

- Tasks that ask you to write in specific forms will require you to understand the structural and stylistic conventions of those forms.

- Questions that ask you to write for specific purposes will require you to understand how the purpose can affect the style and structure of your writing.

Sections 2 and 3 will show you how to apply these key skills to specific question types and coursework tasks.

1 Conventions of speeches

Learning objectives

- To understand the key conventions of different forms of speech.
- To use some of these conventions in a speech.

Speeches are usually formal spoken presentations for a particular purpose – often to persuade an audience to support an idea, or to explain or describe an interesting topic or past event.

Checklist for success

✔ Make sure a strong, lively sense of your own voice or viewpoint comes through.

✔ Structure your speech to get your listeners interested straightaway, keep their attention with new points or ideas, and finish strongly.

✔ Speak directly to the audience by using inclusive pronouns (*you*, *we*) and rhetorical devices. **(See page 88 for more on rhetorical devices.)**

✔ Use informal language, shorter sentences and questions to make a personal connection with your listeners and keep them interested.

✔ Use humour, personal 'everyday' references and powerful imagery or emotive language, as appropriate to your topic and audience.

Exploring skills

① Read this opening to a speech by a school student. Note how a strong personal voice is evident.

Key terms

rhetorical question: a question that is used for effect and does not require an answer

first-person voice and present tense —— *I'm here, interrupting your tasty school lunch, for a simple reason – to ask you to vote for me.*

reason for speech is clearly stated —— *Most of you know me well, I think. I've shown you I can be trusted as a friend and relied on*

friendly abbreviated style —— *as a student in class. I'll listen to your worries, report your wishes and represent you faithfully on the school council. Let's face it – would*

rhetorical question —— *anyone else do the same?*

② Discuss the questions below in pairs. Then write one sentence to describe the overall effect created by this opening. Is it friendly and informal, or hard-hitting and serious?

- What is the speaker's purpose?
- Who do you think the audience is? How does this speech 'speak directly' to them?
- What examples of informal language can you find?
- What examples of humour or personal references are there?

Building skills

That was the first part of a speech. The structure was very clear.

- The **opening topic sentence** set out what the speaker wanted and tried to get the audience's attention.
- The rest of the paragraph kept students' attention by offering reasons **why** they should vote for him.

(3) Now read the following extract from the opening to a speech given by Hillary Clinton in China in 1995.

(4) In pairs, discuss these questions.
- How does the list in paragraph 1 immediately engage with the audience?
- What other examples of the annotated features can you find in the text? What is the effect of each technique?
- How would you describe the speech's overall effect? Is it hard-hitting, inspiring, emotional, funny?

formal opening to conference organisers

sets out the context for why she is speaking

provides further reasons why she is speaking

use of personal pronoun connects with the audience directly

pattern of three sets of images creates vivid idea of togetherness

short sentence for impact

develops and provides further detail on the speech's purpose

rhetorical device: anticipating argument, then answering it

Mrs Mongella, Under Secretary Kittani, distinguished delegates and guests: I would like to thank the Secretary General of the United Nations for inviting me to be part of the United Nations Fourth World Conference on Women. This is truly a celebration – a celebration of the contributions women make in every aspect of life: in the home, on the job, in their communities, as mothers, wives, sisters, daughters, learners, workers, citizens and leaders.

It is also a coming together, much the way women come together every day in every country. We come together in fields and in factories. In village markets and supermarkets. In living rooms and board rooms.

Whether it is while playing with our children in the park, or washing clothes in a river or taking a break at the office water cooler, we come together and talk about our aspirations and concerns. And time and again, our talk turns to our children and our families. However different we may be, there is far more that unites us than divides us. We share a common future.

By gathering in Beijing, we are focusing world attention on issues that matter most in the lives of women and their families: access to education, health care, jobs and credit, the chance to enjoy basic legal and human rights and participate fully in the political life of their countries.

There are some who question the reason for this conference. Let them listen to the voices of women in their homes, neighbourhoods and workplaces. There are some who wonder whether the lives of women and girls matter to economic and political progress around the globe. Let them look at the women gathered here and at Huairou – the homemakers, nurses, teachers, lawyers, policymakers and women who run their own businesses.

It is conferences like this that compel governments and people everywhere to listen, look and face the world's most pressing problems.

repetition of simple refrain, 'Let them.'

powerful emotional appeal

1 Conventions of speeches

Developing skills

As you can see, when you write a speech you need to use techniques that:

- make an impact on your audience
- create an appropriate and convincing voice and style for your audience and topic.

(5) Write down answers to these questions.

- What is Hillary Clinton's message (her **purpose**)?
- Whom is she talking to (her **audience**)?
- How do we know this is a speech rather than a written report in a magazine (the **form**)? Think about the use of tenses, grammar and kinds of sentences used.

As you answer each question, identify the features or techniques that make the speech effective for the purpose, audience or form.

Applying skills

The **structure** of your speech is vital whether you are speaking about world issues or a favourite pastime. You could begin with an **opening** that captures the audience's attention. It could start with an interesting fact or item of information. For example:

> *Did you know the common goose flies thousands of miles to…?*

> *We all remember moments that changed our lives. I first became interested in bird-watching when my father bought me some toy binoculars…*

Or you could begin with yourself and why you are speaking (perhaps referring to your audience).

You need a **middle** that develops your ideas, perhaps using questions to engage listeners.

> *And what about the swallow? Well, it travels an incredible 200 miles a day … (insert more facts) From our roof, I used to watch the swallows overhead, setting off on their incredible journey … (insert more personal **anecdotes**)*

Your **ending** needs to conclude things memorably.

> *Birds are miracles of engineering: no oil needed, no airport; just air, light bones and a sense of direction honed over thousands of years…*

Top tip

Higher-achieving students consider and select different ways of beginning a speech.

Key terms

anecdote: a brief account of an incident in your or someone else's life that makes your argument more believable

> *And that's why I became Head of the World Wide Fund for Nature – to travel the world, describing these miraculous creatures – so you can share my passion.*

Top tip

Make each of your points clearly, using rhetorical language or an anecdote to strengthen your view not to take you off course.

6 Look at this speech task.

> ***Write a speech for your classmates, persuading them to do more physical exercise and/or sport.***

- Decide:
  - who the audience is
  - what the purpose is.
- Look back over Hillary Clinton's speech and the first speech on page 62. Then draft your opening two paragraphs (up to 75 words).
- Try out your opening on a partner. How well did you do?
- If you wish, complete your speech, building on what you have learned.

Sound progress	Excellent progress
<ul><li>You use the first person ('I') and the second person ('you') and make your main point clearly.</li><li>You match your style to your audience.</li></ul>	<ul><li>You engage your audience straight away through personal reference or surprising information.</li><li>You use humour, powerful ideas, imagery, rhetorical questions and repetition to make your point.</li><li>You use a range of sentence lengths for effect.</li></ul>

2 Conventions of dialogue and interviews

Learning objectives

● To understand the key conventions of dialogue and interviews.
● To write effective dialogues and interviews based on given information.

It is important to understand that **dialogue** and interviews have their own conventions. For example, have you ever listened carefully to two friends as they speak? How would you show their conversation as a written text?

Exploring skills

1 Read the dialogue below between a mother and daughter. Then discuss the following with a partner.
   ● What is this dialogue about?
   ● How are Sandra and her mother's reactions to the trip different?
   ● Would you know who was speaking if their names weren't shown? How?

> Sandra: (*eagerly*) It's so exciting! My plane leaves in 24 hours...
>
> Mum: Are you sure you've packed properly? Have you got your visa, travel sickness pills...? You need to prepare properly.
>
> Sandra: (*not listening*) ...and soon I'll be in Paris! I'm so looking forward to it.
>
> Mum: You'll need your phrase book, too. And an umbrella – it's bound to rain. I was looking at the forecast and, although it says it'll be sunny, you never know. Your father and I went to Berlin last year and we got drenched on the first morning.
>
> Sandra: Oh, stop fussing. I'll be fine. Travel is about freedom, not boring plans and 'what ifs'.

Building skills

Dialogues have their own patterns, layout and style.

Content and structure

(2) Reread the dialogue on page 66 and answer these questions.
- How is the dialogue set out on the page?
- What conventions are used to show who is speaking, how they speak and what they are like? (Look at the punctuation and use of italics.)
- Sandra's line when she is '*not listening*' is not a direct response to the line before. Which earlier line does it carry on from?

Style

(3) With a partner, reread the text aloud. Then discuss this question.
- How does this dialogue differ from other kinds of writing? Think about what happens when two people talk together and their speech overlaps and how points are picked up or developed. Also look at the use of more informal phrases.

Developing skills

Sandra is going with a travel company that promises to show her the 'real' Paris. However, her mum has read a travel leaflet that advises visitors to Paris to:
- look out for pickpockets near visitor sites
- purchase 7-day Metro passes as they cost less.

(4) Write the next eight to ten lines of dialogue to continue the script, including both of Sandra's mum's points. How could you also develop Sandra's argument about travel being about 'freedom'?
- Keep the same character style for Sandra and her mother.
- Make the dialogue realistic with some interruptions and overlapping speech.
- Don't just have 'ping-pong' talk of short lines followed by short replies.
- Use the key conventions, including names, punctuation and stage directions.

> **Top tip**
>
> Remember that for directed writing tasks you will need to develop the material you are given to work with. You will often have to construct an argument or present two different viewpoints.

Conventions of dialogue and interviews

Applying skills

5 Read the text below about the Siberian tiger from a conservation website. Next, read the interview in which a conservation expert discusses these issues with a reporter.

- Only 350–400 tigers left
- Used to be in NE China, Mongolia and Korean Peninsula
- Poaching and cutting down trees for logs are main problems; need vast forests to survive
- Body parts used in traditional medicine

Reporter: So – with just under 500 tigers still in the wild, it seems like conservation efforts have failed, haven't they?

Expert: Well, it's true that numbers have dwindled. There were once many more tigers in China, Mongolia and Korea. Places such as the Eastern Himalayas were ideal for them but it's a fragile landscape.

Reporter: (*interrupts*) You haven't answered my question. Have efforts failed? I have been reporting for years on this issue and it's just not improving.

Expert: There are so many problems – we can't do everything. Many, many organisations are committed to protecting different tiger species, but it's a monumental task.

Reporter: So what would you say is the biggest threat to them?

Expert: It's difficult to single one out – but loss of habitat is clearly a huge issue. Once hunting grounds have disappeared, it can take literally hundreds of years to recover them.

Reporter: Right – I get it. No trees, no tigers.

Key terms

synonyms: words with very similar meanings: for example, *cross* and *angry*

Then write brief answers to these questions.
- How are the roles of the reporter and expert shown to be different?
- Where have synonyms or paraphrases been used?
- In what way is this obviously an interview?
- What information was not used in the interview?

On one tiger charity's website, they list some solutions for saving the tiger:

- Identify high-priority tiger populations – larger areas are better, as tigers need 1000 square kilometres free of human activity.
- Train and fund enforcement officers and guards to protect tigers from poachers.
- Develop local community-based conservation programmes.
- Continue well-managed captive breeding (for instance, in game parks) for the most at-risk tigers.

6 Write the interview between the reporter and the manager who runs the charity, using some of the content above. Make sure:

- the reporter continues to speak in the same style
- the charity manager is forceful and tries to get his/her message across about what needs to be done.

Sound progress

- You use the conventions of dialogue and interviews clearly and accurately.
- You provide some sense of the speakers' different characters or voices.

Excellent progress

- You use the conventions of dialogue and interviews correctly and develop ideas to their full potential, making your point of view clear to follow.
- Your dialogue is convincing, with overlapping speech and other realistic elements.
- Your speakers' voices have distinct characters and maintain the reader's interest.

3 Conventions of diaries and journals

Learning objectives

- To understand the key conventions of diary and journal writing.
- To write effective diary entries based on prior information.

A **diary** or **journal** is a personal record of things that have happened to the writer. It can also record the writer's thoughts or feelings.

Exploring skills

(1) Read this diary extract. Who do you think is writing?

> Monday, 11 March
>
>   What a day it's been! I overslept and missed the school bus and then, when I finally arrived, I found out the whole class was on a science trip and they had already left. I felt such a fool. I had to sit on my own outside the head teacher's office all day. It was so boring!
>
>   I'm back home now, sitting in my room. I haven't told mum or dad I missed the trip. If I do, they'll go mad. Dad's home. I'd better pretend I'm asleep.

- date of entry
- use of the first person and past tense
- recounts events that have happened that day
- reference to time/sequence
- personal feelings
- present tense gives sense of things happening now
- future tense shows worries

Building skills

(2) With a partner, discuss the following.
- **Content:** What incident made this student record his thoughts at the end of the day?
- **Structure:** How does the structure reveal what he feels about the situation? Identify three different emotions felt at different times of the day.
- **Style:** How does the style of the writing match the likely age of the person writing?

Checklist for success

Diaries and journals:
- ✔ give a sense of the writer's personality and explain their feelings or changing emotions
- ✔ focus on key moments or incidents in their world
- ✔ (usually) provide a sense of time or sequence.

Developing skills

Your diary entries should aim to develop and extend ideas fully.

(3) How does the following diary entry do this? It is written by Tanya Saunders, a woman who lives in Kenya, East Africa.

> Yesterday, it was cloudy and rainy all day, the crocodiles starved of any sunlight and barely any warmth… then today we awoke to a totally different morning: back to the scorching heat and the crocodiles returning in droves to bask on the sandbanks, while the Goliath Heron, too hot even to finish washing, just sat down in the river and stayed there (and who could blame it?) I had to take a cold shower at midday, just to fortify myself for the onslaught of the afternoon heat.
>
> Tonight, as might be expected, the thunder and lightning are raging again, huge storm clouds fomented in the heat of the day, now towering overhead… and the rain continues, and the bugs multiply, and the flowers prepare to launch into their reproductive cycles once again… the tiny pretty blue *commelina* flowers are already blooming everywhere you look (including on our nascent lawn) and the *sansevieria* we transplanted into our garden (both on the balcony and outside) are sending up a proliferation of shoots, the new spikes breaking the surface of the earth like spiky aliens, and reaching up towards the light…

Tales from Kulafumbi: The Diary of a Nature Lover blog

(4) Answer these questions with a partner.
- What does the writer focus on? Is this like the student's diary? Why/why not?
- How does she use words or phrases related to time and sequence to structure her entry?
- How are tenses used in different sections to show what has happened and is happening?
- How does she use detailed description of the natural world to develop a vivid picture of the weather, and the flowers and plants in the garden?

Applying skills

(5) From reading the second diary, what picture do you get of the writer and her interests?

(6) Write the beginning of a new entry for the next day in which you:
- refer to the time(s) of day and how the weather affects you
- give a very detailed and well-developed observation of some aspect of nature.

Sound progress	Excellent progress
• You write in the first person and give some sense of the person writing.	• You capture the voice of the person and their world.
• You use time references and tenses mostly correctly.	• You provide a vivid portrait of what has happened or is happening to them.
	• You use tenses fluently to move between past, present and future.

4 Conventions of reports

At many times in our lives, we will have to report on situations and events. **Reports** usually tell the reader about an event that has taken place. The writer may analyse or observe these events, or offer a more personal perspective.

Exploring skills

Reports are always written for a particular **audience**. They must be clear and sound convincing.

1 Read this short extract from a report. Then, with a partner, discuss the following.
- What is the subject or topic?
- Who is the likely audience?
- Why is the report split into two paragraphs?
- What sort of report is it?
- Where might you read it?
- Does the report sound convincing?

> The school fundraising day was a great success thanks to you all. Three things made the day such a success: the weather, your hard work and the generosity of visitors and parents.
>
> The day began well, with clear blue skies, but it wasn't too hot. As our families arrived, it began to get really busy. I was working on a stall selling cold drinks. We soon ran out and needed more supplies desperately! I must thank Kiki in particular who cycled all the way to the shop and back with baskets full of lemonade and soda. She's been my best friend since Grade 2 and now you all know why. In fact, just as we restocked, the Mayor appeared and we were able to serve him a wonderfully cool drink.

Building skills

Understanding your audience will make your report sound realistic.
For this, choose the right content, style and structure.

2 Copy and complete the grid based on the extract you have read.

Report to classmates in school magazine about charity day	
Content	It gives clear information, but also covers…
Structure	It could be in time sequence, but could also jump around to topics such as the weather, money raised and number of people there.
Style	

Developing skills

3 Read the longer report below and discuss these questions.

Content

- What is the purpose of this report? How do you know?
- What evidence is there of varied content (use of statistics, expert comment) to support this purpose?

Structure

- How effectively does the report use paragraphs?
- Does it have a strong beginning and ending? Why/why not?

Style

- Is it clear **who** the report is for?
- How formal or informal is it?
- Does it use a variety of sentences to engage listeners?

Top tip

Put different points into separate paragraphs for clarity. Write a strong opening and a powerful conclusion to draw points together.

Top tip

Even for a report aimed at fellow students, you should stick to formal, standard English. And always use the information from any texts you are given.

> Getting students to give to charity is one of our school's biggest challenges, and it's time we and readers of this magazine did something about it.
>
> Recent research I have carried out shows that one in five students has given to charity, although slightly more (two out of five) have been directly involved in some form of fundraising. As our head teacher Mr Marquez said, 'Getting good results and working hard is, of course, vital. But if we are to show that we are a caring community, we must do more, right now, for those less fortunate than ourselves.'
>
> The good news is that since the start of the year, we have raised over $2000 for charity, so we can do it. But is it enough? Surely we can do more.
>
> Tomorrow at 3 p.m. there will be a meeting in the school hall for any teachers and students who wish to organise fundraising events in the coming term. Let's hope it is well attended. Watch this space!

Applying skills

4 Imagine the meeting has taken place. Write a follow up report of at least 100 words including:

- facts or statistics about who and how many attended
- the outcome of the meeting and your views on this, good or bad.

Oxfam

Sound progress	Excellent progress
• You cover the main points of the topic in paragraphs.	• Your text is well ordered with a strong sense of beginning and end.
• You provide some sense of audience and appropriate style and language.	• Your report sounds convincing and real with an excellent sense of audience.

5 Conventions of news reports and feature articles

- To understand the key conventions of newspaper and magazine articles.
- To write reports and articles, using the conventions.

News reports and articles, whether online or in newspapers or magazines, are vital sources of information.

They usually fall into two types. Those that report the main facts or information about very recent specific incidents are **news reports**. Those that discuss, analyse or investigate a topic are called **feature articles**.

Exploring skills

1. Sometimes the headings give clues about what sort of report or article the text is. Try to identify which of the headings belong to news reports, and which to feature articles. Then discuss your answers and explain your decisions with a partner.

> **Top tip**
>
> Succinct vocabulary in headlines can capture an idea immediately.

Temperatures dip to –30° for coldest night on record ——— news article: it is a specific single happening that has just occurred

Why are our winters getting colder?

Ice causes chaos on motorways

Snow go – 36 hours stuck on train

How to predict cold winters

This news report has a very clear structure, which is indicated in the annotations.

Mountain Goat Kills Hiker

by Alex Robinson 19 October 2010

ROBERT BOARDMAN, 63, was hiking with his wife and friend in Olympic National Park on Monday when he was attacked and killed by a mountain goat. The trio was hiking up a popular switchback trail and decided to stop for lunch when the goat approached them and started acting aggressively.

Boardman tried to scare the goat off, but instead of running away, it charged him goring him badly in the leg. More hikers came to try to help Boardman, but the goat stood over the man's body and wouldn't let any other hikers come to his aid.

An hour after the attack, rescuers finally arrived at the scene but Boardman died from his injuries.

Park officials eventually shot and killed the goat.

Apparently, that specific goat had shown aggressive tendencies in the past. 'It has shown aggressive behaviour, however, nothing led us to believe it was appropriate to take the next level of removal,' park spokeswoman Barb Maynes told the Associated Press. 'This is highly unusual. There's no record of anything similar in this park. It's a tragedy. We are taking it extremely seriously and doing our best to learn as much as we can.'

The goat is being examined by scientists to see if it had any diseases that could have caused it to act so aggressively.

Annotations:
- simple headline sums up what happened
- how the incident ended
- main event/ news
- 'expert' comment often with direct quotation
- how the incident happened and what led up to it
- current situation and what is happening next

(2) Read the article. In pairs, discuss and answer these questions.

Content and structure (what is in the article)
- News reports often have the 'who, what, where and when' at the start of the story. Is this the case here? If so, note down each aspect. For example, 'who' is Robert Boardman?
- Expert or witness comments in direct speech are often included to give weight to a story. What do we find out from Barb Maynes? Why wouldn't this be the first paragraph of the report?
- What does the final paragraph focus on?

Style (how it is written)
- To make the report sound objective, writers of news articles tend not to use 'I'. Is this the case here?
- News reports often report events in sequence: what happened, what happened next. Identify any time connectives in the article (for example, *first, later, finally*).
- Most verbs about what happened are in the past tense (for example, *goat* **approached** *them*), but what do you notice about the headline and the last paragraph? Why do you think these are different?

Developing skills

Checklist for success

Feature articles are often more complex than news reports. They:

✔ are often personal (the writer refers to him or herself)
✔ cover wider ground or more complex ideas
✔ offer a distinct viewpoint
✔ have an unusual perspective on the topic
✔ explore ideas more deeply.

Glossary

Bill Sikes: a violent bully and criminal in Charles Dickens's novel *Oliver Twist*
Bull's Eye: Bill Sikes's dog, a Bull terrier, which is brutalised by Sikes
American boxer: a breed of dog often viewed as dangerous

3 Read the opening to this feature article. Then, working in a small group, discuss answers to the questions on page 77.

Why do men love 'dangerous' dogs?
Robert Crampton

— article title explains the topic

There are two problems trying to interview aggressive men with aggressive dogs, one practical, the other ethical. The practical problem is that genuinely aggressive men with genuinely aggressive dogs don't want to be interviewed, still less photographed. These **Bill Sikes** characters tend to disappear, swearing, with **Bull's Eye** around a corner as you approach. Appearances can in any case be deceptive. You find some likely-looking candidate togged up in Lonsdale and adidas, teeth missing, shaved head, 80 lb of canine energy straining at the leash, and he turns out to be a sweet guy with a sweet dog.

— opening sentence is about problems interviewing certain dog owners

— descriptive detail paints picture of dog owner

One such was Lee Randall, 36, an asbestos remover by trade, whom I met in Bow in East London, his **American boxer** Che at his feet. 'Some people are scared of her, but it's not the dog, it's the owner. It's like a baby, or a computer. You get out what you put in. It's the same as anything. A dog is only aggressive if it's taught to be.' Che is fine around people, says Randall, although squirrels are another matter.

— personal involvement of writer

— interviewee's comments

Randall wouldn't want to be seen walking around with a toy poodle, but that doesn't mean he has a boxer to be aggressive, or macho, or as a status symbol. It means he has a boxer because he likes the way boxers look and behave. It's a similar story with Staffordshire bull terriers, the most popular dog in London, according to the Kennel Club. A lot of people think they're ugly, but beauty is in the eye of the beholder. A lot of people think Staffs must be nasty too, because of the way they look, but they're actually renowned for their good temperament, especially around children.   *The Times*

— writer widens the discussion

Structure and content

- Is this feature article about a news event that has **just** happened? Check the opening paragraph and see if it describes a particular incident.
- Compare the mountain goat news report with this one. How is the structure different? For example, think about how the report recounts information about the event.

Style

- What word from the headline makes it clear this is a feature article rather than a news report?
- What can you **infer** about the viewpoint of the writer based on the language he uses? (For example: why does he put '"dangerous" dogs' in inverted commas and what does he say about 'Staffs'?)

> **Key terms**
>
> **infer**: to work out a viewpoint or subtle meaning from clues in the language used or information given

Applying skills

4 Write your own feature article on 'dangerous animals'. Include:

- some of the ideas or facts from the goat report and the dangerous dogs article
- a clear viewpoint: whether you think it is humans or animals that are to blame for most attacks.

You could start with the goat attack but don't make it the whole focus. For example, you could begin:

> The recent death of a hiker, gored by a mountain goat, might make us think that animals are a real threat to humans, whatever the species. However...

Sound progress

- You use relevant information from what has been supplied.
- Your language is mostly accurate with simple sentences explaining your main ideas.
- Your style is mostly appropriate, including a mix of factual and personal content.

Excellent progress

- You show clear understanding of the information you have been supplied and use the material in an original way.
- You use a wide range of factual and personal language, and show that you have inferred meaning from the material supplied.
- Your style is convincing with appropriate tone and register.

Conventions of letters

- To understand the key conventions of two types of letter.
- To write a letter, using these conventions, to suit a particular purpose and audience.

When was the last time you wrote a letter? Perhaps you use text messages or email when you want to contact someone. However, in some areas of life, written letters are still very important.

Checklist for success

When writing letters make sure you:
- ✔ think about the **audience**. (This will change your style and possibly the layout.)
- ✔ focus on **purpose** (why you are writing and what information you need to reveal).
- ✔ match your **style** to both. (Decide how formal or informal you should be.)

Exploring skills

(1) Here are two short letters. Compare their style, tone and structure. What is similar and different about them?

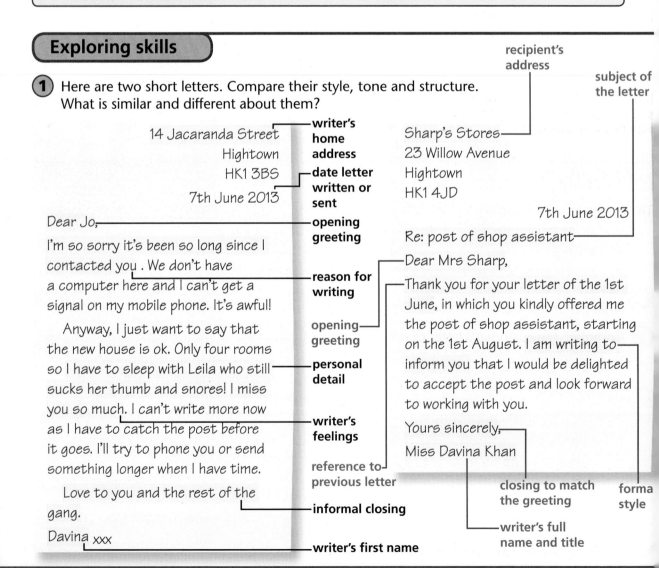

14 Jacaranda Street
Hightown
HK1 3BS

7th June 2013

Dear Jo,

I'm so sorry it's been so long since I contacted you . We don't have a computer here and I can't get a signal on my mobile phone. It's awful!

Anyway, I just want to say that the new house is ok. Only four rooms so I have to sleep with Leila who still sucks her thumb and snores! I miss you so much. I can't write more now as I have to catch the post before it goes. I'll try to phone you or send something longer when I have time.

Love to you and the rest of the gang.

Davina xxx

Sharp's Stores
23 Willow Avenue
Hightown
HK1 4JD

7th June 2013

Re: post of shop assistant

Dear Mrs Sharp,

Thank you for your letter of the 1st June, in which you kindly offered me the post of shop assistant, starting on the 1st August. I am writing to inform you that I would be delighted to accept the post and look forward to working with you.

Yours sincerely,

Miss Davina Khan

Labels: writer's home address · date letter written or sent · opening greeting · reason for writing · opening greeting · personal detail · writer's feelings · reference to previous letter · informal closing · writer's first name · recipient's address · subject of the letter · formal style · closing to match the greeting · writer's full name and title

Building skills

(2) With a partner, discuss what you notice in particular about the different styles used in the letters. Consider:
- choice of vocabulary
- abbreviations and sentence types **(see pages 38–41 for more on this)**
- punctuation
- openings and closings.

Developing skills

(3) Unfortunately Davina makes a poor start to her first day when dealing with a customer. The customer has now written a letter of complaint to Mrs Sharp.

makes the reason for writing clear ———

Dear Mrs Sharp,

I'm writing to complain about the unsatisfactory level of service I received when I visited your store yesterday.

develops and begins to explain in what areas the shop failed ———

As you are aware, I am a regular customer and expect high levels of courtesy and advice from your staff. Unfortunately, your new assistant, Miss Khan, did not meet my expectations in either regard.

links to and develops the previous point, beginning to specify the bad service she received ———

Firstly, it was extremely disappointing that when I approached the counter…

Applying skills

The customer then explains:
- the first specific problem with Davina (perhaps she ignored her or was reading a magazine rather than paying attention)
- the second specific problem (perhaps Davina was unable to help her in some way)
- what action the customer would like Mrs Sharp to take.

(4) Complete the customer's letter of complaint, developing the points in the plan into full paragraphs. Make sure you write with an appropriate level of formality.

Sound progress	Excellent progress
• You use basic conventions (how letters start, end and so on) correctly. • Your text presents the main points in simple sequence.	• You use conventions well and adapt the level of formality appropriately to audience and purpose. • You develop and link ideas fluently in a sequence of paragraphs. • Your sense of voice is convincing and sustained.

Writing to analyse

Learning objectives

- To understand the key devices and techniques for analytical writing.
- To use these techniques in writing.

Exploring skills

When you analyse something you look closely at it in an objective way, usually to find the answer to a question. For example, you might have to analyse factors for the best venue for a party. Analysis often involves making a judgement based on evidence and sometimes weighing up different interpretations.

Checklist for success

In an analysis:
- ✔ **select relevant information**, viewpoints and data to act as **evidence**
- ✔ focus on **specific details** and base **judgements** on evidence
- ✔ explain **how** and **why**, using the **vocabulary of analysis**
- ✔ **synthesise** (draw together) your findings to come to a conclusion.

Here, a teacher writes a report analysing a student's first day of work experience in a shop.

> My first impression of how Andre is coping with the work has not been very positive. I arrived early to meet him on his first day, but he was late and arrived wearing clothing that was far too casual for the smart appearance demanded by the shop owner Mrs Duvalle. Although this is a shop selling groceries, herbs and spices, it has a strong local reputation and needs to maintain it.

1 What do you think is the main purpose of this analysis?
- ○ To describe what the shop sells.
- ○ To tell the reader about Mrs Duvalle's character.
- ○ To explain why Andre's work experience did not start well.

Any analysis must come across as fair and objective with judgments based on evidence.

2 Identify the **analysis** and the **evidence** in the two statements below.

> *The number of passengers using the ferry has declined from 50 or so each day to just a handful (five to ten), which suggests the rise in fares has put travellers off.*

> *Young people clearly want more portable devices, as sales of iPads and other tablet PCs have rocketed in the last year.*

Building skills

Structure

How you structure your analysis is vital. By explaining specific events or information, you can build towards a general conclusion in which you weigh up what has occurred.

Topic sentences can help to structure your analysis. These can naturally set up what comes next. For example, here the teacher who is assessing Andre's performance at work experience comments on his second day at the shop:

The next day, the impression Andre made was not much — topic sentence introduces the second mistake
better. This time, the problem was not punctuality, but his —
lack of focus. An important local customer came in and — summarises the new problem
asked for brown sugar, butter beans and okra. It took Andre
far too long find the okra, so when he came to give the — explains how it happened
customer her sugar, he was hurried and gave her a bag of
cumin powder instead. Clearly, it would be a public relations
disaster for the shop and for Andre if the customer ended — conclusion explores the consequences
up using the wrong product in her cooking.

(See pages 46–47 for more on topic sentences.)

In other words:

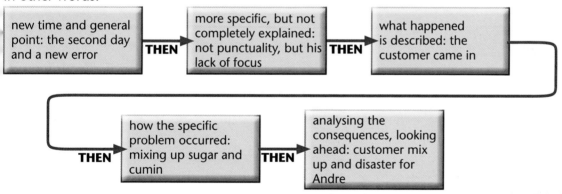

In this way, you can see that the writer is building an analysis of how successful the work experience has been, organising it in time order.

(3) The third day of work experience comes along. Write the paragraph, completing the topic sentence and adding specific details:

As if the cumin mistake wasn't enough, on the third
day, matters... Having been late, and then made a
foolish error, this time he... What happened was that
he... but/so/and as a result...

> **Top tip**
>
> Notice that the first sentence of the third paragraph links back to paragraph two by referring to the 'cumin mistake'. This kind of internal structuring is a feature of high quality writing.

7 | Writing to analyse

Explaining logically how and why something happened is key to analysis. The following linking phrases can be very useful and will help you to **structure** your analysis logically.

Cause and effect connectives

These show or explain the results of actions or ideas:

- *thus, therefore, in this way*
- *this shows/means that*
- *as we can see.*

Conclusive connectives

These types of words or phrases indicate what can be **inferred** or **deduced**:

- *as a result*
- *the evidence demonstrates/reveals/suggests/implies that*
- *one can conclude/surmise/infer/deduce that.*

(4) With a partner, quickly analyse your classroom surroundings. Using analytical words or phrases, explain what the effects of the conditions might be on the class's education. Your analysis can be humorous like the following example:

> *The cracks in the paintwork* **demonstrate** *the school's efforts to create a traditional, comforting environment.* **As a result,** *students feel at home...*

Developing skills

Style

Using language subtly, for instance by making slight changes to the verbs used to explain or analyse, can have an impact on meaning too. Read these two sample analyses:

A

The data shows a rapid decline in the number of tigers roaming freely in our area. In 2000, there were 43 individual animals sighted and recorded; by 2008, this had dropped to just seven. When measured alongside the amount of deforestation over the same period – up by 80% – then there is a clear correlation between the two.

B

The data seems to show a decline in the number of tigers in our area. In 2000, there were perhaps 43 individual animals sighted and recorded; by 2008, this had dropped to seven. When measured alongside the amount of deforestation over the same period – up by 80% – then it might be argued that there is some correlation between the two.

(5) With a partner, discuss these points.

- How does the highlighted vocabulary in B suggest a different conclusion from A?
- What words have been omitted from B? What effect has this had on the tone of the analysis?
- Analytical, numerical language can lend authority to texts. Find examples of it in A and B.

Top tip

Try to make your analysis sound authoritative. To create an impersonal tone for an analysis, avoid using 'I'. This will make what is said sound more objective.

Applying skills

The best analysis will **synthesise** (draw together) different pieces of evidence in a conclusion, but without repeating earlier information word for word. For example, here Andre himself analyses his own performance on work experience:

> Looking back, I think it is fair to say my work experience was very challenging. I made several mistakes, but that is to be expected in a new job, and confronting problems and overcoming them is part of growing up. Perhaps working in a shop isn't for me – but at least I know that now.

Top tip

This synthesis of information in analysis is particularly relevant to directed writing tasks where you are asked to adapt the text provided in your own writing. **(See pages 34–36 for more on synthesis.)**

(6) How does this paragraph draw conclusions? Think about how specific events are summed up in a few brief words.

(7) Now try drawing your own conclusion. Read these two short paragraphs from an analysis of mobile phone usage. Then write a paragraph to sum them up **without** repeating ideas directly.

> The increase in mobile phone usage can partly be attributed to size. In the mid to late 90s, mobile phones were the size of small bricks and could hardly be called 'portable'. You certainly could not put them in your pocket. Now, however, technology can be packed into something not much bigger than a small bar of chocolate.
>
> Another factor relates to cost. Whilst mobile phones were originally an expensive investment, in many countries nowadays it is possible to buy a phone for as little as 20 dollars, even one with quite a few features. Consequently, even small children now have access to them.
>
> To conclude, we can see that...

Sound progress	**Excellent progress**
• You make points clearly, with some attempt at an appropriately informative style and a sense of ending.	• You make points logically, with a clear sense of structure leading to conclusions. • You use analytical vocabulary to give a sense of authority and clear judgement.

Writing to explore and discuss

● To understand how to explore or discuss a key topic or issue.
● To apply these skills to your own writing.

If you are asked to discuss a topic, you need to show you have thought about it in depth by taking into account other viewpoints and by including anecdotes, as well as a range of evidence, such as factual information.

Exploring skills

1 What issue or subject is being discussed in the opening to this article below?

Last week I was taken to a new restaurant in my local town by a friend, and was astonished to see on the menu such things as 'yarrow flower shortbread' and 'nettle soup'. These rather weird items are representative of a new craze – food that has been 'foraged', or gathered in the wild, and then cooked in often quite posh restaurants. There are at least three other restaurants locally that serve strange sounding things that you would normally regard as weeds or wild plants. My friend reckons foraged food is the future. 'It's natural, it's unusual, and it tastes great!' he says. I'm not so sure.

2 Find examples of each of the following:
● a personal anecdote (a story about something that has happened to the writer)
● data or factual evidence about the issue
● comment or viewpoint on the issue from others.

A key element of an article that discusses or explores a topic is to draw on a range of well-chosen evidence or ideas. Here are some further pieces of information about another issue: the benefits of eating chocolate.

100g dark chocolate per day could reduce the risk of a heart attack or stroke by 21%. (*British Medical Journal* research)

Dr Miles Better: 'Eating chocolate is fine, provided it is in moderation and you stick to dark chocolate.'

I bought a large bar of chocolate recently and finished it all in one go, and I felt really guilty, especially when the dentist told me a week later that I needed two fillings!

3 Identify the expert comment; the personal anecdote; the factual information.

4 Now create one paragraph which links all three of these elements together. Copy and complete the rest of the section below starting with the anecdote, then using the factual information and finally adding the expert comment.

> I bought a large bar of chocolate recently and finished it all in one go, and I felt really guilty, especially when the dentist told me a week later that I needed two fillings! However, recent research by ...
>
> In addition, Doctor ...

Top tip

Facts and statistics are great, but don't let them dominate your writing. You need variety in your articles – personal views as well as factual information – otherwise it could become very boring.

Writing to explore and discuss

Conclusions

The 'meat' of your essay will be the detailed evidence and your own and others' viewpoints, but it is always important to end well. This is not 'argue' or 'persuade' writing, so a more general ending, which raises questions or sums things up, can work very well, even if it hints at the personal viewpoint of the writer. For example:

> So, is chocolate the secret to long life or a dangerous addiction? On the evidence provided, it could be both, but I for one won't be abandoning chocolate altogether, at least not yet ...

Discuss the following with a partner.
- What two phrases in the conclusion sum up the two sides of the argument?
- What seems to be the viewpoint of the writer, based on his final phrase?
- How is it toned down by the final few words?

Developing skills

Imagine you have been asked to write an article about the health benefits and risks of eating chocolate for your school magazine.

5. Discuss with a friend which of these personal anecdotes would be the best way to begin. Think about:
   - the audience (who will read your text)
   - what the subject of the article is
   - the purpose – to entertain and inform.

> Every break-time, I notice hundreds of students tucking into their favourite chocolate bar. But do they really know what effect that chocolate is having on them?

> On the way to school today, I passed a shop with long queues of students outside. I wondered if they were waiting to stock up on chocolate for the day ...

> I love chocolate. It's great. And nothing is going to persuade me to stop eating it.

Applying skills

The particular task you complete may give some information from
a passage to base your own writing on. For example, here is some
more detail about chocolate and what is good/bad about it.

- Chocolate usually contains large quantities of anti-oxidants
  (chemicals that can prevent the build-up of harmful
  pollutants in the body and lower blood-pressure)
- Contains caffeine which can help make you more alert
- Typical ingredients in a chocolate bar – butter, sugar, cream
  or milk, lots of calories that can make you put on weight

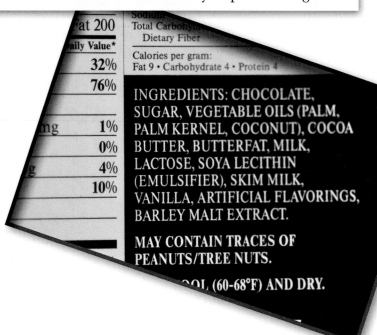

6 Write the first two paragraphs of an article
discussing chocolate and its benefits or disadvantages.
Make sure you:

- start with an appropriate personal anecdote (use the
  one from 'Developing skills' or make one up of
  your own)
- use at least one of the pieces of evidence provided
- if you can, add a comment from either an expert or someone
  with an interest in chocolate (for example, a shopkeeper,
  parent or school student).

Sound progress

- You discuss several aspects of the issue
  using some evidence to support what
  you say.

Excellent progress

- You explore the issue in real depth,
  addressing different viewpoints and
  providing a full range of evidence.

Writing to persuade

- To understand the key techniques writers use to persuade others.
- To learn how to write a persuasive text.

When you write to persuade, you are writing to change someone's beliefs or point of view. To achieve this, you will need to make them understand the benefits of what you are proposing. There are a range of persuasive techniques that can help you do this.

Exploring skills

Read this extract from a parent writing to the Principal of a school:

> Just picture the street by our school if you were to ask the council to ban cars. Instead of huge metal monsters belching out smoke, grinding their gears and skidding to a halt with a screech of brakes, all you would hear would be the happy chatter of little children and their parents.

1 Discuss the following with a partner.
- What is the writer trying to persuade the Principal of the school to do?
- Which senses does the extract appeal to?
- How is this approach effective? What is being promised if the Principal does as the writer suggests?

Building skills

Rhetorical questions

Persuasive texts are often strengthened by making direct appeals to the reader in the form of rhetorical questions that are difficult to argue with. For example:

After all, what could be more important than the safety and well-being of our precious children?

It would be very difficult for the Principal of the school to disagree! But a balance must be drawn between direct appeal and being rude or aggressive.

2 Which of the following would make the most suitable and powerful final sentence?
- **a)** *Wouldn't it be great to limit cars near the school?*
- **b)** *Do you really want to gamble with the health and happiness of your pupils?*
- **c)** *Do you want to be seen as that annoying man who wouldn't ban cars?*

3 Think of two more suitable rhetorical questions to end this paragraph.

Developing skills

You also need to include clear evidence for your viewpoint, in the form of facts or statistics, expert opinion or a personal anecdote. All of these can strengthen the point you wish to make.

End your point with a call to action – giving a clear sense of what you want to happen next – as shown below:

The benefits of a traffic-free zone outside school are clear. ——— clear topic sentence to introduce the point

Recent research has shown that once cars are banned, up to 70% of parents walk their children to school; ——— factual evidence to support the point

which would be incredibly beneficial to our children's health. ——— specific benefit from the evidence

This is why I am asking you now to contact the local council to create a 'Traffic Free Zone' outside the school. ——— call to action

(4) Discuss the call to action with a partner.
- What exactly does the writer want to be done now?
- Which of these other calls to action could end the paragraph?
  - (a) *So please act now and contact the local council to create a 'Traffic Free Zone' outside the school.*
  - (b) *I suppose the next step could be to contact the local council.*
- Which phrases make one suitable and the other unsuitable?

Applying skills

(5) Write a further two paragraphs to the Principal in which you put forward the benefits of the 'Traffic Free Zone'. You could mention:
- how parents who drive their children to school often argue over parking
- the benefit to children socialising on their walk to school.

Alternatively, use your own ideas or arguments.

Checklist for success

✔ Begin by grabbing your reader's attention with a 'promise' or an 'image'.
✔ State what you want to happen.
✔ Support this point with evidence.
✔ Use imagery or other sensory detail to create an impact.
✔ Appeal directly to the reader using personal pronouns and strong adjectives.
✔ End with a rhetorical question or include a final call to action.

Sound progress	Excellent progress
• You make clear, logical developed points using a limited range of persuasive techniques.	• Your points are logical and developed, but also powerfully expressed, using the full range of persuasive techniques.

10 Writing to argue

- To understand the key techniques writers use to argue a viewpoint.
- To learn how to write an argumentative text.

Exploring skills

It is an important to have the right skills to **put forward an argument** that considers the facts and ideas around an issue, and then reaches a **conclusion** in which you state your viewpoint. **Structuring** your argument logically is a vital part of this.

Checklist for success

Clear structure

✔ Make points clearly and develop them logically.
✔ Vary sentence lengths and types to achieve different effects.
✔ Write strong openings and endings.

Content

✔ Consider arguments for and against (even when arguing for one point of view).
✔ Add **evidence** or examples to support the points made.
✔ Include expert **opinions** and direct quotations.
✔ Where appropriate, use **rhetoric** or **anecdote** to support your case.

---

1 Read this opening to an argument text:

> It is clear that the school day is much too long. Classes full of half-asleep students, teachers checking their watches and poor-quality work all make this very obvious.

Key terms

opinions: something the writer believes or feels: for example, whether he or she likes something

Discuss these questions with a partner.

- What is the writer's point of view? Where is it expressed in the text?
- How does he or she support their viewpoint with evidence?
- Which, if any, of the features in the checklist are used by the writer?
- How successful is the use of these features?

Building skills

Structure: arguments for and against

There are different ways of structuring argument texts, where you need to consider both sides of the argument. Let us look at these, using the issue of bike rental schemes and whether they should be introduced into a particular place.

The simplest structure is as follows:

> **Paragraph 1:** introduction – the issue: what bike rental schemes are
>
> **Paragraphs 2–4:** points for bike rental schemes in your town
>
> **Paragraphs 5–7:** points against bike rental schemes
>
> **Paragraph 8:** conclusion: you weigh up the points, and give your opinion.

However, there is a more interesting approach: you decide what your opinion is, and use the technique of counter-argument/rebuttal to argue your case.

Read this extract from a bike rental scheme example response:

> **Bike rental schemes** are very popular right now, but are they really worth it? After all, it costs a lot of money to build the **docking stations**, create and plan signage and run the schemes. However, think of the income generated. In London in 2011, a bike scheme raised £7 million in one year. Money well spent, in my opinion.

(2) Note down the **counter-argument against bike rental schemes** that is put forward.

(3) Now identify the **rebuttal**, and the word which introduces it.

(4) Find the short sentence that emphasises the writer's own personal view.

This approach can be summarised as follows:

> **Paragraph 1:** introduction – the issue
>
> **Paragraph 2:** point 1 plus counter-argument
>
> **Paragraphs 3–4:** points 2 and 3, with counter-arguments alongside
>
> **Paragraph 5:** any further points which strengthen your key view but don't have counter-arguments
>
> **Paragraph 6:** conclusion – summing up the evidence

Using evidence

Good arguments use evidence. This might be statistical or based on ideas or others' opinions. Read the next paragraph of the same article:

> As for the idea that you need to be earning a lot of money to hire a bike, just think of the alternatives. As **commuter** Jon Devani says, 'I used to have to pay to park my car at the station and then for my rail ticket – now I'm paying less for the bike and I'm getting fitter too.' Research has shown that, of 100 people questioned who use bike schemes, over 65% said they were good value compared to other forms of transport. It's hard to argue against that, isn't it?

5 Now note down two types of evidence the writer uses to rebut the argument being challenged in the paragraph.

6 How does the use of longer sentences to provide this evidence help to put it across convincingly?

7 Now write the third paragraph. Try to match the style of the first and the second.
- Start with a new problem (for example, you live too far to cycle all the way to work).
- Suggest the solution (it could be to take the bus so far and then pick up a bike).
- Finish the paragraph with a short sharp sentence, or a rhetorical question.

> **Top tip**
>
> Rhetorical questions in 'argue' texts tend to be slightly less emotive than in a 'persuade' text and are used more to sum up or round off a point.

Checklist for success

✔ One point introduced → Counter-point introduced → Conclusion drawn

Developing skills

8 Using a variety of connectives is also vital in structuring your argument. Which of the following phrases could replace the ones in bold in the argument text below? Rewrite the paragraph using suitable connectives from the list provided.

firstly	however	this means that	in this way
thus	to begin with	yet	in contrast

> **On the one hand,** we could argue that wolves are violent predators who will prey on any weaker creatures they come across. **On the other,** we can see the evidence of a place such as Yellowstone Park. When wolves were reintroduced there, much to the consternation of many local people, they brought down the elk numbers. **As a result,** the balance of the eco-system was restored as the destruction of willow trees, which elks eat, was reduced.

9 Now read these points related to making the centre of a local town pedestrianised.

Joni Muller, 35, mother of 2 young children: 'I would definitely go into town to shop if there weren't any cars – it would be so much safer.'

even when weather is bad, people won't be allowed to park

safer – less traffic

more space, no cars, trucks, vans

10% drop in sales when similar scheme introduced in nearby town

difficult for senior citizens who are less mobile

encourage families, healthy – less pollution, car fumes

difficult for shop owners to take deliveries

estimated 70% improvement in air quality according to research by local environment group.

shopkeeper, Raj Kapoor, 52: 'At the moment my older customers can park nearby, but that will change. I worry they won't bother to come in.'

(10) Sort these arguments into those 'for' and those 'against' pedestrianisation, using a table like the one below.

For	Against
Safer – less traffic	10% drop in sales for similar scheme in another town.

Applying skills

(11) Now write an article for your local paper in which you argue for or against the pedestrianisation of your local town. You will need to:

- weigh up both sides of the argument
- decide which one you will support
- select the order of the points you want to make from your for/against table to make a logical and developed argument
- consider counter-arguments and then 'knock them down'
- use a range of connectives to logically support or argue against one view or another
- use rhetorical questions, if appropriate, to support what you say
- use a range of short and long sentences for effect: for example, to stress your point of view or put evidence across convincingly.

Sound progress	Excellent progress
• You include arguments for and against, but your expression is a bit weak and you don't use the full-range of argumentative techniques.	• You synthesise all the key points, evidence, personal opinions in a fluently-expressed text using the full range of argumentative techniques.

11 Writing to inform

- To understand the key features and purposes of writing to inform and explain.
- To write an informative piece of text.

Being able to provide clear and logical information to help your reader understand a process or find out more about a subject is a vital skill for life and learning.

Top tip

Including clear and logical information can also be a useful way to strengthen an argument or persuasive piece.

Checklist for success

✔ Make sure you include the most important information required and use a range of different types of information.
✔ Organise the information in a way that is clear to follow, using connectives and paragraphs.
✔ Make the text accessible and interesting to read.

Exploring skills

1 Read this short extract from a magazine providing information about a new 'app'. Then make notes on whether:
- the main information about the 'app' is provided and where
- the information is provided in sentences that are clear and easy to follow.

TrakkMeNow

Price: $2.00. Produced by TrakkWebAppsLtd

TrakkMeNow is a new app that allows the user to utilise the cell phone as a personal coach and training partner. It includes built-in GPS to track the user's running, cycling, canoeing, skiing. It also provides data on distance travelled, speed and calories burnt. In addition, it has audio feedback for every 5 km travelled. For iPhone, Blackberry and most other devices.

Building skills

You will note that in this text the information provided is **impersonal** and quite **formal**. There is no real sense of the writer or their viewpoint as the purpose is to provide clear, unbiased information.

The following text about another cell phone 'app' is rather too informal and has too much personal **opinion** for an information text.

Key terms

opinion: something the writer believes or feels: for example whether he or she likes a building

Dragon Hunter King 2020

Price: $10. Produced by DragonHKEnterprises

This fantastic, cool new app makes you – yes, YOU – King of the Dragon Hunters. You can download MILLIONS of superb locations (mountains, castles, palaces, swamps – you get the idea), track down the baddies (the dragons) and stab 'em, shoot 'em or zap 'em! Turn into magical new shapes or become invisible in a flash.

(2) Rewrite the text so it is an information text only. Start:

This new app…

Developing skills

Of course, there will be occasions when you are writing to inform **and** writing for another purpose: for example, when persuading a friend to visit you. Here is the opening of a letter that combines **fact** and opinion.

Dear Rosa,

You must come to see us! There's so much to do here and I can't wait to show you round. Our castle has been here for 1000 years (it's perched at the top of the hill just behind our house), and there's the old harbour full of fishing boats.

However, don't worry! We do have modern attractions too. Our cinema has five screens. It's a ten-minute walk from here, so we can go whenever you like.

Shahena

> **Key terms**
>
> **fact**: something known to be true: for example, the date a building was built

> **Top tip**
>
> Topic sentences such as 'You must come to see us!' and 'We do have modern attractions too.' help introduce the information and opinions that follow. This sequencing helps to make the text clear and logical.

(3) Identify the factual information and the opinions.

Good informative writing also makes links and connections between ideas clear by using connectives.

Applying skills

(4) Imagine you are the organiser of a local festival or event in your area. Write two paragraphs of a letter informing businesses in other towns about the event, inviting them sponsor it in some way. Your main purpose is to give clear, accurate information. You could include information about:
- the event or festival
- advertising or other business opportunities (such as taking a stall).

Sound progress	Excellent progress
• You include the relevant information but not in a particularly logical or clear sequence.	• You include the relevant information, introduced in a logical sequence and linked by clear connectives.

12 Writing to review

- To understand the key features and aims of writing to review.
- To write a review combining information and opinion.

We all have opinions about the stories we read, the television programmes we watch and the computer games we play. But to review effectively, it is important to interest others and provide information at the same time.

Exploring skills

Here is a short review of a film. Note how it provides information and a personal opinion.

The Fisherman's Friend (PG)

Director: Danny Spielstein.   Running time: 1 hr, 30 mins.

This charming, coming-of-age movie features Brad Jolina as the lonely boy, Joe, befriended by ageing fisherman Morgan Freebody. When he's made an orphan, Joe runs away from the chaotic, grimy children's home run by Mrs Mallock (a truly frightening Jennifer Anybone). Hunted by the police, Joe hides out in an old boat. Sentimental, but somehow incredibly touching, so don't miss this tear-jerker. Bring plenty of tissues!

adjective expresses the writer's opinion

noun phrase sums up the type of film and story

actors and their roles summed up in the same sentence

first part of the plot told in present tense verbs

expanded noun phrase to cram in information

end sums up the opinion and style of film all in one

(1) With a partner, discuss any film, story or television programme you have seen or read recently. Sum up the main story and give your opinion of it as concisely as possible and without giving away the ending.

Building skills

Adding detail through the use of adjectives and adverbs is key to conveying your opinion in reviews.

(2) Complete the sentence on page 97 by adding:
- adjectives that show a positive or negative viewpoint or opinion
- adjectives to describe the character, the role the actor plays and other details
- adverbs to suggest how well or convincingly something is done.

Key terms

noun phrase: the combination of a noun and adjectives: for example, *coming-of-age movie*; it can be expanded to create a descriptive phrase: for example, *action-packed, drama-rich, challenging movie*

You can make the details up!

> This … (*adjective*) comedy stars Matt Le Blond as an … (*adjective*) school teacher who … (*adverb*) falls in love with … (*adjective*), … (*adjective*) nurse Jemma Jones.

Developing skills

It is also important to make sure that all the key elements of a text, film or game are covered. For a book, these might be characters, plot, setting and themes.

Here, a student describes reading *The Tempest* by William Shakespeare.

> Reading <u>The Tempest</u> for the first time, I was struck by the powerful themes and plot. Set on a magical island, it tells the story of the exiled Duke of Milan, his daughter Miranda and the mysterious Prospero, who conjures up a storm with his magic spirit Ariel to get revenge on his enemies.
>
> This timeless play also explores themes of government and politics, as well as mercy and justice, all reflected in the wonderful poetry and dialogue.

3 Read the student's writing and note down:
- how each paragraph deals with slightly different aspects of the play
- how paragraph 2 links back to the first
- how complex sentences are used.

Applying skills

4 Choose any story, play, programme or film and make brief notes about its plot, characters, themes and key features. Then jot down some viewpoint adjectives and adverbs (like *charming, exciting, ridiculous, implausibly*). Finally, using your notes, write the opening two or three paragraphs of a review.

Checklist for success

✔ Discuss the main elements (but not the ending) of the text being reviewed.
✔ Include your viewpoint, using adjectives/adverbs to convey opinions.
✔ Write mostly in the present tense: for example, *This play explores...*

Sound progress

- You include the main elements of what you are reviewing but do not combine opinion and information in a fluent and entertaining way.

Excellent progress

- You combine key elements of what you are reviewing with opinion so the reader is well informed, but also gets a strong sense of your viewpoint through well-chosen vocabulary.

13 Writing to describe: atmosphere

- To understand how to create atmosphere in descriptive writing.

The best descriptive writing transports the reader to another time, place and experience by using the senses to paint a picture, convey taste, smell, touch and sound, and suggest movement or gesture. Creating a memorable or **evocative** atmosphere is the key.

Exploring skills

Read these two openings to a text that begins: *Stepping onto the beach I see …*

> … through my tired eyes, rain lashing the rusty old boats in the harbour, the rotten hulks of decaying dinghies, like sleeping, weary beasts, and the fishermen, rolling damp cigarettes under the grey, looming curtain of clouds.

> … the sparkling light of the early sun, shimmering like strings of pearls, across the placid surface of blue. At the water's edge, I smile at the sight of the slim young men, their ankles ringed with whitened salt, as they step from their canoes onto the ivory sand and laugh together as they carry their pots of pink crabs to the shelter of the trees.

Key terms

connotations: the associated ideas that a word brings to mind

Specific words and phrases in descriptions create **connotations** in your mind. For example:

```
dark, shaded room ─┐
                    ├─ grey, looming curtain ─┬─ flat, long screen
┌───────────────────┘     of clouds          └─
└─
```

1. Copy the spider diagram and add two more connotations.

2. With a partner, discuss the following questions.
   - What overall **effect** or **atmosphere** is created in each description? (Use adjectives such as *dull, joyful* or *gloomy*.)
   - What clues do we get (if any) to the writer's **mood** or **emotions**?
   - Which words and phrases help to achieve both of these?

Top tip

Writers create associations for readers by using imagery such as **similes** or **metaphors**. For example: linking *decaying dinghies* to *weary beasts*.

Building skills

(3) Now choose one or more of the following ideas and write a further sentence to add to one of the texts on page 98. Try to create connotations and to sustain the atmosphere throughout.

- Other people or children on the beach
- Buildings such as a cafe, bar, houses, hotels or fishing huts

> ### Checklist for success
>
> ✔ Create vivid associations with **imagery (similes** or **metaphors)** to add atmosphere.
> ✔ Use sensory language to describe shape, sound, feel, taste or smell, as appropriate.

Developing skills

Here are some notes a writer made on a different descriptive topic: *A trip to a remote place.*

- pathway through deep rain-forest
- me and what I was wearing
- ancient, ruined temple
- leaving camp/what I had for breakfast
- my companion and what he/she is like
- spider that I see on a tree
- sky seen through the trees
- heavy rain which begins to fall

(4) Note down:

- which elements are **most important** and could create a **powerful overall atmosphere**
- which elements you might leave out.

Now read these alternative extracts from a text on the same topic:

A I gasped at the myriad colours of the spider which sparkled in the raindrops falling like a shattered necklace through the amber branches …

B My companion stepped back, blood draining from her face, as the spider fixed her with its tiny black eyes, its body no more than an inch or two away on the twisted limbs of a tree which bent over us …

(5) For each extract, list any details which help to create the mood. Look particularly at:

- the **spider's colours** and **the appearance** of the **raindrops** in text A
- the **tree's shape and position** in text B.

Applying skills

(6) Write at least two paragraphs from this piece describing the scene and mood on your arrival at a remote place. If you wish, use opening sentences A or B and/or the notes above.

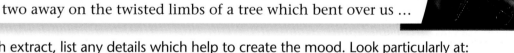

Sound progress	Excellent progress
• You include a range of descriptive details and create a particular atmosphere.	• Your descriptions are vivid, and create powerful associations in the mind with an overall atmosphere.

14 Writing to describe: structure

Structure is also vital for an atmospheric description. Making sure you include a range of ideas, represent the writer or character's perspective and use a variety of sentence types can enhance your writing.

Exploring skills

Take this task:

> **Describe an exciting moment or special event.**

Imagine you have chosen to write about a party or dinner given for a special guest, relative or friend of the family. You could describe or write about:

- your home and what it is like
- preparations where the party took place
- the food and refreshments
- the way people behaved: their movements and gestures.

(1) Add any other ideas that might complete the description of this event.

Of course, simply listing these ideas is not enough. You have already seen that the best descriptions are specific, focused, vivid and reveal emotions subtly. So, how can you develop each of these ideas? Here is an example of how to expand upon the place where the party will happen:

> The special event took place at my parents' apartment on Pineapple Gardens. We live in a small three-roomed flat, overlooking a dusty street which is permanently busy with cars and trucks with grinding gears, as well as cattle, stray cats, dogs, and chickens. So, you can imagine my father's anxiety when rich Uncle Sarfraz announced he was coming to visit us.

— specific small details, like the street or city

— specific focus: not just 'home' but the number of rooms and size and where it was

└ what it is like to live there (traffic, vehicles, animals)

There are two key sentences here. The first is the long second sentence, which is built up from the simple clause 'we live in a … flat' by many extra details to 'fill in' the picture. The second is the final sentence of the paragraph.

(2) What does this final sentence do?

> **Top tip**
>
> Make sure you do not slip into simply recounting events, as if this were a narrative. Focus on describing the setting and atmosphere.

Structuring paragraphs to move from the general (uncle's visit) to the specific (parents' anxiety) is very effective. The next paragraph could build on the first, focusing on a further aspect of the visit: for example, the parents' panicky preparations for Uncle Sarfraz's arrival.

(3) Write a long sentence that describes how the parents prepare the living room or eating area for Uncle Sarfraz, focusing on specific things they do (putting out the best plates, making special dishes). Do not stray into giving background information about Uncle Sarfraz, but stick to detailed description of the preparations and the room. Start: *My mother raced around the living room …*

Building skills

Using a variety of sentence structures is very important when trying to describe a specific atmosphere or mood such as fear, excitement or tension. Here is an example of an extract from a task titled: *Describe a performer or entertainer who amazed or held your interest.*

> As night fell, he emerged onto the stage. For a moment, all was quiet. He stood in the pool of light. Next to me, someone stifled a cough. He stared directly at the audience, gazed from one side to the other, and then seemed to fix his ice-blue eyes on me, as if looking into my very soul.

The paragraph works because **the order** helps to build tension and, importantly, reveal the narrator's own emotions: the performer appears, the audience waits, the performer connects with the audience as a whole, and then finally focuses in on the narrator.

(4) Discuss the following with a partner.
- How do the short sentences at the start of the paragraph create tension?
- How does the longer last sentence move the focus from the audience to the narrator?

(5) Read this next paragraph from the same text. It is detailed but its sentences are all the same length and lack tension or interest.

> Suddenly, after two hours, the performance came to an abrupt end as he sang the last words of his final song and disappeared offstage. We stared wide-eyed towards the stage as the arena lights came on and bathed us in brightness. The place seemed ordinary now and was no longer the magical site of a few minutes before. But the lights went down once again and everyone exploded into excited cries. A beam of yellow picked out a thin figure at the side of the stage who was holding a guitar, and without warning a beautiful melody began.

6 Rewrite the paragraph on page 101. You will need to:
- create some short sentences for impact and surprise
- cut out unnecessary words when you create these shorter sentences.

Developing skills

To create a description that is well-structured and atmospheric, a distinct sense of time, place, people and their different perspectives is vital. How can this be done?

Consider this description task title: *The old, abandoned school.*

Here is a possible list of things that might be included:

- The **past** and **present**: the school as it once was, and the school now
- The **time of day** of the description: for example, a late winter's day would change the description
- The **narrator's point of view** or **other perspectives**: for example, a former pupil revisiting the school in the present and remembering the past
- The **senses**: how the school looks, the sounds, the feel of the place, its smells

Now, here is the start of one writer's plan using some of these key ideas:

Paragraphs 1–2:   Old man in the present, staring from outside at the old school, describing how it looks. A description of the weather to add to atmosphere of cold and old age …

Paragraphs 3–4:   Old man in classroom, looking at the place he sat at as a younger man – include description of school before it was abandoned …

7 Can you continue the plan? Add notes for paragraphs 5 and 6. What elements are missing and could be included? Don't just think of random ideas. Decide what would fit logically (perhaps someone younger's point of view).

Here are the written up paragraphs 3 and 4 from the plan above.

> As dusk fell, he entered the derelict classroom. He walked to the wall at the back, where his name and hers were still carved, a clumsy love-heart between them. He sighed, brushed the dust away and sank into a chair.
>
> Now he could hardly stand or sit; back then, he used to race off at lunch and later run like the wind around the playground. He looked out of the window. The bulldozer stood ready. Soon his past would all be gone.

(8) Discuss these questions with a partner.
- What do we learn from the first paragraph about the time, the place and the man in the room? What **senses** does the language appeal to?
- In what way does the second paragraph **contrast** the character now and then?

(9) Now bring in another person's perspective – the driver of the bulldozer. Read the start of a possible paragraph 5 which contrasts what the driver thinks with the old man's thoughts:

> Outside, as the driver of the bulldozer turned off his machine, he stared at the old man. What was he doing in there? No one wanted this leaky, tatty school anymore. He wanted his children to be taught in …

Complete the paragraph by writing a contrasting description of a modern school with a completely different look and feel from the old one.

Top tip

The best descriptions often convey the inner life and thoughts of characters through things described in the outer world. For example, the names carved in the wall suggest the old man's feelings of loss.

Applying skills

(10) Select any **one** of the following descriptive writing tasks and write the complete text.
- Write a descriptive piece which begins, 'Stepping onto the beach I see …'.
- Describe the scene and atmosphere as you arrive at a remote place.
- Describe an exciting moment or a special event.
- 'The old, abandoned school' – write a descriptive piece with this title.

Sound progress	Excellent progress
• You include a range of ideas, and create a specific atmosphere with use of senses, imagery, and sentence variety.	• You create vivid connotations and a powerful atmosphere, using contrasts, different perspectives and revealing the inner life of characters.

15 Narrative writing

- To understand the key features of a good storytelling.
- To write an effective narrative.

Exploring skills

What makes a good short story? Is it what happens or how it's told? Is it how much it shocks you, makes you sad or makes you laugh? Perhaps it is all of these things – and more!

> ### Checklist for success
>
> Some basic advice is useful, however, for all short narratives.
> ✔ Have a limited number of developed characters (only one or two, but others can be mentioned in passing).
> ✔ Don't try to cover too many actions, timespans or events.
> ✔ Develop a convincing voice or style for your main character(s).
> ✔ Make your story memorable through its structure and language (such as unusual imagery or lively dialogue).
> ✔ Capture your reader's attention from the start.

1. Discuss the checklist with a partner and add any more narrative features you can think of.

2. Read this short plan done for a story called 'A disappointing night'. With a partner, discuss what could be changed or improved. Remember, the story must be interesting.

- **Introduction**: we meet six school friends, their names, what they're like
- **Development**: a school talent contest is announced
- **Complication**: there is not much time to rehearse
- **Climax**: the night of the talent show; none of them win
- **Resolution**: they meet in a cafe the next day and agree to enter next year

---

> **Top tip**
>
> The narrative structure in the plan is a useful way of planning a story, but it can be varied. For example, the plot could include several complications.

3. Try to improve the plot and the details. Consider changing:
   - the main ideas, characters, storyline
   - the structure. For example, start later in the story and flash-back to earlier events.

4. Note down your ideas and then present them to your group, or the rest of the class.

Applying skills

Narratives, then, combine excellent characterisation with a plot the reader wants to follow. However, there are other key elements of narrative that lead to really compelling stories.

Vivid imagery and description

In telling your story, vivid touches of descriptive detail can make it really come to life. For example:

Similes: *The lights of the school hall **glared at me like accusing eyes** – I had no right to be on stage and would definitely make a fool of myself.*

Metaphors: *Her **poisonous remarks wounded me** deeply, **arrowing** straight to my heart.*

'You haven't got what it takes!' she spat out.

Variety of sentences for effect

For example, use long and short sentences for effect:

I stepped onto the stage, the lights glaring at me like accusing eyes, the audience – including my parents – somewhere out there in the darkness, waiting for me to open my mouth. Then the words came. I began to sing. I was going to be all right.

(See pages 38–41 for more on sentence types and using them for effect.)

(12) Plan and write a first draft of your own narrative. Choose one of the following titles:

> ***Write a story in which a 'dare' or 'challenge' is central to the plot.***
> ***Write a story entitled:*** A Disappointing Night.

Top tip

Try to avoid **stereotypes** in characterisation. Not all old people are weak and frail, and not all school teachers are bossy!

Top tip

Ending with a short sentence can be very effective – if your plot has built up to it.

Sound progress

- You create a simple, clear story with one or two main characters.
- You build in some variety in sentence type and vocabulary use.
- You use some vivid language and description.

Excellent progress

- You tell a compelling story with a complex plot that might surprise the reader with a stimulating start and a powerful ending.
- You focus on and develop one or two interesting main characters.
- You use vivid language and description which keeps the reader interested throughout.

Section 2 Applying Key Skills in Examinations

In Section 1, you learnt a range of key reading and writing skills:

skimming and scanning	inferring and deducing implicit meanings
selecting information	writing in a range of forms and genres
understanding explicit meanings	writing for a range of purposes

These can be applied in a number of contexts, both in everyday life and in your examinations.

	Everyday life	Assessment situations
Skimming and scanning Selecting information	When you need to find specific information: for example, looking up a film time at your local cinema.	Short answer questions that require you to find specific information.
Understanding explicit meanings	When you need to work out the obvious meaning: for example, reading a set of furniture assembly instructions.	Closed questions that require you to explain simple events, actions or statements by offering synonyms.
Inferring and deducing implicit meanings	When you need to 'read between the lines': for example, reading a newspaper article about a political scandal and recognising bias.	More open questions that invite you to offer your interpretation of information or your subtle understanding of emotions or attitudes.
Summarising	When you need to pull together information from a number of sources and present it succinctly: for example, reading a number of travel guides and then summarising the key points to persuade someone else to go there on holiday with you.	Tasks that ask you to focus on specific aspects of a text, first listing those ideas and then summarising them in a few concise paragraphs.
Writing in a range of forms	At work when you might be asked to write, for example, a speech saying farewell to a colleague.	Extended response or directed writing tasks that require you to select points from a text and use them to create a new piece of writing. Composition tasks.
Writing for a range of purposes	In personal situations where you may need to write an explanation (for example, an insurance claim) or make an argument (for example, writing to your local council about improving leisure facilities).	Extended writing or directed writing tasks that offer you the chance to select points from a text and then use them to create a new piece of writing Composition tasks.

Summary questions

A specific type of assessment task will require you to write a selective summary of what you have read.

To answer this type of question you will need to:

- locate the particular section of the passage that the task or question refers to
- understand the specific focus of the question
- understand the specific meanings of words and phrases in the passage
- understand the implicit meanings and attitudes in the passage
- select, analyse and evaluate what is relevant to include
- note the key points to include in your own words
- write in an appropriate style for a summary, concisely and using your own words.

1 Understanding summary questions ⓒ

- To understand what is required for the note-making part of summary questions.
- To be able to break down the question.

Summary questions will ask you to make notes on one or two aspects of a single passage and then use them to write a selective summary of the passage.

Exploring skills

Read this passage from a traveller's account.

> People were friendly and hospitable. I remember, for example, the small group of men who insisted on taking us dynamite fishing one afternoon. This involved planting explosives in the bed of a shallow lagoon, detonating them, and diving down into the pleasantly tepid water to catch the stunned fish – which we then tossed at random into the waiting boat. This was not very environmentally friendly, but I admit it was fun.
>
> Afterwards we were invited back to one man's house, a squat, flat-roofed building situated in a fragrant orange grove, where we sat on the roof in the evening sun, sipping mint tea, before being served a delicious stew of fish, crab and squid. Dessert consisted of fresh local oranges, apricots and bananas. It seemed strange, however, that while my wife and I ate with the men, and were served first, the men's wives who had cooked the food ate indoors, and only after we and the men had been served. This reflected what we found elsewhere. We rarely met women: they were always at home or in the fields.

1. What do you learn from this passage about the following? Discuss your answers with a partner.
   - The local people and their customs.
   - What the climate is like in this area.
   - How the men fish with dynamite.

Building skills

Now, suppose you are asked to respond to this task.

> *What does the author describe himself doing in the passage.*
> *Write your answer using short notes.*

Your notes should include the key facts. They do not need to be written in sentences. Do not include anything not asked for. Here are some sample notes on 'what the author describes himself doing'.

- Goes dynamite fishing
- Helps by diving down and throwing fish in boat
- Drinks mint tea
- Eats meal with his wife and fishermen

These notes correctly select what the author actually does. They do not, for example, say what he thinks.

(2) Below are bullet-point notes made in answer to the question, 'What do we learn about the work and home lives of the fishermen in the passage?' Sort them into relevant and irrelevant points. Then put the chosen points into a logical order.

- Work in small group
- Sometimes fish using dynamite
- Use boat
- Have to dive into water
- Friendly and hospitable
- Bad for environment but fun
- Flat-roofed house in orange grove
- Eat fish stew and local fruit
- Writer and wife eat with the men
- Men and women eat separately
- Wives cook
- Writer and wife don't meet women much

Developing skills

Your notes should just contain key words and phrases. For example, you should write 'Work in small group' rather than 'The fishermen work in a small group' or even 'They …'.

It is not essential to use your own words in the notes, but if you do, you will find it easier to do so in your summary later. For example, instead of 'not very environmentally friendly, but fun' you could say 'bad for sea-life, but enjoyable'. This is also more **concise**: it says the same thing in fewer words.

(3) Find a concise way to say, in note form, 'This involved planting explosives in the bed of a shallow lagoon', using your own words.

(4) You can save words by finding one word for a group of things. (For example, 'dogs, cats and hamsters' are all 'pets'.) Write a concise note on what the author was given to eat.

Top tip

If you don't understand a word, guess its meaning from the sentence. If water is **'pleasantly** tepid', then 'tepid' cannot mean 'freezing' or 'boiling'.

Key terms

concise: brief and to the point

Applying skills

(5) Consider the question below. Make notes on the key points. Then put the relevant points into a logical order.

What do we learn about the people and their customs from the passage?

Top tip

If there is no obvious alternative for a phrase such as 'mint tea', just use it.

Sound progress

- You understand how to make notes on the key information.
- You understand how to put your notes in a logical order.

2 Preparing to answer summary questions (C)

Learning objectives

- To find and select information to answer the question.
- To organise the information.

To write a summary, you have to make notes on the text and then put them into the best order, in sentences.

> **Checklist for success**
>
> ✔ **Locate:** find key points from the text, using skimming and scanning. (See pages 8–13.)
> ✔ **Select:** choose the most relevant points from those you've found.
> ✔ **Order:** put these points in the best order to answer the question, using your own words.
> ✔ **Write** your summary in sentences using your own words where possible.

Exploring skills

You will be asked to make notes on one or two aspects of a passage and then summarise it. There will be ten key points that you could select and you need to include most of them to do well.

Read the passage below about Malakhara wrestlers in Pakistan from *A Game of Polo with a Headless Goat* by Emma Levine.

> The wrestlers wore the baggy trousers of their *shalwar kameez*, with the bottom of the trousers pulled up and tucked into the waist, looking like short baggy bloomers which ballooned from their bottoms. They [...] wore a turban on their heads. Before the fight, they carried out a sacrosanct ritual particular to this sport. Each took his *sundhro*, which is a very long piece of green material, and with the help of his opponent twisted it into a long rope. Then each wrestler wrapped his *sundhro* round his waist and tied it securely.

1. Scan the passage for information on what the wrestlers wore. Then cover it and, in pairs, take turns to describe what they wore.

2. How did you do? Scan the passage to see if you left out anything relevant. You should **not** have included what the wrestlers **did**.

3. Write notes on what the wrestlers wore.

Building skills

Read how the account continues.

The rule of this form of wrestling, which is quite unique, is for each man to aim to get his hand inside the back of his opponent's *sundhro*, and then throw him to the ground from that position. (Some believe that this is the origin of *sumo*.) Other than this move, the arms may not be used to perform any type of wrestling grip, the legs being more important and used to trip and overbalance the opponent and eventually floor him.

It was very different from the *rhiji* [another kind of wrestling …] much faster and more of a frantic scrap, with several matches continuing simultaneously on the field. They darted, each trying to grab at the other's waist, snatching their necks, trying to spin them round to overbalance them. The pair nearest to me grabbed each other's arms, trying to fling each other around, legs kicking in a kind of clumsy waltz; after a few minutes of this, one eventually got his hand in the other's *sundhro*, grabbed it, pulled it and flung his opponent on his back. He hit the ground with a tremendous wallop.

Such force meant that the fallen wrestler suffered not only defeat, but also it seemed to me severe concussion. He lay motionless on the ground with no one overly concerned except me. The victor went over, slapped him around to revive him and poured water over his face, so if he didn't die by knock-out it would probably be through drowning.

(4) Make notes on the rules and aims of Malakhara wrestling. Be selective. Do not, for example, give details of what happens when a wrestler is knocked out.

Developing skills

In your summary, you must order your information logically. It does not have to follow the order of the passage. For example, you could describe what the wrestlers wore starting with the turban. The important thing is that the order should be clear.

(5) Place the points you have noted for the rules and aims of Malakhara wrestling in a clear order. Consider whether there are other equally good ways to order them.

> **Top tip**
>
> Stick to the information you are asked to give. From this text, you are looking for the best seven points to include in your summary.

Applying skills

In an examination, the passage is likely to be longer than the one given here and will probably contain up to ten possible key points.

(6) Make notes on what happens in a typical match. Follow the first three steps in the Checklist on page 112: locate key points, select and order. Then write your summary using your own words and keeping to a word limit of 75 words.

Sound progress

- If the question asks for two types of information, you provide both.
- You only include relevant information.
- You keep to the word limit.

Understanding summary questions E

Learning objectives

- To understand summary questions.
- To learn how to select information.
- To learn how to order information.

Summary writing is a useful skill in everyday life – whether it helps you to jot down notes from the newspaper or sum up the plot of a film or a book. Summary questions will ask you to make notes and then summarise information from a passage. You will be asked to focus on one or two aspects of the passage.

Exploring skills

Checklist for success

✔ Select the actual information requested.
✔ Make short notes to summarise the key points.
✔ Use longer sentences where possible to write your summary.

Glossary

thwarts: crossbars
cinched: tied
bow: front

Read the passage below from Martin Douglas Mitchinson, *The Darien Gap: Travels in the Rainforest of Panama.*

I opened a jar of beans as the sun set. I sliced a fresh tomato, and the sky went dark. As I tore off a piece of bread, I thought of how Paul [my brother] would appreciate this picnic menu. By the time I finished eating, drift logs were bumping and then hammering into the dugout. I couldn't see them coming in the dark. I tied the packs and baskets to the **thwarts** and I **cinched** the strap on my glasses so that the frame pressed into my face.

I should have done even more. I should have untied the bowline right then, but I didn't want to lose the distance I'd paddled that afternoon. I thought that I could survive the worst of it if I stayed low in the boat. By the time I fully understood my mistake, the river was racing out and the current began dragging the dugout from one side to the other. After little more than an hour, I'd already lost control. Uprooted trees hooked onto the **bow** and then let go with a shudder, and the low branch I'd used to tie the bowline was already too high to reach.

1 What do you learn from this passage about the following aspects? Discuss your answers with a partner.

- How the writer intended to spend the night.
- What he did wrong.

2 Make bullet-point notes on the problems experienced by the author.

3 Now read the continuation of the passage below.

> Dragging a machete beside me, I began inching forward on my belly to cut the rope. As my weight shifted to the left or right it sent the dugout shooting off in one direction and then correcting hard to the other side. When I was still a few feet from the bow, I felt the dugout veer hard to the right, then tip even farther, and then farther still as the river grabbed the **gunwale** and water flooded over the bow.
>
> The current washed me back until my feet hit a thwart. For a split second we were under completely. I gripped the sides and waited. Fully submerged, I thought of my brother again. I thought of the loose paddle and the glasses strapped to my face. And then we levelled off. The boat was filled to the top, the current racing and washing over the gunwales whenever we dipped to one side even slightly.

Make notes on what the author did to try to get out of danger and what happened to him and his canoe. Discuss with a partner if there are any details you should leave out of your notes because they are irrelevant.

Building skills

Summarising involves grouping together some details to save space. Therefore it is important to be selective, even at the note-making stage. For example, if asked what Mitchinson *does* and *thinks* in the passage, you would include his meal, but not every detail.

4 Write two bullet-point notes summarising (a) what kind of meal Mitchinson had, and (b) what it made him think.

5 Another two aspects of this passage could be the dangers of tidal canoeing and how Mitchinson tries to cope with them. In groups, make a list, spider diagram or mind map to show what points you would include for these two aspects.

Now suppose you are asked:

> **What are the dangers of tidal canoeing as experienced by Mitchinson, and how does he try to cope with them?**

You will have to make brief notes on these two aspects and then turn these notes into continuous writing using your own words as far as possible, and in sentences. Your summary should not include anything you are not asked for, such as your opinions.

6 Below is a short notes summary responding to this task. What irrelevant information is included?

- Tide goes out very fast.
- Speed of current drags canoe side to side – could capsize
- Logs and uprooted trees hit the canoe
- Water washing over sides – canoe could flood
- He could drown
- Mitchinson has tied canoe to branch
- As level drops, branch becomes too high to reach
- Ties possessions to crossbars
- Has simple picnic
- Secures his glasses
- Thinks about brother
- Cuts rope so canoe can go with flow
- He must really love danger

Developing skills

Try to use complex sentences instead of shorter, simpler ones. For example, here is a complex sentence:

> Finding that the river level has dropped to the point where he can no longer reach the branch, Mitchinson has to crawl to where he can cut the rope in order to free the canoe.

This combines four ideas in one sentence (the river has dropped; he can't reach the branch; he has to crawl to cut the rope; this will free the canoe), taking fewer words than separate sentences would and improving the writing style by linking ideas in a continuous flow.

7 Write a summary of the dangers of tidal canoeing based on this passage. Use the notes on page 116 if you wish, but be sure to include only the relevant points. Write about 50 words, in two or three complex sentences, using your own words as far as possible.

Applying skills

8 Look back at the notes you made for activity 4. Write two complex sentences, which each include at least two of your points.

Top tip

You can often guess the meaning of a word from the sentence. For example, the canoe *veers* to the right, so veering must be something to do with changing direction.

Sound progress

- You focus on the aspects of the passage identified in the question.
- You identify at least 15 relevant points in your notes.
- You attempt to use your own words and some complex sentences in your continuous summary.

Excellent progress

- You focus on the aspects of the passage identified in the question.
- You identify at least 15 relevant points.
- You use your own words to write complex sentences, which contain two or more points.
- You do not include introductory or concluding sentences but get straight into the summary.

4 Preparing to answer summary questions (E)

- To find and select information to answer the question.
- To collate and order the information.

To write a summary, you will have to locate and select relevant information and present it in the best possible order. You will have to collate information from different paragraphs, gathering facts together.

Exploring skills

When you start to respond to summary questions in the exam, you should already have read the passage carefully. Your skimming and scanning skills will be useful in finding relevant information to include in your notes. **(See pages 8–13 for more on skimming and scanning.)**

To do as well as possible, try to include 15 relevant points.

Read Passage A, part 1 from 'Something Approaching Enlightenment', in which Rolf Potts describes a bus journey in northern India.

> While still within the fog of my initial inspiration, it was fairly easy to rationalise a three-day bus ride through the remote Himalayas. Once I was actually en route to Kaza, however, I immediately realised that my whimsical pilgrimage could very well get me killed. The copy of the *Hindustan Times* that I'd bought in Shimla, for instance, devoted an entire front-page story to grisly mountain bus crashes. 'At least 40 people were killed when a bus plunged into a tributary of the Ravi River yesterday evening,' the article read. 'Earlier in the day, eight people died and thirteen were injured when a truck carrying them fell into a gorge 35 kilometres from Manali.'
>
> The Indian highway signs were not much more encouraging. In lieu of shoulders or guardrails, dangerous curves on the mountain featured boulders with white-painted slogans that read 'O God help us!' or 'Be safe: use your horn'. I kept staring out at the river valley 300 metres below and imagining our driver cheerily honking the horn as we all plummeted to certain death.

> **Top tip**
>
> As you scan the passage, look carefully for **key words** or **phrases** that relate to the focus of the question. Missing these key words may lose you marks.

1 Use your reading skills to list key phrases that tell you what worries the writer about going on a Himalayan bus journey. Begin with 'get me killed'. You should find another three or four key phrases.

Now read Passage A, part 2.

The most alarming part of the Himalayan bus ride, however, was the road itself, which seemed to be buried under massive mudslides at 30-kilometre intervals. Indeed, every couple of hours, our bus driver would screech to a halt and I'd peer out the window to see what had formerly been the road lying in a crumpled crust 20 metres down the mountain. Invariably, several dozen Indian highway workers would be making a frenzied effort to carve a makeshift dirt track into the flank of the mud wall in front of us. My fellow passengers would disembark and smoke cigarettes at the edge of the cliff, watching disinterestedly until the labourers gave a shout and our bus driver would rumble across the improvised mud road. Along with the other passengers, I'd then follow on foot at a safe distance, climbing back into the bus once the normal highway resumed. My main solace amidst all this was the promise of Kaza and the serene Buddhist environs that hopefully awaited me there.

After two days of nonstop travel, I'd made it deep into the Tibetan border region before the transmission dropped out of the bottom of my bus near a town called Pooh. Folks in Pooh informed me that there were no more onward buses that day, but I might be able to find transportation out of Kob, 10 kilometres further up the road. Feeling optimistic in the early-afternoon sunshine, I set off for Kob on foot.

② Use a table like the one below to list key phrases in the passage that relate to the problems with the Himalayan roads and how the bus services attempt to cope with them. In the right-hand column, put your chosen phrases into note form.

Original	Note form
'buried under massive mudslides at 30-kilometre intervals'	Roads often covered by fallen mud

Top tip

Time will be tight for writing your summary in an examination, but practising putting original phrases into your own words now will mean this skill comes more naturally.

Developing skills

Read Passage B from 'Egg Child' by Sarah Levin.

Pulling my scarf tightly around my head, I worked my way into the van. There was no room to sit, so I hunched over and grabbed onto the back of a seat, accidentally yanking on a young girl's hair as we rolled over a pothole. She turned and smiled gently, took the bag I was holding and nestled it in her kilt-clad lap as we braced ourselves for the next lurch.

The bus station was teeming with merchants selling bottles of orange-pink juice, rows of biscuits, tired battery-powered stereos and used T-shirts. Ticket-sellers crowded around me, yelping East African destinations in rapid succession: 'Nairobi!' 'Tanga!' 'Dar es Salaam!' Buses groaned into motion, spewing brown gobs of exhaust; men ran after them, hitting the sides, leaping into the doorways as they took off down the narrow streets. I muscled myself into the minibus bound for Moshi and looked into the horde of dark faces that had almost simultaneously turned to stare at the white girl. A pain seized my stomach and I breathlessly slipped between two elderly women, willing the Loperamide to soothe my intestines.

The bus grew more crowded. A toddler was deposited on my lap, my shoulders squeezed between the two soft women beside me. They spoke to me in slow, easy Swahili, asking where I was from and where I was going. They touched their hands to mine, and we swayed together on the long road.

The women waved, imitating my gesture, when I got off at the stand in the town of Boma a ya Ngombe. The merchants again surrounded me, more desperate this time, because there were never white faces here. I shook my head slowly, over and over, glancing through their bony forms for the next bus. The wait here was never longer than five minutes, though the ride was more cramped. I was pulled on, prodded towards the window across from a man holding a chicken by the legs. The bird squawked, its eyes beady, its white feathers brushing my fingertips in a frenzied escape attempt.

It was past noon; sunlight poured through the glass like untouchable fire. I wiped the sweat from my eyebrows. My teeth chattered. The man across from me watched with bloodshot eyes, his chicken trembling on his knees.

At Sanya Juu I crawled over seven laps, the plastic bags tied to my wrists trailing behind me. The sun had disappeared by now, its yellow beams shrouded in clouds. I dodged a puddle and headed toward a small kiosk by the side of the road. I asked to use a bathroom; the woman pointed behind me to a guesthouse. Crossing the road, I was met with the upturned glances of children, their dusty bellies poking out beneath too-small shirts. One boy took my hand as I crossed. His feet were bare, as wrinkled as a 40-year-old's. His hand was moist in the heat and warmed my own.

3 Find seven key phrases in this passage that show the problems the author had with road travel. This time try to put them directly into your own words. For example, you could replace 'muscled' with *pushed*. This is one of several phrases showing that the bus was crowded. In a summary, you could write: *She has to push her way onto the crowded bus.*

Applying skills

The information you select from the passage must be in a logical order in your summary. You do not have to put it in the order in which it appears in the passage.

4 Put your notes from activity 3 into a spider diagram. Then use a different coloured pen to number the points in an order that a reader will be able to follow. Discuss different options with a partner.

5 Now use your own words and phrases from activity 3 to write a summary of the author's problems. You should write 100–150 words. Try to use some complex sentences.

Sound progress

- You provide the information the question asks for, using your own words.
- You cover all the main relevant points.
- You write in grammatically correct sentences.
- You try to use some complex sentences.

Excellent progress

- You combine points, using your own words, in complex sentences that are well punctuated and fluent.
- You structure your summary logically.
- You write tightly and succinctly.
- You do not include introductory or concluding sentences but get straight into the summary.

Exam-style questions and sample responses: summary questions

Key skills

You will need to show the following skills when answering summary questions:

- demonstrate understanding of explicit meanings
- demonstrate understanding of implicit meanings and attitudes
- select for specific purposes
- articulate experience and express what is thought, felt and imagined
- sequence facts, ideas and opinions
- use a range of appropriate vocabulary.

Exploring responses: summary questions

A high quality response will show an understanding of the passage. You will need to stick to what you are asked to do in the question; note and then order the important points; then write a fluent summary in your own words.

1 Read the following passage from Bruce Chatwin's *In Patagonia*, about the voyage of John Davis in his ship the *Desire*, in 1593.

> The fleet entered the Magellan Strait with the southern winter already begun. A sailor's frostbitten nose fell off when he blew it. Beyond Cape Froward, they ran into north-westerly gales and sheltered in a tight cove with the wind howling over their mastheads.   5
>
> [...] In a storm off Cape Pilar, the *Desire* lost the *Pinnace,* which went down with all hands. Davis was alone at the helm, praying for a speedy end, when the sun broke through the clouds. He took bearings, fixed his position, and so regained the calmer water of the Strait.   10
>
> He sailed back to Port Desire, the crew scurvied and mutinous and the lice lying in their flesh [...] He repaired the ship as best he could. The men lived off eggs, gulls, baby seals, scurvy grass and the fish called *pejerry*. On this diet they were restored to health.   15
>
> Ten miles down the coast, there was an island, the original Penguin Island, where the sailors clubbed twenty thousand birds to death. They had no natural enemies and were unafraid of their murderers. John

Davis ordered the penguins dried and salted and stowed fourteen thousand in the hold. [20]

On November 11th a war-party of Tehuelche Indians attacked [...] Nine men died in the skirmish, among them the chief mutineers, Parker and Smith [...]

The *Desire* sailed at nightfall on December 22nd and set course for Brazil, where the Captain hoped to provision with cassava flour. On January 30th he made land at the Isle of Plasencia, off Rio de Janeiro. The men foraged for fruit and vegetables in gardens belonging to the Indians. [25]

Six days later, the coopers went with a landing party to gather hoops for barrels. The day was hot and the men were bathing, unguarded, when a mob of Indians and Portuguese attacked. The Captain sent a boat crew ashore and they found the thirteen men, faces upturned to heaven, laid in a rank with a cross set by them. [30] [35]

John Davis saw pinnaces sailing out of Rio harbour. He made for open sea. He had no other choice. He had eight casks of water and they were fouled.

As they came up to the Equator, the penguins took their revenge. In them bred a 'loathsome worme' about an inch long. The worms ate everything, iron only excepted – clothes, bedding, boots, hats, leather lashings, and live human flesh. The worms gnawed through the ship's side and threatened to sink her. [40]

2 Read the following exam-style summary question and the sample responses that follow.

(a) What difficulties were met by Davis and his crew, and how did they try to cope with them? Write your answer using short notes, aiming to find 10 points. [10]

(b) Now use your notes to write a summary of the difficulties met by Davis and his crew, and how they tried to cope with them.

Your summary should be in continuous writing and use your own words as far as possible. It should include all 10 of your points from (a) and it must be 100 to 150 words. [5]

Exam-style questions and sample responses: summary questions

Response 1A

• Very cold	• Some crew mutinous	Portuguese
• Man's nose fell off	• Attacked by Indians	• Penguin worms ate
• Storms and gales	twice; lost many men	men
• Crew got scurvy and	• Thirteen men killed	• Should not have killed
lice	by Indians and	all the penguins

Feedback

This response includes nine points but only five are clear and relevant (cold, storms, scurvy, mutiny, Indians), and it only covers the difficulties, not how Davis and his crew tried to cope with them. The point about the man's nose is a detail rather than a key point. The point 'Penguin worms ate men' is unclear, and the final point is an opinion, which should not be included in a summary response.

Response 1B

It was really cold, as we see when the man's nose falls off. Probably near the South Pole. There was storms, scurvy, which is from lack of Vitamin C and mutiny, which is when the men won't follow orders, maybe wanting more pay. The men had 'the lice lying in their flesh'. Luckily two leaders got killed by Indians. The Pinnace got lost and sank in a storm. Also they was attacked by Indians twice. In a way the penguins get their own back with the worms. The men should not kill so many.

— unnecessary explanations and guesswork

— quotes passage rather than using own words

— more or less true, but not clearly relevant to question

— relevant point, concisely made, but with poor verb agreement

— opinion, which is not needed

Feedback

This response makes five clear points (cold, storms, scurvy, mutiny, Indians) but is too short and only covers the difficulties, not how Davis and his crew tried to cope with them. It wastes time on evidence (the nose), explanation (scurvy, mutiny), guesswork ('Probably...') and opinion (last sentence). The phrase 'the lice lying in their flesh' is not in the response writer's own words. The sentence 'The Pinnace got lost and sank in a storm' is partly true but shows a misunderstanding as the passage does not say that the ship sank because it was lost. There is also one incorrect verb agreement.

Recommended Band: 4 (Core)

Response 2A

• Winter, very cold, gales and storms	• Tried to get fruit and vegetables
• Took shelter in cove	• Some crew mutinous
• Davis prayed and navigated Desire into calmer Strait	• Attacked by Indians; lost 22 men
• Crew unhealthy – scurvy and lice	• Only had foul water, and not much of that
• Improved diet – eggs, gulls, scurvy grass, etc.	• Worms bred in penguins ate almost everything

Feedback

These notes include 10 relevant points, covering both parts of the question: difficulties encountered and how Davis and his men tried to cope. There are no irrelevant points.

Response 2B

Davis and his crew suffered from severe cold, storms and gales, but they took shelter in a bay. Davis prayed and navigated the 'Desire' into calmer waters, though the 'Pinnace' sank in a storm.

— relevant points concisely made

— fluent complex sentence

The crew were lice-ridden and suffering from scurvy. They began to mutiny, but they regained their health by adding eggs, meat and scurvy grass to their diet. They also managed to gather fruit and vegetables from the Indians' gardens. Going ashore to get materials for new water barrels a few days later, they were attacked by Indians and Portuguese and fled without water.

— effective, concise sentence using own words

Having little water, and none of it fresh, Davis headed towards the open sea to look for water elsewhere. Finally, the penguins they had preserved for meat became the breeding ground of worms, which ate everything except iron, and ate into the ship, almost sinking it.

— complex sentence concisely combining points

Feedback

This response mentions 10 clear, relevant points, blending both aspects of the question into coherent paragraphs which take us through the difficulties and coping strategies in chronological order, using connectives and some complex sentences. It makes good use of the available word limit.

Recommended Band: 1 (Core)

Exploring responses: summary questions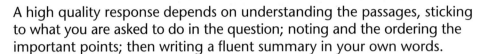

A high quality response depends on understanding the passages, sticking to what you are asked to do in the question; noting and the ordering the important points; then writing a fluent summary in your own words.

 Read the following passage.

From *A Walk in the Woods* by Bill Bryson

There was a sound of undergrowth being disturbed – a click of breaking branches, a weighty pushing through low foliage – and then a kind of large, vaguely irritable snuffling noise.

Bear!

I sat bolt upright. Instantly every neuron in my brain was awake and dashing around frantically, like ants when you disturb their nest. I reached instinctively for my knife, then realized I had left it in my pack, just outside the tent. Nocturnal defence had ceased to be a concern after many successive nights of tranquil woodland repose.

There was another noise, quite near. 'Stephen, you awake?' I whispered.

'Yup,' he replied in a weary but normal voice. 'What was that?'

'How the hell should I know? It sounded big.'

'Everything sounds big in the woods.'

This was true. Once a skunk had come plodding through our camp and it had sounded like a stegosaurus. There was another heavy rustle and then the sound of lapping at the spring. It was having a drink, whatever it was.

I shuffled on my knees to the foot of the tent, cautiously unzipped the mesh and peered out, but it was pitch black. As quietly as I could, I brought in my backpack and, with the light of a small torch, searched through it for my knife. When I found it and opened the blade I was appalled at how wimpy it looked. It was a perfectly respectable appliance for, say, buttering pancakes, but patently inadequate for defending oneself against 400 pounds of ravenous fur.

Carefully, very carefully, I climbed from the tent and put on the torch, which cast a distressingly feeble beam. Something about 15 or 20 feet away looked up at me. I couldn't see anything at all of its shape or size – only two shining eyes. It went silent, whatever it was, and stared back at me.

'Stephen,' I whispered at his tent, 'did you pack a knife?'

'No.'

'Have you got anything sharp at all?'

He thought for a moment. 'Nail clippers.'

I made a despairing face. 'Anything a little more vicious than that? Because, you see, there is definitely something out here.'

'It's probably just a skunk.'

'Then it's one big skunk. Its eyes are three feet off the ground.'

'A deer then.'

I nervously threw a stick at the animal, and it didn't move, whatever it was. A deer would have bolted. This thing just blinked once and kept staring.

I reported this to Katz.

'Probably a buck. They're not so timid. Try shouting at it.'

I cautiously shouted at it: 'Hey! You there! Scat!' The creature blinked again, singularly unmoved. 'You shout,' I said.

'Oh, you brute, go away, do!' Katz shouted in merciless imitation. 'Please withdraw at once, you horrid creature.'

2 Read the following exam-style summary question and the sample responses that follow.

> **(a)** What makes the author anxious and how do he and his friend respond to the situation?
>
> Write your answer using short notes, aiming to find 15 points.   [15]

> **(b)** Now use your notes to write a summary of what makes the author anxious and how he and his friend respond to the situation.
>
> Your summary should be in continuous writing and use your own words as far as possible. It should include all 10 of your points from a) and it must be 200 to 250 words.   [5]

Response 1A

- Bryson hears sound out of tent
- Reaches for knife but it's outside
- Katz is weary
- Bryson gets backpack
- Shines torch and finds knife
- Even a skunk sounded like a stegosaurus
- Appalled at how wimpy knife is
- Shines torch outside and sees eyes
- Asks Katz if he has a knife
- Katz not bothered: thinks it's a skunk or deer
- Bryson tells animal to scat
- Katz only shouts sarcastically

Feedback

These notes only make 12 points, not 15. Of these, one is irrelevant because it is not about what makes Bryson anxious or how he and his friend respond ('Even a skunk…'). In some cases it is not clear that the writer has understood the point, because they quote the actual words in the passage ('weary', 'Appalled', 'scat').

Recommended Band: 3 (Extended)

Exam-style questions and sample responses: summary questions

Response 1B

Bill Bryson hears a loud sound outside his tent and reaches ——— **makes a point but could be clearer**
for his knife but it's outside. His friend just responds ———
wearily when asked for something sharp. Bryson gets his └── **uses words taken from the passage and unnecessary detail**
backpack and looks for a knife but he is appalled at how
wimpy his is – more use for buttering pancakes than self-
defence. He comments that even a skunk sounds as loud as ——— **not strictly relevant**
a stegosaurus out here in the woods. When he shines the ———
torch outside he sees frightening eyes, so he asks Katz if └── **effective sentence**
he has a knife. Katz, however, couldn't care less as he thinks
it's just a deer or skunk or some other harmless animal.
Bryson is not convinced. He thinks it's much bigger because
its eyes are high up. He's obviously a bit of an anxious type ——— **unhelpful speculation**
and not used to the great outdoors at all. However, he tells
the animal to scat. The creature just blinks, so he asks Katz ┌── **fairly accurate interpretation but quotes text and interprets unnecessarily**
to shout. But Katz just shouts 'Oh, you brute, go away do!' ───
sarcastically, probably just keen to get some sleep.

Feedback

This response makes a number of correct points with reasonable fluency, but does not fully cover how the author responds, speculates and gives irrelevant details (the skunk sounding like a stegosaurus). The information is poorly structured and is sometimes in the original words ('appalled at how wimpy'), even quoting some of the text directly. It is too short, because some key points have been omitted.

Recommended Band: 3 (Extended)

3 How could this response be improved to make it Band 1? In pairs decide, using the Excellent progress box in the Check your progress table on page 130 as a guide. Now read a Band 1 example.

Response 2A

• Bryson and friend Katz camping at night • Shines torch and finds knife
• Hears sound outside tent – could be • Dismayed at how small knife is
large animal • Shines torch outside and sees eyes
• Thinks it's a bear • Asks Katz if he has a knife
• Reaches for knife but it's outside • Katz offers his nail clippers
• Asks friend what noise was • Katz not bothered: thinks it's a skunk
• Katz not pleased to be disturbed   or deer
• Bryson unzips tent, looks out, gets • Bryson shouts at animal
backpack • Katz shouts ironically at animal

Feedback

These notes include 15 clear and relevant points, placing the passage in context ('camping at night') and giving an appropriate amount of detail. Paraphrasing ('dismayed' for 'appalled') makes it clear that the writer understands the key point.

Response 2B

Camping with his friend Katz in the woods one night, the author is alarmed to hear what sounds like a large animal pushing through the branches and leaves, then drinking at a nearby stream. Immediately thinking that the animal must be a bear, Bryson sits up fearfully and reaches for his knife. Realising that it is in his backpack outside, he quietly unzips the tent, gets the pack and takes out the knife, but on opening the blade is dismayed as it is too small to use as an effective means of self-defence. — *concise summary setting context* / *good use of own words*

Bryson shines a torch at the animal and is disappointed at its weak beam. However, it illuminates the animal's eyes just staring back, apparently unafraid. The eyes are three feet off the ground, revealing its size, which adds to Bryson's fears. Katz seems unperturbed, answering in a voice that shows tiredness rather than fear. Bryson, finding that his friend has no weapon other than nail clippers, throws a stick at the animal, then shouts, though not with any great force. When it does not go away, he asks Katz to shout as well, which he does – though in a way suggesting that he is ironically mocking Bryson for being so timid and cautious. — *good vocabulary* / *effective complex sentence, giving clear, logical sequence* / *sums up effect of Katz's words without quoting them*

Feedback

This response covers all the important points for both aspects of the question, in a balanced way, with no irrelevance. It uses complex sentences in a fluent and well-structured response, paraphrasing without quoting directly from the passage. It shows understanding of inferred meaning (final sentence). The response makes good use of the available word limit.

Recommended Band: 1 (Extended)

Sound progress

Content

- I can identify and note the main points in a passage.
- I can identify which points are relevant to the question.
- I can guess the meanings of some difficult words from their sentences.
- I do not waste time on explanation or opinion.
- I can answer the whole question.

Style

- I can express information clearly in my own words.

Sound progress

Content

- I can identify and note the main points in a passage.
- I can identify which points are relevant to the question.
- I can guess the meanings of difficult words from their sentences.
- I do not speculate or give opinions.

Style

- I can express information fluently in my own words.

Excellent progress

Content

- I can identify and note all the main points of a passage.
- I can judge which points are the most important.
- I can understand implied meaning and express it in my own words.

Style

- I can convey a sense of the tone of a passage.
- I can combine several pieces of information into complex sentences, using clauses and my own words concisely and fluently.
- I can structure my summary logically in a way that makes it easy for the reader to follow.

Instead you need to explain by using an alternative word or synonym that means the same thing. So a better answer would be:

> It tells us that the girls were extremely happy and almost
> overwhelmed with joy.

(2) Complete the table below with synonyms for the words given.

Original word	Synonym
shimmering (sequins)	shining and catching the light
(beautifully) manicured (nails)	
slicked back (hair)	

Developing skills

Sometimes a question will require more than a literal explanation of a word or phrase and its meaning. It may call for you to make an inference. This means that you have to read between the lines. (See pages 20–27 for more on this reading skill.)

Read the extract below:

> We were stars for the night! Some teachers were like paparazzi. They lined the red carpet, all dressed up themselves, lenses zooming, making us blink with the flashes and calls for smiles. Others formed a human shield, bossily holding back the cheering Year 7s, as if they were bouncers at a film première, keeping us away from mere mortals.

(3) Now read this question and copy and complete the table below. Then add two more example words / phrases and add their meanings and what you infer from them.

How did the teachers behave at the prom?

Word	Meaning	Inference
like paparazzi	Taking photographs	
formed a human shield		Protective of the prom goers – didn't want the photos spoilt.

Applying skills

(4) Using your own words explain the teachers' behaviour towards the younger students watching the prom guests as they arrive at the school.

Sound progress

- You can locate and select suitable words and phrases.
- You can show understanding by explaining the meanings of words using synonyms.
- You sometimes offer inferences as well as literal explanations.

3 Understanding writer's effects questions: explaining meanings

- To understand what questions about the meanings of words and phrases mean.
- To practise answering questions in your own words.

Language questions that focus on the effects created by the writer come in two parts, so there are two key skills that you will need to master:

- locating specific words or phrases in a text
- explaining what they mean in your own words.

Exploring skills

In order to explain meanings in your own words you need to be able to:

- find the given word or phrase in the text and understand the **context**
- if you know the meaning, explain it in new words or phrases, perhaps thinking of **synonyms**
- if you don't know the meaning, try to work it out using a range of skills and strategies.

Key terms

context: the details around a word or phrase that help determine its meaning

synonym: a word or phrase that is very similar in meaning to another one: for example, *angry* and *cross*

Read this short text and the question that follows:

> I realised as we entered Paris on the coach that I knew practically nothing about the city or its past. I had been a fool – why hadn't I prepared? After all, I was the teacher. Now, fifty expectant students stared wide-eyed at me, waiting to be enlightened about the French Revolution, the paintings in the Louvre and the history of Notre-Dame.

Explain using your own words, what the writer means by the word in **roman:**

(i) 'Now, fifty **expectant** *students stared wide-eyed at me'.*

1. Even if you know the meaning of 'expectant', go through this process with a partner.
   - First, think about the context or situation: what is the writer's job and why is he worried?
   - Now, consider the word 'expectant'. Is it like any other words you know? It is an adjective so who or what is it describing here? Do you know any synonyms for it?
   - What other clues are we given? If the students are 'wide-eyed', does this suggest they are interested?

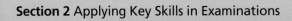

Building skills

(2) Taking all this into account, decide which of the following answers is the best, and why. Remember, the best answers do not use words from the text.

- excited and expecting a good time
- hopeful and eager to hear from him
- irritated by him

Developing skills

(3) Now, write your own answer to the following question on the same text:

Explain in your words what the word in roman *means in the selected text below:*

(i) students stared wide-eyed at me, waiting to be **enlightened** *about the French Revolution, the paintings in the Louvre, and the history of Notre-Dame.*

Go through the same process as before.
- What is the context or situation? (You already know this.)
- Who are 'waiting to be enlightened'?
- What other similar words come to mind?

Applying skills

Finally, read this longer passage that follows on from the one above and answer the questions that follow:

We snaked our way along the street to the entrance to the museum. A man in a smart suit approached. 'Do you need a guide, monsieur? I know everything there is to know.' I gave him a grateful nod of the head and we followed him in. One of my pupils, Billy, came up to me. 'Why aren't you doing it, sir? You're a French teacher, aren't you?' he asked in an accusing way, looking me straight in the face.

> **Top tip**
>
> Take care. Sometimes words that have similar spelling have little in common. For example, 'grate' as in the tray that catches ashes from a fire, has nothing to do with the adjective 'grateful'.

(4) Explain, using your own words, what the words in *italics* mean in each of these examples:
- We *snaked* our way along the street to the entrance
- I gave him a *grateful* nod of the head
- he asked in an *accusing* way, looking me straight in the face.

Sound progress

- You show you understand the word in general terms but you occasionally reuse the original word in your explanation.

4 Preparing to answer writer's effects questions C

Learning objectives

● To understand how particular words and phrases suggest ideas and emotions.
● To apply what you have learned to a text.

Often, when being asked to respond to a text, you will have to not only explain the meaning of the words selected but also explain how these same words suggest a particular idea, emotion, feeling or aspect of character.

Exploring skills

(1) Read this opening to a chapter from *Q & A* by Vikas Swarup.

> The sun seems weaker, the birds less chirpy, the air more polluted, the sky a shade darker.
>
> When you have been **plucked** from a beautiful big bungalow and **dumped** in a crumbling house where you are **forced** to live in a crowded dormitory with dozens of kids, I suppose you do acquire a somewhat jaundiced view of life.

Read this example response to a question which asked students to:
● explain the meaning of the words in bold
● say how they suggest the writer's feelings of helplessness.

Word/phrase	Meaning	How it suggests a feeling of helplessness
'plucked from a beautiful big bungalow'	Taken suddenly without warning	The verb 'plucked' suggests the writer was like a small creature or item taken from above without knowing why.

This is a very good answer. But what could have been added to this to make it even better? Discuss with a partner each of these ideas. (Remember, it is the **word in bold** that is being explained.)

● The response could have mentioned how the bungalow meant he had a home once and he doesn't any more.
● The response could have explored the idea that an unknown outside force grabs him, as we don't know who takes him and this adds to his 'helplessness.'

> **Top tip**
>
> Think of 'suggest' as meaning 'what comes into your mind'. For example, the word 'crumbling' might bring to mind pieces of a biscuit or bread. Also, by using the present participle form, '...ing', it suggests the process is actually taking place in front of your eyes.

Building skills

(2) How would you describe the atmosphere created in the extract above? Use adjectives in your answer.
● Start by putting in the normal meaning of the word in column 2.
● Add a longer explanation about how it suggests 'helplessness' in column 3.

Word/phrase	Meaning	How it suggests 'helplessness'
'dumped in a crumbling house'		
'forced to live in a crowded dormitory'		

Developing skills

The very best explanations of how writers suggest ideas through language often refer to the grammatical function of a particular word. In this further example response to the question on page 138, it is helpful to know that the person who 'does' an action in a sentence is called the 'subject'. Usually, we are told the subject but here, this isn't the case.

> The writer's feeling of helplessness is increased by the fact we do not know who 'plucked' him from his home. The lack of a 'subject' makes the act even more frightening.

3 Discuss the following with a partner.
- What types of word are the other words in bold?
- Is the same true of them – that they have no subject?

4 Choose either 'dumped' or 'forced' and rewrite your answer from column three, making sure you refer to the type of word used.

Applying skills

Now read this further extract from *Q & A* in which the narrator finds himself living in a Juvenile Home:

> It is **cramped**, noisy and dirty. It has just two toilets with leaky washbasins and filthy latrines. Rats scurry through its hallways and kitchen. It has a classroom with **ramshackle** desks and a **cracked** blackboard.

5 Write about how each of the three words in bold suggests the Home is an unsuitable place for education and learning.

Checklist for success

✔ Make sure you are clear about the meaning of the selected word.
✔ Consider what images or ideas come into your mind.
✔ Refer to the correct language term, if relevant (such as 'noun' or 'verb').

Sound progress

- You explain the meaning of the word, and can say what effect it creates.

5 | Understanding writer's effects questions (E)

● To understand what is required when answering questions on writer's effects.

When responding to questions about the language used by a writer in a text, you may be asked to select particular words and phrases and explain their effect, for example in conveying atmosphere, setting, someone's appearance or character.

A typical question might be:

> *Reread the descriptions of:*
> *(a) the earthquake in paragraph 4*
> *(b) the beach at Kare Kare in paragraph 5.*
> *Select four powerful words or phrases from each paragraph. Your choices should include imagery. Explain how each word or phrase selected is used effectively in the context.*

Exploring skills

When writers create effects, we as readers are made to feel particular emotions or have a sense of 'being there' first hand. These effects are **not** accidental – writers have deliberately set out to make us feel that way.

Read the following passage:

> I found myself on Kare Kare beach many times that winter staring at the cliffs on either side, as the westerlies whipped the waves up and hurled them onto the land. Like the sea, my mind raged. I had lost everything – my home, my wife, my children. Could I start all over again?

(1) With a partner, discuss whether any of the comments below have selected a 'powerful word or phrase' and commented on the effect it creates.

It's clear the writer wants us to feel angry with the man – he's just self-pitying and should get on with his life.

The phrase 'like the sea, my mind raged' is very effective as it directly compares the stormy sea with the writer's confused state of mind using a striking image.

'whipped the waves up' is a good phrase. It means that it is very stormy.

Building skills

Writers use a range of techniques to achieve effects. For example:

- **well-chosen vocabulary:** *'When you have been **plucked from a beautiful big bungalow** and **dumped in a crumbling house...**'*
- **imagery:** *'the moon shone weakly, **like a sick patient's eyes**, on my prison cell...'*
- **sentence variety:** *'We approached it with caution, steering our little raft through the narrow gaps between the cliffs, wondering where it was and when we would see it and beginning to think it didn't exist. Suddenly, I saw a thin strip of gold! The beach.'*

(2) With a partner, discuss what **other** techniques writers use to create effects.

Developing skills

Often, the writer suggests a feeling or idea. For example, we might say: *The writer implies that the man is in a hopeless position, as even the moon seems unwell and unable to help him.*

(3) Choosing one of the other quotations above, write one sentence saying what is implied or suggested about the narrator or situation in the extract on page 140.

Applying skills

Now read this extract from *Q & A*. Then read the question that follows.

They didn't come for me in a jeep with a flashing red light. They came in a blue van with wire-meshed windows. Like the type they use to round up stray dogs. Except this one was for rounding up stray boys. If I had been younger, they would probably have sent me to an adoption home and put me up for sale. But since I was eight years old, I was sent to the [...] Juvenile Home for boys, in Turkman Gate.

The Juvenile Home has a capacity of seventy-five, and a juvenile population of one hundred and fifty. It is cramped, noisy and dirty. It has just two toilets with leaky washbasins and filthy latrines. Rats scurry through its hallways and kitchen. It has a classroom with ramshackle desks and a cracked blackboard. And teachers who haven't taught for years. It has a sports ground where grass grows as tall as wickets and where, if you are not careful, you can graze yourself against stones the size of footballs.

Reread the descriptions of:

(a) how the writer is picked up by the authorities in paragraph 1

(b) the Juvenile Home in paragraph 2.

Select four powerful words or phrases from each paragraph. Your choices should include imagery. Explain how each word or phrase selected is used effectively in the context.

(4) Write a paragraph to answer part (a) as fully as you can. Where possible, refer to the writers' techniques mentioned above. You can also answer (b) if you wish.

Sound progress

- You locate and select suitable words and phrases.
- You show some understanding of effects by explaining the meanings of your selections.

Excellent progress

- You locate and select the most appropriate and powerful words and phrases.
- You analyse the effects of these selections, referring to specific techniques.

6 Preparing to answer writer's effects questions (E)

Learning objectives

- To locate the correct section of a passage and select relevant words, phrases or other examples.
- To analyse the effects of the language chosen by the writer.

In order to understand how writers achieve their effects, it is useful to follow a clear process. This is especially important as some of the effects created are quite subtle and require you to look for **implicit meanings (see pages 20–27)**.

Exploring skills

Checklist for success

✔ Understand and explain the meaning of particular words and phrases.
✔ Respond to the sensory or emotive appeals the writer makes to the reader.
✔ Read between the lines for implied or suggested meanings.
✔ Draw conclusions and inferences about the atmosphere and tone created.

Read this story opening about a young man who has arrived late at night and is searching for 'Fourwinds', a house deep in the countryside.

> It was not silence I heard: my feet trod steadily on the stony road; I heard the hooting of an owl, the screech of some unseen creature in the verge, the faintest rustle of grasses sighing against each other. It was on a high, open road, curving over the swell of hillside that I saw as the flanks of some prehistoric animal, deep in slumber. I could see quite clearly my road curving ahead, and the clump of trees, inky black, that marked my turning point.
>
> Linda Newbury, *Set in Stone*

1 How well do you understand the basic meaning of the text? With a partner, put these two phrases into your own words, thinking about possible **synonyms** you could use:

- 'the screech of some unseen creature on the verge'
- 'the faintest rustle of grasses'.

Key term

synonyms: words with a very similar meaning: for example, *angry* and *cross*.

Of course, a text cannot simply be understood by explaining specific words and phrases. We need to look deeper.

(2) Select and note down **four words or phrases** from the passage that create a sense of unease or mystery.

(3) With a partner, discuss **why** you think these particular words or phrases create this feeling.

(4) Write a paragraph about the four words or phrases and why you feel they create a feeling of unease.

The same character now continues his journey in a new paragraph. Read the next part of the story.

> Fourwinds, the house at which I was to take up employment, apparently lay in a very isolated spot, for I could see no sign of habitation, no plume of smoke from a shepherd's humble croft. I felt very conscious of travelling from one stage of my life to the next: every step away from the road carried me farther from London, my mother and sister, the art school and my friends there; each tread brought me nearer to the house and its inhabitants, of which, and of whom, I knew very little.

— the writer is alone

— repetition of 'no' is negative and empty

This passage:

● **builds** on what we were told in the previous paragraph and increases our sense of foreboding and anticipation

● **adds** new information and implies more about the narrator.

(5) Write further notes about the extract to analyse the effects or feelings created. Think about symbolic ideas, where what is described reflects bigger or wider issues.

(6) Share your annotations with a partner. Then, using the feedback, write your own short response to the paragraph describing what effect is created by the selected words and phrases. Is the effect still one of unease or do you sense other feelings now?

Developing skills

When responding to a question, you may have much more to say about one aspect of the passage than the other. For example, powerful imagery or descriptions can be relatively easy to write about, but where clues are more subtle, it can be more difficult. However, it is important to answer as fully as you can on both aspects or parts of a text.

Read the following extract from a story by E. Annie Proulx. In it, a man is hunting grouse.

> The first morning of the season was cold, the frosted clumps of tussock grass like spiral **nebulae**. I went up the hardwood slopes, the trees growing out of a cascade of shattered rock spilled by the last glacier. No birds in the grey monotony of beech and maple, and I kept climbing for the ridges where stands of spruce knotted dark shelter in their branches.
>
> The slope levelled off; in a rain-filled hollow, a rind of ice imprisoned the leaves, soot-black, brown, umber, grey-tan like the coats of deer, in its glassy clasp. No birds.
>
> I walked up into the conifers, my panting the only sound. Fox tracks in the hoarfrost. The weight of the somber sky pressed down with the heaviness of a coming storm. No birds in the spruce. Under the trees the hollows between the roots were bowls filled with ice crystals like moth antennae. The birds were somewhere else, close hugging other trees while they waited for the foul weather to hit, or even now above me, rigidly stretched out to imitate broken branch stubs in the web of interlacing conifers, invisible and silent, watching the fool who wandered below, a passing hat and a useless tub of steel tied to the ground by the earth's inertia.
>
> What, I thought, like every **grouse** hunter has thought, what if I could fly, could glide through the spruce leaders and smile down into the smug, feathery faces like an old ogre confronting the darling princess. The view from the ground was green bottlebrushes, impenetrable, confusing, secretive, against a sky the colour of an old galvanised pail. No birds.

(7) Remember, it can be the combination of different elements that create effects. But first, focus on the elements themselves. Make notes on:
- what happens (if anything) in this passage as a whole
- the weather and the environment, and particular words or phrases that stand out
- the birds and how they are described.

Glossary

nebulae: an interstellar cloud of dust and gas
grouse: a type of game bird bred for hunting

Top tip

Focus on words or phrases that catch your eye or are especially powerful or evocative. Imagery, in particular, is worth analysing.

Applying skills

Now look at this question based on the passage.

> *Reread the descriptions of:*
> *(a) the birds in paragraphs 1 and 3*
> *(b) the narrator's fantasy in paragraph 4.*
> *Select four powerful words or phrases from each paragraph. Your choices should include imagery. Explain how each word or phrase selected is used effectively in the context.*

There are 10 marks for this answer, so 5 marks, more or less, for each of (a) and (b).

When answering, remember to:

- **locate** the sections referred to
- **select** specific words and phrases related to the two aspects you must answer on and make sure one includes use of **imagery**
- **analyse** and **explain** why they are effective.

You will need to consider the different techniques used by writers, as explained on pages 16–33, such as:

- particularly powerful vocabulary (for example, connotations of particular verbs or nouns)
- emotive language (expressing strong emotions or feelings)

- imagery
- sentence variety
- contrast
- repetition
- information that is left out or implied.

Here is the first paragraph of a sample response to part (a) of the question.

The narrator's first mention of the birds is their absence: 'No birds in the grey monotony'. This void, and the link to dull colours and unchanging nature, is effective because it implies stalemate and inaction.

— right focus
— has already interpreted the effect
— further synonym for 'absence'
— explains effectiveness of quoted words
— sums up combined effect of description

(8) Using this approach, reread the 'grouse' passage, select a word or phrase from paragraph 3 and write a similar response. Then write an answer to part (b) of the question.

Sound progress

- You select appropriate words and phrases to answer the question.
- You explain meanings at a basic level.
- You say something about the effectiveness of the choices, but without much detail or understanding of what is implied.

Excellent progress

- You choose words and phrases carefully to answer the question.
- You explain, but also interpret meaning in your own words, making a judgement about combined effects or the particular effects of the selected words or phrases.

Exam-style questions and sample responses: comprehension and writer's effects questions

Key skills

You will need to show the following skill:

- demonstrate understanding of how writers achieve effects.

Exploring responses: comprehension questions

1. Read the following passage. It comes from Sarfraz Manzoor's autobiography, *Greetings from Bury Park*, which describes growing up in Luton, in the United Kingdom, as a young British Pakistani boy in the 1970s and 1980s.

My brother passed his driving test at the third attempt and was soon scouring the pages of the *Luton Herald* for a cheap second-hand car. He eventually found a gold Vauxhall Viva which my father bought for seventy pounds. Dressed in his stonewashed denim jacket and jeans, his face bristling with stubble and wearing mirrored sunglasses, Sohail would take the Viva for 5
aimless drives into town with the windows down and bhangra bursting from the speakers. At the weekends he would lovingly repair the bodywork, filling dents with gauze and letting me help with the vacuuming. When he replaced the old car stereo he gave the old one to me. My friend Ben explained how I could wire speakers up to it and have my own music system in the bedroom I 10
shared with my brother.

Sohail no longer played sports for the college but he went weight-training three times a week; he also bought body-building magazines and the walls of our bedroom were plastered with images of past Mr Universes. The men all had the same expression of concentrated serenity, the arms would be either 15
outstretched like a Greek god or posed to display the bulging biceps. Sohail read books on body building; we knew Arnold Schwarzenegger when he was a body builder. When he caught me looking at the magazines Sohail would insist that I felt his biceps. 'Can you feel that? Does it feel hard?' he would ask proudly. 'Don't you wish you had muscles like that?' 20

I loathed being thin. At junior school I was convinced a tapeworm was getting to my food before me; it was the only explanation for why I remained rake thin no matter how much I ate. The photographs of body builders on the bedroom wall did nothing for my self-esteem. My father believed the best cure for low self-esteem was public ridicule. This meant that whenever anyone 25
came to visit there was an inevitable moment when they would ask how the children were. It was particularly pointed when Shuja came to visit because my father had known him since childhood and the longer my father had

known someone the freer he felt to humiliate his children in their presence. Although he was the same age as my father, Shuja seemed older; his eyes were deep set and he looked like he was wearing eyeliner, but in fact it was charcoal. The henna in his hair had turned it orange. 'Manzoor sahib, is your son eating correctly? He looks painfully thin. Not like his brother at all.' 30

'Yes, he is very thin. We tell him to eat more, but nothing seems to work. Son, pull your shirtsleeves up. Let him see your arms. Do you see how thin they are? Practically sticks.' 35

(2) Read the following exam-style comprehension questions and the sample responses that follow.

(a) *State how many times Sohail took his driving test. (paragraph 1 'My brother … brother')*

(b) *Explain, using your own words, what the writer tells us about the way Sohail treated his car? ('At the weekends … vacuming.' (lines 7–9))*

(c) *What does the writer means by the phrase 'public ridicule'? (line 26)*

(d) *What does the writer tell us about how Sarfraz thought and felt about being thin? (paragraph 3 'I loathed … at all.')*

(f) *Why did Safraz's father embarrass him in front of Shuja? (paragraph 3 'I loathed … at all.')*

Response 1, task (a)

Sohail took his test twice and passed it the third time which shows he wasn't very good.

Feedback

This sample answer is too long and contains a comment as well as a slightly unclear response. Clearly the writer of the response has understood that the test was taken three times but says he 'took his test twice', which is confusing and could cause this response to fail to score a mark.

Recommend: no mark

Response 2, task (a)

> Three times.

Feedback

This answer is all that is required. The prompt word 'state' means that a quotation is acceptable and no comment or explanation is needed. It does not matter that the answer is not a full sentence.

Recommended: full marks

Response 1, task (b)

> He drove it aimlessly and played loud music in it.

Feedback

This answer misunderstands the focus of the question, which is on Sohail's treatment of the car rather than how it is driven. It also uses a word close to one from the original text ('aimless') but does not explain what this term means.

Recommended: no marks

Response 2, task (b)

> Sohail mends the car, cleans it and buys new equipment for it.

Feedback

This sample answer is brief but by using synonyms shows a clear understanding of what 'repair', 'vacuuming' and 'replaced the old car stereo' mean.

Recommended: full marks

Response 1, task (c)

> The writer means that he looks stupid in front of everyone.

Feedback

This answer is partially correct as 'in front of everyone' is a fair explanation of 'public'. However, the comment 'he looks stupid' does not explain what 'ridicule' is. It is an explanation for looking ridiculous.

Recommended: half marks

Response 2, task (c)

> That his dad makes fun of him in front of other people

Feedback

From this answer it is clear that the writer of the response has understood that ridicule is a process 'done' by the father. '[M]akes fun of' is a fair synonym and 'in front of other people' is acceptable for 'public'. A full sentence answer would have been preferred.

Recommended: full marks

Response 1, task (d)

> He 'loathed being thin'.

Feedback

This answer is correct but there are actually three possible answers in the lines specified. No reference is made to his confusion as to why he was thin or to his low self-esteem.

Recommended: award 1 of 3 possible marks

Response 2, task (d)

> We are told that he 'loathed being thin', 'was convinced a tapeworm was getting my food' and had 'low self-esteem'.

Feedback

This is a full answer covering all of the boy's thoughts and feelings.

Recommended: full marks

Response 1, task (f)

> Because he'd known him a long time

Feedback

This sample answer is incorrect. The text says that the embarrassment was worse in front of old friends but the main point is that the father thought humiliation was a solution for low self-esteem.

Recommended: no marks

Response 2, task (f)

> Because he thought that public ridicule would cure
> Sarfraz's low self-esteem

Feedback

This is a correct answer. It is not in the writer's own words as this is not required by the question.

Recommended: full marks

Exploring responses: writer's effects questions

1 Read the following exam-style writer's effect questions and the sample responses below them.

> (e) (i) Re-read the first and second paragraphs ('My brother passed' to 'Don't you wish you had muscles like that?'). Explain using your own words, what the writer means by the words in italics in three of the following phrases:
>
> (a) 'aimless drives into town with the windows down' (line 6)
> (b) 'lovingly repair the bodywork' (line 7)
> (c) 'the walls of our bedroom were plastered with images of past Mr Universes' (line 14)
> (d) 'Sohail would insist that I felt his biceps' (line 19)
>
> (ii) Sohail is very keen to make the most of his appearance and show off his car and his looks. Explain how the words and language in each of the phrases you have chosen help to suggest Sohail's vanity.

Response 1

Word/phrase	(i) Meaning	(ii) How this suggests Sohail's vanity
(a) 'aimless'	no real aim to his driving as if he has no place to go	It suggests this because he doesn't have a purpose, just want to show his car to others.
(b) 'lovingly'	with kindness and affection, he likes doing the bodywork on the car he bought very much	The word 'lovingly' tells us he likes the car more than anything else, even people, which isn't very normal, and means he is a show-off about having a car.
(c) 'plastered'	wrapped tightly on the wall all over like wall-paper	This shows that posters of body-builders are very important to Sohail otherwise he wouldn't have covered his wall with them, and he is a body-builder too.

Feedback

(a) While the explanation is broadly correct it uses a very similar word to the one in the text, and misses the point that it is not that he has 'no place to go' as such, but that he chooses not to go somewhere. The further explanation gets close to a good explanation when it says he 'want to show his car to others' but there is nothing to say that the car is an extension of himself and the verb does not agree correctly.

(b) The explanation is close to the meaning, but 'lovingly' suggests something stronger than 'kindness and affection'. The further explanation needs to focus on the pride Sohail feels, and also how the car reflects his own personality.

(c) Quite a good explanation of the word 'plastered' and a better further explanation which suggests how important body-building must be to Sohail. The response begins to make the connection to Sohail's own body-building but needs to go further.

Recommended Band: 3 (Core)

Response 2

Word/phrase	(i) Meaning	(ii) How this suggests Sohail's vanity
(a) 'aimless'	without a goal or end point of the journey in mind	This adjective suggests the journey is less important than him showing off to the world. Because it is a drive without an end, it means he can spend more time showing himself off.
(b) 'lovingly'	adoringly	The adverb 'lovingly' suggests he acts towards the car as if it is a part of him, and that by making it look good it suggests he is making himself look good too.
(c) 'plastered'	stuck tightly/ overlapping each other	The verb 'plastered' suggests these pictures completely cover everything in sight. As Sohail is a body-builder too, it is like he has images of himself all over the room, which is very vain.

Feedback

(a) The explanation is very good – the key is that the journey has no end point. The further explanation enlarges on this by explaining how this gives Sohail more time to show off.

(b) The explanation is spot on. 'Lovingly' is a very strong adverb and suggests adoration of the object – in this case the car. The response has cleverly linked the way Sohail treats his car with himself – it is his car and by pampering it, he is making himself look good.

(c) This is very good explanation of the word, although 'plastered' is perhaps even stronger as an idea than 'stuck tightly'. The further explanation links Sohail's desire to be surrounded by the 'body beautiful' with his own image.

Recommended Band: 1 (Core)

Exam-style questions and sample responses: comprehension and writer's effects questions

Exploring responses: writer's effects questions Ⓔ

1 Read the following passage from a short story called 'Honeymoon' by Charlotte Wood. Mandy, 21, is on her honeymoon with Matthew at a house by a lake. Each morning she takes a kayak (a type of canoe) out onto the lake. One morning she sees the small red swatch of a kite high in the air.

When she and Cathy were small their father had had a brief kite-flying craze, driving his reluctant girls to the highest of the bare hills near the town. He would lift his kites, delicate creations of dowl and bright tissue paper, from the boot of the car. Mandy would huddle in her nylon parka, hair whipping her face in the freezing wind. 'I told you to wear something warmer,' her father growled while he untangled a cord. But Mandy had insisted on her pink tartan skirt and bare legs, and the wind was icy. The girls had to stand, each holding a skein of nylon line in both hands, while their father strode up the hill ahead of them. Then he would throw up each of the kites and shout, 'Run!', and they had to run over the knobbly tussocky ground, holding the lines high above their heads.

The kite would mostly swirl once or twice and arrow straight towards the stony ground. But sometimes, sometimes, it would lift, and the spool would whirl and tumble in her hands, the purple kite lifting higher and higher, and Mandy would begin to smile, and Cathy's green box kite would lift and she would shriek, her head thrown back and her mouth wide open, and their father would stand and watch his children falling in love with the high space above that small town, with the possibilities of flight.

Now Mandy looks up at the distant red kite in the blue sky above the lake, anchored to somewhere on the distant shore. She remembers the rhythmic tug on the line, calibrating its pull against the weight of her own body, the pleasure of letting out the line, then resisting. She turns from it then, and paddles towards the centre of the lake. But all morning, it seems the kite stays with her, always above her, there in the outer corner of her sight.

The wind rises. She churns back through the water towards the house, breathing deeply and rhythmically, pushing the high end of the paddle forward with all the strength of one arm as she dips deep and pulls the low end through the water with the other hand, the choppy little waves slapping over the prow of the kayak.

Afterwards she walks up the garden, her arms and legs pleasantly jittery from the last long stretch of effort.

When she slides open the glass door Matthew is reading the paper at the table.

'I said I was going to come with you,' he says crossly. 'But you didn't wake me up.'

The room feels small and airless after the wide gusty space of the lake, the red star of the kite stamped on the sky.

'Oh sorry,' she says, as she passes his chair. 'I forgot.'

(2) Read the following exam-style writer's effects question and the sample responses that follow.

> *Re-read the descriptions of:*
>
> *(a)   the kites in paragraph 2 and paragraph 3, beginning, 'The kite would mostly swirl once or twice …'*
>
> *(b)   Mandy's return to the lake house from 'Afterwards she walks up the garden …' to the end of the passage.*
>
> *Select four powerful words or phrases from each section. Your choices should include imagery. Explain how each word or phrase selected is used effectively in the context.*
>
> *Write about 200 to 300 words, allowing for the size of your handwriting.*
>
> *Up to 10 marks are available for the content of your answer.*

Response 1

(a) 'swirl' and 'arrow': these give a clear image of the kite's rapid movements and how it changes direction unexpectedly. ⟵ **specific focus on individual words**

'Lifting higher and higher' suggests the kite is almost disappearing from view into the air. It is like it ⟵ **suggests symbolism but not developed** represents the children's enjoyment which gets higher with it.

'distant red kite' is an image which links back to the kite Mandy saw in childhood. It reminds her of being a child again, but this time she is not in charge of the kite. Its colour is bright, like it is reminding her of something.

'rhythmic tug' is effective because it makes me think the kite from childhood was like music, perhaps a ⟵ **good suggested link, but effect not really explained** symbol or metaphor of a heartbeat.

(b) 'pleasantly jittery': this suggests she's feeling happy, but 'jittery' also suggests nerves, like butterflies in the stomach, like when you're in love, which is effective because it fits the honeymoon. — **good links and explanation**

'the room feels small and airless'; the size of the room and the fact it is enclosed contrasts with the wide open space of the lake which is described well by 'wide gusty space' and seeing the kite. It implies Mandy wants to escape from the room and the situation. — **good comparison but effect needs to be explored more fully**

'stamped on the sky' – makes us think of something like a strong mark which can't be forgotten.

Feedback

(a) The words and phrases are well chosen, and explained in clear terms. On occasions, the response goes beyond the literal – the vivid movement of the kites, for example – to the symbolic and how they represent the children's enjoyment or how the rhythmic tug links to a 'heartbeat'. However, more on the imagery and these links and connections could have been developed.

(b) The second part of the answer shows some good interpretation of the selected phrases, but more could have been made to connect the 'airless' room with the stale conversation between Mandy and her husband. Perhaps a comment on the combined effect of the kite-flying episode and the later view of the kite and what it represents would help.

Recommended Band: 2 (Extended)

3 How could this sample response be improved to make it a Band 1? Work with a partner to decide, using the Excellent progress box in the Check your progress table on page 156 as a guide.

Response 2

(a) The verbs 'swirl' and then 'arrow' suggest the unpredictability of the kites, through their rapidly-changing movement which is a metaphor for life itself. — **well-chosen verbs to focus on**

'Stony ground', is very powerful imagery as it creates the effect of dreams breaking in hard everyday reality. But dreams do succeed sometimes and the 'possibilities of flight' seems to be a metaphor for the future – the potential for happiness. — **inference from imagery explained very clearly**

The 'distant red kite' is a symbol that creates the — picks up on further symbolism
association of a warning light and suggests all is not
well for Mandy. It is out of reach, yet it follows her
and she can't escape, like a memory of better times. — excellent paraphrase and interpretation in own words

(b) Her return to the lake house emphasises the gap
between hopes and reality.
The phrase 'pleasantly jittery' suggests she is
unsure of herself, as if slightly drunk or nervous, or
like a teenage lover, which is appropriate given it's her
honeymoon.
But the juxtaposition of the 'small and airless' — language term used correctly and link to marriage made clear
room with the lake, only serves to emphasise the
claustrophobia of her marriage.
'The red star of the kite' associates the kite with
something almost heavenly or spiritual, and is a
metaphor that creates an additional contrast with
what is going on down on earth.
The kite 'stamped on the sky' is an effective contrast
to her current situation. It is used as a positive image
in the character's mind, suggesting it is branded on
her memory, like the enjoyment of childhood kite-flying. — excellent link back to earlier symbolism

Feedback

(a) The words and phrases chosen represent the vivid symbols and images of a childhood that is past, when someone else was responsible for her, and when anything seemed possible. The link is made very successfully between the kite's movement and life itself, and later how the image of the kite creates a lasting contrast between the character's current situation and the past.

(b) Language terms are used correctly and help to explain how effective the specific words and phrases are in conveying the contrast between the freedom of the lake and the claustrophobia of her marriage. An opportunity is perhaps missed to pick up on the brutal shortness of the conversation and the metaphor of the kite being like a 'star' and all that suggests, but otherwise this is very impressive response.

Recommended Band: 1 (Extended)

Sound progress

- I can identify the required words or phrases from a passage.

- I can show understanding of the writer's words and phrases.

- I can show some understanding of how writers achieve effects.

Sound progress

- I can locate the correct section or area of a passage.

- I can select appropriate words and phrases where required.

- I can explain the meanings of words and some effects in at least one part of the question.

- I can show some understanding of how writers achieve effects.

Excellent progress

- I can locate the correct section or area of the text referred to.

- I can select appropriate words and phrases where required.

- I can discuss a wide range of language used in the passage, analysing connotations and making inferences.

- I can explain the writer's reasons for using specific words, phrases or other techniques including imagery by referring both to the meaning and associations of the words used.

- I can group examples of the writer's language uses together to give an overview of the intended attitude or meanings.

- I can paraphrase or interpret meanings in my own words in creative ways.

Chapter 6

Extended response and directed writing questions

Some assessment tasks will require you to read one or two passages and select points and details from them to then reuse and adapt to create a new piece of writing on a given topic and for a given audience. This type of writing is often referred to as extended response or directed writing.

To answer these types of question you will need to use both reading and writing skills:

Reading:
- demonstrate understanding of the explicit meanings included in the passage
- demonstrate understanding of implicit meanings and attitudes in the passage
- analyse, evaluate and develop facts, ideas and opinions

Writing:
- articulate experience and express what is thought, felt and imagined
- sequence facts, ideas and opinions
- use a range of appropriate vocabulary
- use register appropriate to audience and context
- make accurate use of spelling, punctuation and grammar.

You will need to use the understanding of different writing forms and different writing purposes that you developed in Chapter 3.

1 Understanding extended response questions Ⓒ

Learning objectives

● To understand what is required for extended response questions.
● To be able to break down the question.

An extended response writing task will follow a passage you have read. It asks you to write a particular text, based on the passage. It is likely to provide details about:

- **what role/voice** you will take on to write the text
- **why** you are writing (the main purpose)
- the **type or form** of writing you must produce
- **who** it is for (the audience)
- **what to include** (information)
- and possibly **how to start** (the opening lines).

It is vital to balance the content (the information you include) with an appropriate **style** for the audience and purpose.

Exploring skills

In the following extended response task, the passage provided was a radio interview with a mountain ranger talking about his job, including why he loves the Rockies, the reasons he gets called out to groups in the Rockies and what he advises people planning to do the walk. (You can read this on page 170.)

Glossary

The Rockies: a range of mountains in North America

> *Imagine you are a student wishing to embark on a walking tour of the Rockies with two friends, which will require time off school. Write a letter to your head teacher requesting time off and reassuring him or her that you and your friends will be safe.*
>
> *You should include:*
> - *why you wish to do the trip despite any concerns from the school*
> - *your preparations for travelling*
> - *how you will deal with any unwanted attention from bears.*
>
> *Begin your letter with:*
>
> **Dear Mr/Mrs (head teacher's name)**
>
> **I know that you are concerned that I wish to take several weeks off school, walking with two friends in the Rocky Mountains, but...**

1. Note down the words and phrases from the question that tell you:
   - what **role or voice** you will take on as you write (the **viewpoint** you are writing from) **(See pages 56–60 for more on voice and role.)**
   - what sort of text you have to write (the **form**)
   - the **purpose** of the text (why you are writing)
   - who it is for (the **audience**)
   - what to include (the **content** or key points).

   Compare what you have written with a partner's answers. Do you agree?

Building skills

The information you gather from identifying the key words in the question is vital.

2. Copy and complete the table below.

Key part of question	Key words and phrases	What this means for your answer (both content and structure)
Who you will be when you write	Student	You are not an expert so you will write about the advice you have been given and the preparations you have made. Your 'voice' will not be that of an experienced guide, but of a younger, quite excited traveller.
Type of text	Letter	It is likely to have a structure in which you make clear what you are writing about first, followed by further explanations.
Purpose of text		
Audience		
What to include		

Developing skills

3. Here is one student's letter opening. How well do you think they have read the question? Pick out the good and bad points.

> Hi Carl!
> You cool with us going? This trip I'm gonna do is AWESOME, dude! Just think – wild animals ready to rip us to shreds, weeks without food – how great is that? Only kidding – I heard this expert guy on the radio who pretty much gave me all the info on what to do if a bear attacks me. Basically – run like mad!!

Applying skills

4. Rewrite the opening paragraph above using a more appropriate style.

Sound progress

- You focus on the correct content from the source text or passage.
- You use this content in a way that makes it clear who you are and why you are writing.
- Your style is generally appropriate for the given voice and audience.

Developing an extended response

Learning objectives

● To use the skills you have learned when answering an extended response task.

Exploring skills

1 Read the following passage, which describes an 84-year-old man's plans to sail from the Canary Islands to the Bahamas on a raft. As you read, imagine you are the man's grandson and what you might be feeling about the trip.

> In his tiny flat in West London, Anthony Smith is racking his brain as to what might possibly go wrong with his next big adventure. But try as he might, he can't think of anything, other than to observe that 'the most dangerous things are the ones you haven't thought of.'
>
> You and I might beg to differ. In fact, if you weren't lucky enough to 5 have met him, you'd probably think he was off his rocker. He is, after all, 84 years old, with a gammy leg and still recovering from a near-fatal car accident. And he is planning to sail nearly 3000 miles across the Atlantic with three other men in their later years. On a raft made of gas pipes.
>
> 'Why a raft? Because it's interesting and it's safe and it's easy,' he says. 10 Rafts, he says, are stable, impossible to overturn, surprisingly easy to steer and have a remarkable safety record. 'On the 50 or so big rafting expeditions I know of, only one person has died. But he was 64 and he was depressed and his expedition had failed.' In other words, Smith seems gently to be implying, the poor fellow had it coming to him. [...] 15
>
> He says having an older crew should prevent any unnecessary risk-taking. 'Older people are more cautious about themselves. They're not as stupid as young people. On the Kon-tiki expedition, some of them went swimming and almost died because the raft drifted off faster than they could swim. Well, we're going to be more sensible. Swimming's banned.' 20
>
> *Saga Magazine*

Building skills

2 Now read the following question and note down the key words, which will help you complete the task below.

> *Imagine you are Anthony Smith's grandson. You have been invited onto a news programme to talk about your grandfather. Write the conversation that you have with the presenter. You should include:*
> * *what your grandfather is intending to do*
> * *your concerns about the trip*
> * *the reassurances your grandfather has given you.*

Developing skills

You should now be clear about:

- the different **'voices'** and **styles** you need: the grandson and the adult TV interviewer
- **what to include** from **the passage** and **what you can add** (your own ideas about the grandson's feelings).

Do not simply reproduce what is in the passage. You need to go further and **infer** what sort of person the grandfather is and how this will affect the grandson's point of view.

(3) List the objections the grandson might have.

> - If something does go wrong, will he be fit enough to cope?
> - I'll miss him!

The bullets in the question will provide a structure for your answer:

> Interviewer: So, can you tell viewers about your grandfather's incredible plans?
>
> You: Well, he's aiming to...
>
> (Add follow-up questions to develop this section.)
>
> Interviewer: And what do you feel about his wish to venture across the Atlantic?
>
> You: I guess it's good that he...
>
> (Add follow-up questions and answers.)
>
> Interviewer: But how do you feel personally? You must be worried!
>
> You: Of course...

— these questions reflect the first two bullets in the question

— this question moves the interview towards the third bullet in the question

Applying skills

(4) Now draft a response to the question.

Checklist for success

✔ Base your interview on what is in the passage but use your own words.

✔ Include Anthony Smith's perspective, making inferences about his character and relationships from what you've read.

✔ Develop the voices of the interviewer and grandson so they seem 'real'.

> **Top tip**
>
> Make sure you use the features of good **dialogue** (see pages 66–69). Structure the interview so that the discussion **develops**, for example, with the interviewer asking increasingly pressing questions: *Surely you would not deny your grandfather the chance to enjoy himself?*

Sound progress

- You base your content on the source texts and your own details.
- Your style is generally appropriate to the voice(s) and audience.
- You structure your response to reshape the material from the text.

3 Developing an extended response

Learning objectives

- To understand what is required for an extended response writing task.
- To be able to break down the question and respond to the passage.

For this type of question you will usually have to read a passage of about 650–750 words. You will then write a text based on details from the passage.

Checklist for success

Read the question carefully and make sure you are clear about:

✔ **what role/voice** you will take on to write the text
✔ **why** you are writing (the main purpose)
✔ the **type or form** of writing you must produce
✔ **who** it is for (the audience)
✔ **what to include** (selecting and adapting information from the text(s) provided, inferring meaning and adding your own details).

Exploring skills

1 Read the following extract from *The Old Patagonian Express* by Paul Theroux. In this extract, the author, from the USA, has been taken to a football match between El Salvador and Mexico by his friend Alfredo. **Touts** are trying to sell them tickets.

'Take your watch off,' he said. 'And your ring. Put them in your pocket. Be very careful. Most of these people are thieves. They will rob you.'

I did as I was told. 'What about the tickets? Shall we buy some **Suns** from these boys?'

'No, I will buy **Shades**.'

'Are they expensive?'

'Of course, but this will be a great game. I could never see such a game in Santa Ana. Anyway, the Shades will be quieter.' Alfredo looked around. 'Hide over there by the wall. I will get the tickets.'

Alfredo vanished into the conga line at a ticket window. He appeared again at the middle of the line, jumped the queue, elbowed forward and in a very short time had fought his way to the window. Even his friends marvelled at his speed. He came towards us smiling, waving the tickets in triumph.

Glossary

Touts: people who sells tickets at high prices outside grounds
Suns: tickets for places in the sun
Shades: tickets for places under cover or out of the sun

We were frisked at the entrance; we passed through a tunnel and emerged at the end of the stadium. From the outside it had looked like a kettle; inside, its shape was more of a **salver**, a **tureen** filled with brown screeching faces. In the centre was a pristine rectangle of green grass.

It was, those 45,000 people, a model of Salvadorean society. Not only the half of the stadium where the Suns sat (and it was jammed: not an empty seat was visible); or the better-dressed and almost as crowded half of the Shades (at night, in the dry season, there was no difference in the quality of the seats: we sat on concrete steps, but ours, being more expensive than the Suns, were less crowded); there was a section that Alfredo had not mentioned: the Balconies. Above us, in five tiers of a gallery that ran around our half of the stadium, were the Balcony people.

Balcony people had season tickets. Balcony people had small rooms, cupboard sized, about as large as the average Salvadorean hut; I could see wine bottles, the glasses, the plates of food. Balcony people had folding chairs and a good view of the field. There were not many Balcony people – two or three hundred – but at $2000 for a season ticket in a country where the per capita income was $373 one could understand why. The Balcony people faced the screaming Suns and, beyond the stadium, a plateau. What I took to be lumpish multi-coloured vegetation covering the plateau was, I realised, a heap of Salvadoreans standing on top or clinging to the sides. There were thousands of them in this mass, and it was a sight more terrifying than the Suns. They were lighted by the stadium glare; there was a just-perceptible crawling movement among the bodies; it was an ant-hill.

The writing task you will be set requires you to show you have read the passage carefully and understood both **explicit** and **implicit** meanings. **(See pages 16–27 for more on these.)**

(2) Note down the explicit information given in the passage (the basic 'facts'). For example:

* Writer goes to football match.
* He thinks about buying tickets from touts.

3 Developing an extended response

Building skills

(3) In a small group, discuss the implicit information: what is revealed about the writer, Alfredo and their attitudes through the language and content. Then independently, answer these questions.

- What image of Salvadorean society is provided by the description of the Suns, Shades, Ant-hill and Balcony people?
- What are the author's feelings about the crowd? Does he find the experience funny, for example?
- What can we infer about Alfredo from what we are told? For example, think about how he gets the tickets.

Share your answers with the class. What picture, if any, emerges of the author and Alfredo?

Developing skills

(4) Read this task based on the passage and note down the key words so that you are absolutely clear what you have to do.

> *Imagine you are Alfredo. Write a journal entry about the day. Make sure you include:*
> - *details of the events that took place and what happened*
> - *your view of the stadium and experience*
> - *how you think Paul, the author, reacted and felt.*
> *Begin: Today, I took my American friend Paul to a football match...*

(5) Before you write your answer, discuss in pairs how Alfredo might write differently about the experience from Paul. For example:

- In what way does he seem to 'know his way around'?
- How does he respond to some of his fellow countrymen?
- How does he feel about seeing the game?

What sort of 'voice' might Alfredo have? (For example, jokey or friendly.)

Here is the opening of a sample Band 1 response which uses some of the advice above to good effect.

Today I took my American friend Paul to a football match. It was between us and Mexico and generated the usual frenzy of excitement on both sides as they are our arch rivals. I was so happy to be there: we never get these games here, so it was an experience to savour, although I must admit keeping an eye on Paul made it challenging...

— excellent vocabulary based on accurate content

— Alfredo's voice: his liking for football, how his home town does not get big games

— shows he knows his way around

Applying skills

(6) Spend 5 minutes planning your response and considering what you know about **diary or journal entry conventions. (See pages 70–71 for more on this.)** Try out the following structure to plan the different aspects of the experience.

> Paragraph 1: quick explanation of what I did (basic 'explicit' information about the events)
> Paragraph 2: my excitement about being there
> Paragraph 3: getting the tickets – problems with touts, my warnings to Paul
> Paragraph 4: going into the stadium, Paul's response to what he saw; why it was good we were in the Shades
> Paragraph 5: how I felt about the crowds and my own people
> Paragraph 5: what I felt about Paul's visit and the impressions he got

Or you could begin with overall impressions of Paul, like this:

> Paul is an interesting friend. Today, I expected him to be put off football matches for life, but…

(7) Write a first draft of your journal entry from Alfredo's point of view.

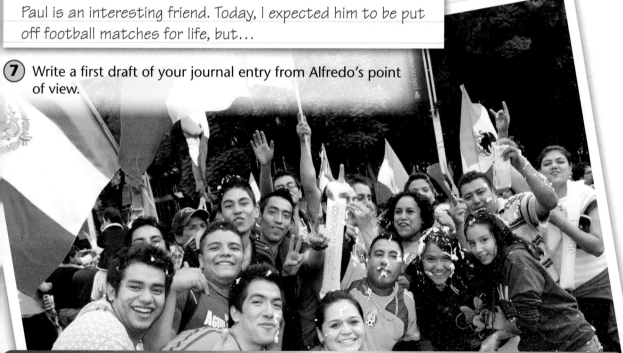

Sound progress

- You cover the basic information given in the passage in a clear way.
- You make an attempt to capture Alfredo's attitude but it is not sufficiently different from Paul's.
- You structure your response to reshape the material from the passage.

Excellent progress

- You draw together different elements and information from the passage in a convincing way, including more subtle or implied meanings.
- You capture Alfredo's voice and his perspective on events in a clear way, making the best use of the journal form.

4 Developing a directed writing response Ⓒ Ⓔ

- To understand what is required for a directed writing response.
- To write an effective plan and response.

Successful directed writing depends on you reading all the information provided carefully, and considering how it can form the basis for your own text.

Exploring skills

1 Read the two texts provided below for a directed writing-style task. As you read them, bear in mind that you will need to make use of them in your response.

> *Here are your notes from an interview you conducted for your school magazine with a student called Paolo. He has set up a scheme at school where young people can text, email or phone for advice if they are worried about crime.*

Interview notes: 'Call me' scheme

- Set up by Paolo's after his cell phone was stolen
- Upset because police didn't follow this up
- 'Call me!' has a special mobile number and email address

- Five boys answer emails, calls and texts
- Boys are volunteers: some with strong personalities, some more gentle/thoughtful
- Open from 4 p.m. to midnight each day
- Average of 3–4 calls a day, 10–12 texts or emails
- Calls have been as much about relationship or family problems as crime
- Only one student has complained about the advice given (on bullying)

Top tip

Even before you look at the writing task, you can begin to **infer** from the information given.
For example, for this task:
- from the interview notes you can infer that not many calls were received, meaning the scheme has not been a great success
- from the letter, when the parent includes the question 'What sort of advice is this?' you can infer that the writer's sense of frustration at the boy's behaviour.

Key term

infer: read between the lines of a text to draw out the **implicit meanings**

Letter to Paolo from a parent concerned about the scheme

Dear Paolo,

I'm contacting you about this new scheme of yours. I am sure it is a good idea in principle, but I feel bound to inform you of my views. Recently, our son came to us and told us he had used your scheme. He was upset about an illness in the family, and didn't want to trouble us, so he phoned the 'Call me' number. Apparently, a very helpful boy talked with him. He had been through a similar experience and made our son feel he wasn't alone. The problem was that the next time our son felt he needed to talk, and tried to phone 'Call Me', there was no answer as it was closed during school hours. Luckily, this time we realised he was feeling upset. So we talked to him and were able to help out. But, what would have happened otherwise? Not all parents recognise when their children are upset.

However, more worryingly, we have recently found out about another call he made to 'Call me'. At the time, he was being bullied at school by some older boys, but on this occasion when he phoned the scheme, he spoke to a boy who didn't show much sympathy and told him to 'deal with it' by taking on the bullies himself! What sort of advice is that? Fortunately, our son had the sense to talk to his teacher, who contacted us, and the bullying was dealt with in the proper way.

To sum up, his first experience of your scheme was positive; I don't know if that first boy had been trained in counselling but at least he was sympathetic unlike the second one!

I am convinced your heart is in the right place, Paolo, but we felt it best to let you know about our son's experiences. He tells us that he would think twice about using the scheme again.

Building skills

The directed writing-style task you will respond to is:

You are a fellow student at Paolo's school and have interviewed him about the scheme. Write an article for your school paper in which you argue whether the scheme is a good idea or not. You will need to:

* *explain the scheme and how it works*
* *explain why and how Paolo set it up*
* *evaluate the scheme and write about what could be done to improve it.*

Use the notes from the interview and the anonymous letter from a parent to Paolo.

2 With a partner, role-play the interview between Paolo and the student reporter. This will help you to see how your ideas about the task and texts provided can be developed through inference.

* If you take the role of Paolo, explain why and how you set up the scheme (building on the information given).
* If you take the role of the student reporter, ask challenging questions, such as: *Do all students working for 'Call me' receive some training? Isn't it a problem if …?*.

Developing skills

3 Look back at the directed writing-style task on page 167:

Highlight or note down from the task:
- what role/voice you have to take on to write the text (thinking about their perspective)
- why you are writing (the main purpose)
- the type or form of writing you must produce (conventions)
- who it is for (the audience).

Content and structure

Here is part of one student's plan for the article. Note how she has begun to make inferences.

> Title: Help at hand, but only sometimes
>
> Paragraph 1: Paolo's scheme – what it is
>
> Paragraph 2: Why he set it up – shopping centre gang, robbery, police inaction, how friends said they'd felt the same
>
> Paragraph 3: How it works – volunteers were all his friends, hence boys
>
> Paragraph 4: My thoughts – surely boys put girls off phoning? Better to select mix
>
> Paragraph 5: Other issues – why open only for 8 hours? More volunteers could mean 24-hour coverage? Not many callers either

4 Add any further ideas or points to the plan. What else needs adding? Refer to the other issues raised in the anonymous letter.

Style

You will need to build on what you already know about:
- **conventions** of newspaper articles **(See pages 74–77 for more.)**
- **explaining** clearly: including key details as your readers will not know about the scheme
- **arguing** a point of view: using persuasive language, such as emotive imagery or rhetorical questions to get the readers onside. **(See pages 88–93 for more.)**

5 With a partner, discuss why the extract from sample Response B seems closer to the style required than Response A shown opposite.

Response A

Only boys. You've got to be kidding, Paolo! Isn't that going to put any frightened young girl off calling – especially if it was a male thug who snatched her phone?

— this is ok, but you'd need to know what 'only boys' is referring to. It is too short and informal

— good use of a rhetorical question but too emotive

Response B

Paolo's decision was to have boys manning the phones. He believes that male voices offer greater comfort and security but the lack of calls from girls suggests this isn't the case. The number of calls is quite low, so does he need to think again? Paolo deserves our support – he struck me as decent, thoughtful and a good role model for our school – but I suggest he needs to do further research and find out who teens really want to answer their calls.

— provides a clear explanation first

— cleverly gets readers on side with a pattern of three about Paolo before making own view clear

> **Top tip**
>
> The secret for success is not to fill your answer with the information you have been given, but to use it carefully to develop your own response.

Applying skills

(6) You already have a basic structure you could follow for this task. Now apply what you know about newspaper articles and their conventions to write your first two paragraphs for the article. You could begin like this:

Fellow student, Paolo Rivera's 'Call me!' scheme has been running for a year now to offer help and support to teenage victims of crime. Open from...
So, I thought I'd find out why he started it and whether...

— makes audience clear

— basic facts: what it is

— purpose of article

Sound progress	Excellent progress
• You include the main points, but they are undeveloped.	• You infer from the information provided to develop a thorough, perceptive, convincing article with clear explanations and argument.
• You show an occasional sense of audience but there are some lapses in style.	• You show an excellent, consistent sense of audience, using a persuasive and appropriate style.
• You use a straightforward but effective argument, though it is not always powerful.	• You structure your response to reshape the material from the text in a way that is extremely appropriate to the form of writing used.

5 Exam-style questions and sample responses: extended response and directed writing tasks

Key skills

You will need to show the following reading skills:

- demonstrate understanding of explicit meanings
- demonstrate understanding of implicit meanings and attitudes
- select for specific purposes.

You will need to show the following writing skills:

- articulate experience and express what is thought, felt and imagined
- sequence facts, ideas and opinions
- use a range of appropriate vocabulary
- use register appropriate to audience and context
- make accurate use of spelling, punctuation and grammar.

Exploring responses: extended response tasks

1 Read the text below. It is the transcript of a radio interview with Dave Ludnor, an expert guide to the Rocky Mountains. Then look at the exam-style extended response task that follows it.

Interviewer:	Delighted to have you on the programme, Mr Ludnor. So do you have any advice for our listeners who are excited about visiting the Rockies?
Dave:	Maybe – but forget 'excited'. Stick to being prepared. I've got a list here of things people should take – the usual stuff: water bottles, compasses, GPS devices and maps – oh, and pepper spray.
Interviewer:	Pepper spray? Is that in case bears attack?
Dave:	It's a last resort. The best thing to advise listeners is to try to avoid them altogether. Travellers should speak to park rangers beforehand about local bear activity and keep their eyes on the trail for droppings and paw prints. And sing or make plenty of noise. Most bears want a quiet life and will keep away. Also, keep the camp site clean as bears are drawn to food and smells. If people do encounter a bear, they should retreat quietly or speak in a calm voice so that the bear is aware they are human.
Interviewer:	Thank you. That seems very clear. Can you tell our listeners what you've brought in?

Dave:	It's a one-ring cooker, but a collapsible one that'll fit into the side pocket on a rucksack. These are the really important things – not bears so much. Eating, keeping warm and dry. Make sure you have top quality waterproofs, shoes or boots, and a bivvy that's light but hardwearing.
Interviewer:	That all sounds obvious.
Dave:	Maybe. But it's amazing how many people forget the basics. They take the GPS device and forget decent outerwear. And they don't prepare themselves physically.
Interviewer:	What exactly do you mean?
Dave:	Well, doing some regular jogging before setting off would help. And oxygen training isn't a bad idea – in case you reach high altitudes.
Interviewer:	That's very useful. Thank you for coming in.

Imagine you are a student wishing to embark on a walking tour of the Rockies with two friends, which will require time off school. Write a letter to your head teacher requesting time off and reassuring him or her that you and your friends will be safe.

You should include:

- *why you wish to do the trip despite any concerns from the school*
- *your preparations for travelling*
- *how you will deal with any unwanted attention from bears.*

Response 1

Dear Mr Khan

I know that you are concerned that I wish to take time off school with two friends in the Rocky Mountains but I will be ok, I promise they will too because we have made lots of preparations. ——— punctuation is incorrect

Like we heard this expert on the radio, Dave Ludnor, and he gave out this list of stuff to take with us – pepper spray, water bottles, compasses, GPS devices and maps and things like that. Plus the usual such as waterproofs, waterproof walking shoes, a bivvy and this collapsible one-ring cooker which is really cool. You can fit it in your pocket would you believe?

——— makes reference to interview but too informal

——— tries to make it personal, but a little informal again

We have prepared really well too. I have done fitness training and so have Ray and Marta and like acclimatisation too by doing some oxygen training. We also went running every day in six months, I can tell you I'm fitter than at school!

——— begins to add own ideas, but poorly-expressed in places

——— incorrect use of preposition

Lastly the bears. this Dave guy reckoned that it is best to avoid them. Check with park rangers as to bear activity. Also, on the trail, check for droppings, paw prints, etc. and talk or sing while walking so bears can get out of people's way. Keep your camp clean as bears are attracted to food and smells. If you do encounter a bear, retreat quietly or speak in a calm voice so that the bear is aware you are human. That should do it.

——— lifted almost word-for-word from the interview; needs to be paraphrased more, for example, refers to 'people's' when it should be 'we/our'

Don't worry, the trip will do us good and we'll all grow up and come back to school with lots of great stories. I also want to work in conservation or something at some point.

Thanks

Jose

——— covers first bullet of the task but in no depth

Feedback

This response just about covers all the aspects of the task, but sloppy punctuation, too much simple repetition of information and not enough on the reasons for the trip keep this answer from being stronger.

Recommended Band: 2 (Core)

(2) How could the response be improved to make it Band 1? Work with a partner to decide, using the Sound progress ⓒ box in Check your progress table on page 188 as a guide.

(3) Now read the second sample response.

Response 2

Dear Mr Khan,

I know that you are concerned that I wish to spend two weeks of valuable school time with two friends in the Rocky Mountains. First, I want you to know this is important to me as I might want to work in conservation or as a ranger when I am older. But I do understand that you want to make sure your students are ok.

    However, I also want to let you know we have made lots of preparations. We have consulted guide books and maps, worked out a route listened carefully to an expert on the radio talk about bears and travel in the Rockies. This seemed a bit frightening but something we needed to check. Don't worry, though, cos I think we have that covered now.

    The expert, Dave Ludnor of the Rockies Route Guide, gave out this very helpful list of basic, lightweight cooking utensils, navigational devices like GPS and suitable outer-wear, which will keep us dry and warm.

    He also provided us useful advice about how to prepare for encounters with bears, which was mostly common sense stuff such as checking for bear activity with park rangers, keeping an eye out for tracks and droppings, and also singing or talking in a normal voice so that bears know we're around. We also need to keep the camp clean and not leave food around as bears will overcome their fears if they get the scent of dinner!

    We learnt from him that if we were to come across bears, we should simply move back slowly and calmly, speaking in our usual voices, so as to provide early warning of our presence. As you know, I find it hard to be quiet in class so this won't be a problem!

    I am aware that all of this might make you feel even more concerned for us, but I am sure you would agree this is a chance of a lifetime. Despite my love of adventure, I believe we will develop skills such as teamwork and learn to cook and clean for ourselves too. Hopefully, the skills we have learned can be used in school and we could also give a talk and show photos to other students, if you like?

Yours,

Marco

- gives reason for trip

- continues clear, formal opening with reference to reason for letter

- paragraph introduces the new point well, but ends too informally

- paraphrases well with most of the basic information included

- good link to new point

- new point introduced

- nice use of humour brings out 'voice' of student

- good inference from interview with expert

- last paragraph develops the first bullet reasonably, although once again more could have been added

5 Exam-style questions and sample responses: extended response and directed writing tasks

Feedback

The response on page 173 is clear and competent. It does not simply list information from the interview but puts it into the writer's own words. Quite a good understanding of the head teacher's concerns is shown. The response also picks up on the writer's love of adventure and hints at a future career, although more could have been made of this. The language used is a little repetitive, but this is a fluent, clear letter.

Recommended Band: 1 (Core)

Exploring responses: extended response tasks **E**

1 The following extended response task is based on the passage 'Alone in the balloon', which is on page 217 of the coursework section of this book. Read the task and then the two sample responses that follow.

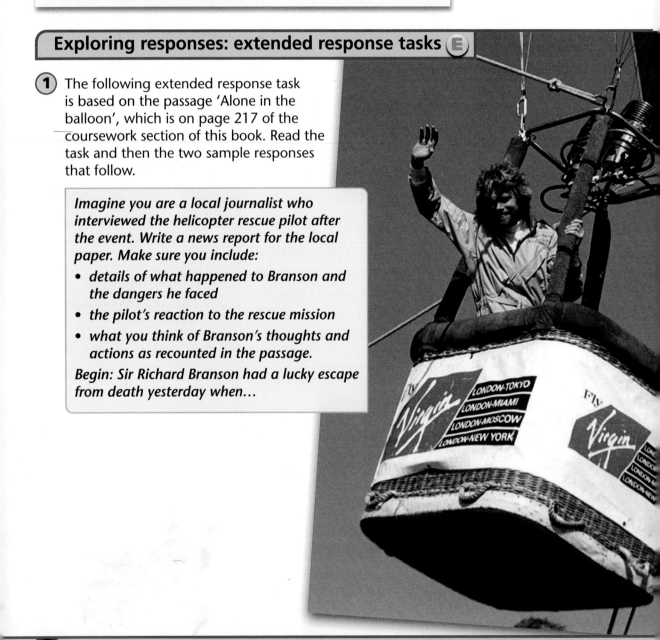

> *Imagine you are a local journalist who interviewed the helicopter rescue pilot after the event. Write a news report for the local paper. Make sure you include:*
>
> - *details of what happened to Branson and the dangers he faced*
> - *the pilot's reaction to the rescue mission*
> - *what you think of Branson's thoughts and actions as recounted in the passage.*
>
> *Begin: Sir Richard Branson had a lucky escape from death yesterday when...*

Response 1

Sir Richard Branson had a lucky escape from death yesterday when the balloon he was flying crashed into the sea. It was awful and he was really lucky. I found this out when I interviewed the pilot of the helicopter that got him.

The pilot said, 'I was coming through the clouds when I saw Mr Branson sitting on top of the capsule waving this rag at me, so I waved back. He must have seen me I think.'

'So what did you do next?' I asked him. He said, 'Well I obviously circled round to see if the capsule had crashed because when he waved he was still in the air coming down, then I saw him. It was a miracle he was alive because those balloons are heavy and there's the gas.'

Of course these celebrities cause lots of problems for rescue teams round here on the coast. In fact not just celebrities but members of the public who don't prepare properly for sailing or other activities. I think it was awful. We have to pay the rescue services and what if they refused to help? Think of that.

Anyway the most amazing thing the pilot said was watching the balloon as it sailed away into the air after Branson released it. 'At first I thought he'd drowned but then I saw him come to the surface of the water. Luckily we got a rope down to him as that sea is icy as you know, otherwise he would have frozen to death.'

So I think the pilot was just doing his job but he did admit that he gets sick of people needing his help all the time, and I agree it's a bit much.

Annotations:

- better to use a more specific verb like 'rescued' or better 'plucked him from danger'
- not really necessary; could have been integrated better
- shows close reading of the text but would be better in the reporter's own words
- again good close reading and use of quotation from pilot, but needs to be more in report style
- shows some sense of local audience
- verb should be 'is' because talking about an ongoing situation
- personal viewpoint and voice of reporter, but style too informal and goes off the point
- picks up on detail from the passage
- tries to bring together pilot and reporter's views

Feedback

This response makes an attempt to take details from the text and integrate them into the report. Unfortunately, the style is inconsistent and the content lacks structure and the sense of audience is missing. Vocabulary is mostly lifted from the original text, although there is some attempt at original ideas, if rather clumsily expressed.

Recommended Band: 4 (Extended)

(2) How could this response be improved to make it Band 3? Work with a partner to decide, using the Sound progress (E) box in Check your progress on page 188 as a guide.

(3) Now read the second sample response.

Response 2

Sir Richard Branson had a lucky escape from death yesterday when the balloon he had used to cross the Atlantic plunged into the icy cold sea just off our coast. His partner, Per Lindstrom, also survived and was rescued by a local helicopter pilot from the coastguard service. — key information provided in first paragraph

Speaking to the pilot after the rescue he explained to me — good lead in to the pilot's experiences

how he had first seen the balloon at about 8000 feet but — shows close reading

it wasn't until he saw Branson clinging to the capsule and waving a rag in the air later on that he realised he was in trouble. Of course he couldn't do anything at first but when Branson crashed the balloon and leapt into the sea he was able to rescue him. 'It was a miracle he was alive,' the pilot — style sounds more like storytelling here than news report

said, given the icy temperature of the water. 'Luckily we got a rope down to him, otherwise he would have frozen to death.'

The pilot talked about how he felt when rescuing people. He told me it was his job and he was proud to do it, although it can be disappointing when people, even members of the public, don't prepare properly for the cold weather off our coast.

My view is that we cannot stop celebrities and members — reporter's view, but not really expanded enough

of the public from taking on challenges such as these.

As a reporter too, I like to hear of exciting stories such — this new point should really have been a new paragraph and developed

as Branson's but I am just pleased when it doesn't end in tragedy. Branson was lucky, more than anything, in my opinion.

The pilot says he will continue to rescue people without — ends with pilot's view and a good quotation

asking questions. 'What else can you do?' he says.

Feedback

This response covers most of the key points requested in the task and is expressed in a clear and structured way. Very occasionally the style slips from that of a reporter and there are also moments when key information or views could have been developed.

Recommended Band: 3 (Extended)

4 The following exam-style extended response task is based on the passage 'Entering the stadium', which is on pages 162–163. Read the task and then the sample response that follows.

> *Imagine you are Alfredo. Write a journal entry about the day you have had. Make sure you include:*
> * *details of the events that took place and what happened*
> * *your view of the stadium and experience*
> * *how you think Paul, the author, reacted and felt.*
> *Begin: Today, I took my American friend Paul to a football match...*

Response 1

Today I took my American friend Paul to a football match between our beloved home nation and Mexico, but what is memorable is the experience of taking Paul to see it. For myself, I cannot believe I was actually there – this sort of spectacle does not come to Santa Ana.

    Anyway, the main thing was that we got into the match. As usual it looked difficult to get tickets but using my charm and determination I pushed through the crowds and got tickets for us. I was worried for Paul. He asked me about buying tickets from those dreadful touts who charge a fortune, and will rob you of your precious belongings as you stand there. I soon told him the facts! He kept well out of the way and sensibly waited.

    Inside the stadium there were the usual groups – the Suns who were happy to have the cheaper tickets; the Shades paying a little bit more – and of course the rich ones. It was worth paying more for our tickets – even though it was evening so there was no sun to hide from – because it wasn't quite so busy. I don't think Paul is used to our concrete steps. I imagine he is used to luxury – soft seats, coca-cola, food served to you as you wait.

    He seemed overwhelmed by the sight. Of course, the rich folk in the balconies caught his eye and I imagine he would have preferred to be with them, away from the excitement and able to drink wine, eat good food. Of course, they are only small boxes really, but I have always wanted to go in one. One day maybe! I didn't mention the balconies to him as it was too expensive for me; naturally, I felt embarrassed.

    As to the mob who watch the game from outside – well, what can I say? I would do the same as them if I could not get a ticket, but they did look crazy – like animals really. I think Paul probably considers many of us animals, and perhaps he is right, but I hope our friendship has shown him Salvadoreans are not all mad!

Annotations (right margin):
- nice phrase makes text personal
- writer's view of the experience
- events from the passage described, but vocabulary a bit repetitive ('got/get tickets' twice)
- new paragraph deals with the Suns, Shades
- begins to develop the viewpoint of writer
- shows inference from passage as Alfredo hadn't mentioned the balconies
- idea of 'haves' and 'have nots' in Salvadorean society could be developed more

5 Exam-style questions and sample responses: extended response and directed writing tasks

Feedback

The journal entry on page 177 sounds convincing. There is evidence of a competent reading of the passage and the writer has done well to select and use some of the ideas and facts. Some of these are developed, but perhaps not sustained sufficiently.

Recommended Band: 2 (Extended)

(5) How could this response be improved to make it Band 1? Work with a partner to decide, using the Excellent progress (E) box in Check your progress on page 188 as a guide.

(6) Now read the second sample response.

Response 2

Today I took my American friend Paul to a football match. It was between us and Mexico and generated the usual frenzy ——— **excellent vocabulary** of excitement on both sides as they are our arch rivals, of course. I was so happy to be there: we never get these games here, so it was an experience to savour, although I must ——— **develops information from the passage** admit keeping an eye on Paul made it challenging. ———

    I was the hero of course. No one expected me to get the ——— **reference from the passage enables development of voice** tickets but by brute force and worming my way to the front I got them! This was just as well as Paul was all for spending all his money on ticket touts who would have robbed him blind! I ——— **Alfredo's voice comes out in this idiomatic phrase** had to remind him to pocket all his valuables and keep hidden. If they spot you are an American, you are easy prey.

    He seemed fascinated by the crowds when we eventually got in. I had bought the more expensive tickets for the shaded section because I knew it would be quieter, even ——— **again, shows close reading of passage** though it was a night-time kick-off. The stadium was obviously unlike anything in the US, with the different groups and divisions. Yes, seeing those in our society who have it all, in the balconies with their fine living and drinking, compared with the beetle-like masses who scrambled to watch the game from outside is difficult to take in. We are used to it of course, but I was glad we were in the Shades and not out

there. Naturally the concrete steps are not luxurious, ——————— infers character and perspective from information
but I could not even consider balcony tickets; even with
my salary of 1200 dollars a year, I would have been
embarrassed to tell him that is almost twice my wages.
    I think Paul liked being in the middle of it all, experiencing the ——————— again, good turn of phrase
wild heart of everything, in any case. He did not complain and ——————
seemed magnetised by the green strip of grass surrounded ——————— offers comment on Paul's attitude
by the chanting, singing masses. I felt strangely both proud ——————
and sad: the first emotion because Paul seemed intoxicated ——————— again, good sense of voice – Alfredo's dual feelings
by the sights; the second because there is so much that is
hard about our lives in this country.

Feedback

This response reveals a thorough reading of the passage, with a good range of the original ideas taken from information that is modified and developed. There is some excellent vocabulary, which creates further vivid detail, too. If there is a weakness, it is that the fear Paul feels when he sees the 'ant-hill' does not come through here.

Recommended Band: 1 (Extended)

Exam-style questions and sample responses: extended response and directed writing tasks

Exploring responses: directed writing tasks Ⓒ Ⓔ

1 Read the passage below, and then the survey notes on the facing page with the sample task, before looking at the sample responses that follow.

> *A former student, who is now a successful business person, has returned to your school and given the following speech in which they have pledged to donate a large sum of money.*

Thank you, everyone, for allowing me to come and speak to you today.

Some years ago, I left this school with excellent qualifications, many friends and memories of great experiences. I also had many hopes and dreams, but when I went out into the world of work I realised I lacked some important skills. These were in Information Technology and how to make the best use of the fast-moving digital world we all now live in. Fortunately, I was able to attend night school and worked for a company that trained me and helped me 'get on'. They had patience and saw something in me – perhaps the skills of friendship and flexibility that I must have learned here, in this building. A few years later, I set up my own business and – well, here I am today – to give something back to the school I enjoyed attending so much.

That takes me back to my point about IT. For all its qualities, this school lacked those resources. I needed to learn how to use computers during my years here; they were expensive and not many people had access to them. So, my gift to you today is to invest in your school's computer system. Without up-to-date hardware, fast computing and access to the internet, it could be argued that school has little to offer to the ambitious student. I was lucky. Someone had faith in me and I learned those skills later, but not everyone will be as lucky as me.

I am determined you will not miss out, as I did. I haven't talked to students, but I can tell that the resources here are not up to scratch and surely a new computer suite will bring the school – our school – into the 21st century? Computers are the future. In fact, they are the present. Who wouldn't like a computer suite that has sparkling new screens and large-memory drives? Whether you are a computer geek or not, you and your studies will benefit from this investment.

Once a new suite is built, I would be delighted to come back and open the suite that my funding has bought.

Thank you once again for allowing me to share my vision.

A survey of students and teachers at the school has come up with these suggestions for how to spend the money.

- improved catering facilities
- better sports facilities
- a counselling area for younger students
- new books for the library
- free textbooks for all exam classes
- new eco-friendly transport: a new minibus running on a hybrid engine
- electronic registering system for staff and pupils
- an extra day's holiday each year: funding teachers' salaries for the day.

You have listened to the speech, but feel this not the best use of the money. Write a letter to the business person, arguing that it would be better if the money was spent differently. You will need to:

- *explain why you think the money should not be spent on the computer system and resources*
- *suggest an alternative area or use for the money, providing reasons for your suggestion.*

Response 1

Dear Aleisha,

    I heard your speech today and I don't agree with you. There are many other things we should spend money on at the school. These are important things that we cannot ignore. I think that spending money on a computer system is a waste of money. Our school system is not bad and there are computers if we need them. Anyway most of us have our own computers at home. Why do we need them in school?

    A second point is that computers go out of date very quickly so if you want to replace these ones then you will have to replace the new ones too. So it is not just spending money now but lots more in the future. You say, 'computers are the future' but I'm not sure. Because actually computers will get smaller and smaller and we will end up having them just on phones.

    I would spend the money on books for the library. Lots of books we use in the classroom are tatty and in bad condition. If you have these books it does not make you want to learn. If you have new books then it is nice to hold them and touch them and you want to read what is in them. Our library also has very out-of-date books. We need new titles about teenage things and stuff we are interested in.

    Of course there are lots of other possibilities too like better food or new sports facilities but I think choosing books is the best idea of all. Everyone will remember how kind you were to the school and be very grateful.

Yours, Yousuf

Annotations:

- This is a rather blunt opening!
- Other than what? It needs to be clear from the start that the subject is the computer suite.
- gives a reason for not needing computers but could develop it further
- offers very good point, but then the rhetorical question weakens it because there is an answer: not every child has its own computer
- starts new paragraph with a clear new point
- tries to anticipate argument, drawing on an idea from the speech, but doesn't answer it very convincingly
- offers own suggestion as requested by question
- choice of vocabulary is dull
- ending needs to sum up main points: why books are a better choice than computers

Feedback

The response does answer the task, but the style and structure of the letter are rather clumsy and not very persuasive, sounding impolite in places. Good points are made, especially in paragraph 3, but elsewhere assertions are made without much supporting evidence. Little reference is made to the speech.

Recommended Band: 4

2 How could this response be improved to make it Band 3? In pairs, decide, using the Sound progress (E) box in Check your progress on page 188 as a guide.

(3) Now read the second sample response.

Response 2

Dear Antonio,

Thank you for coming to school and offering to donate money for new computers. You made a strong case based on your own experiences and it is very kind of you. I am sure everyone is grateful for the offer. However, if I may, I would like to suggest another use for your cash.

— uses appropriate polite style for opening, referring to the speech

The problem with spending money on computers is that it is not just the hardware cost. Even if you put in the best system money can buy, you will need people to look after it and update it. Everything you say suggests that your investment is a 'one-off', but this and issues such as software need to be taken into account.

— gives a clear reason for not choosing computers

— infers this is the case from the speech, but more could be added

An additional problem is that the future is about mobile personal computing. I am not sure schools need big systems any more. After all, even you admit you left 'some years ago' and things have changed. If you could buy all students tablets or netbooks, then that would be fine.

— good link with previous paragraph

However my main suggestion is to spend money on something different. You say that you had wonderful experiences at the school and it made you who you are now. Some of these experiences may have been sports-related, so I recommend that you spend your money on better sports facilities. We need a new sports hall as ours has a leaking roof. I know that some people would say that not all students enjoy sport, so why spend on that? My belief is that a new hall would make more students join in.

— again, good points made but need to be taken further

— anticipates counter-argument and provides answer

I have other suggestions for sports facilities too. Dance is very popular now, so we could have a dance studio. What do you think? Does this sound good to you? It's your money, so you decide.

— questions are a bit sharp, but do engage the reader

Computers are great as you say and they are indeed part of the present and future but the most important thing is health and happiness. This is why I say – improve the sports facilities first. Surely everyone can agree that feeling fitter and being active is better than staring at a screen?

— good rhetorical question and image to end on

Yours, Rahima

Feedback

This response covers the task in a clear, logical way and draws some good inferences from the speech provided. It would be worthy of an even higher mark if some of its excellent ideas had been developed further. In addition, even greater variety of vocabulary and use of persuasive devices would help. However, this is a good response.

Recommended Band: 3

Exam-style questions and sample responses: extended response and directed writing tasks

Exploring responses: directed writing tasks C E

1 The following directed writing task is the same as the one you looked at on pages 166–169. Reread it and then look at the sample response that follows.

You are a fellow student at Paolo's school and have interviewed him about the scheme and seen the anonymous letter from the parent to Paolo.

Write an article for your school paper in which you argue whether the scheme is a good idea or not. You will need to:
- *explain the scheme and how it works*
- *explain why and how Paolo set it up*
- *evaluate the scheme and write about what could be done to improve it.*

Use the brief notes you took at the interview (below) and the letter from the parent (see page 169).

Notes from interview
- Paolo's cell phone is stolen (a present from his brother); he was upset because police didn't follow up
- 'Call me!' has a special mobile number and email address
- Five boys answer emails, calls and texts
- Boys are volunteers: some with strong personalities, some more gentle/ thoughtful
- Open from 4 p.m. to midnight each day
- Average of 3–4 calls a day, 10–12 texts or emails
- Calls have been as much about relationship or family problems as crime
- Only one student complained about the advice given (on bullying)

Response 1

New scheme to support students — appropriate, if rather dull, headline for the article

Paolo Rivera, a student in Grade 10, has brought in a new scheme to help fellow students who are the victims of crime. He has got volunteers to assist by answering calls to a cell phone number or replying to texts or emails. The scheme, called 'Call Me!' has now been running for a year, so how well is it working?

— first two sentences provide the main subject information clearly

— clever use of question 'sets up' rest of the article

Paolo says he set the scheme up after he was attacked by a gang and had a new cell phone stolen. He felt so hurt and angry, and was disappointed when no one was caught but didn't know who to turn to. That was why he set up the scheme, so that students who suffered like him could talk to someone.

— a little obvious – seems to repeat what has gone before

Some people have criticised the scheme, saying that the small number of calls, texts and emails per day show that it is not working. I think the real problem, however, is that it is only available from 4–12 a.m. If you have to check the opening times, then you are just not going to bother. Indeed, one student I spoke to confirmed that whilst the first call had been dealt with well, there was no one available the second time around because of the time, just when they needed someone. Paolo says this is because his volunteers are at school at this time, but surely the solution is to have more volunteers? If the school supports it, then they would be prepared to allow students an hour off once in a while, I think.

— evaluates the scheme using evidence from Testimony 1

— rhetorical question emphasises solution

Perhaps even a bigger issue is training. The volunteers Paolo uses are very willing but may not know how to talk to a younger student who has been bullied or who is involved in gangs or crime. Once again, evidence from the same anonymous letter suggests that this can even be handled badly. Until this has been sorted out I think the service should be suspended. People may be getting bad advice.

— good lead in to new points

— infers information from the letter but sounds a little vague – needs expanding

Of course we should not criticise Paolo too much as this is a good idea and he is trying to help others, but clearly more thought needs to go into this. I recommend Paolo gets a committee of staff and students together, gathers ideas and plans the new service carefully. Then perhaps it will be used more frequently.

— good use of pattern of three to stress solution and round off article

Exam-style questions and sample responses: extended response and directed writing tasks

Feedback

A satisfactory article, which provides a basic evaluation of the different points from the information given, and suggests some solutions. The sense of audience is reasonable although it is not immediately clear that the article is writen for other students. The response is well structured with some use of persuasive devices.

Recommended Band: 2

2 How could this response be improved to make it Band 1?
Work with a partner to decide, using the Excellent progress box from Check your progress on page 188 as a guide.

3 Now read the second sample response.

Response 2

Help at hand – but only sometimes ———————————— clever headline suggests view of writer

Fellow student Paolo Rivera's 'Call me!' scheme has been —— clear introduction covers basic facts
running for a year now to offer help and support to teenage
victims of crime. Open from 4 p.m. till 12 each day and
staffed by five boys from the upper grades, students can
text, email or call for advice and support. But that's just
the problem – few students have used the scheme (just an
average of 3–4 calls per day, for example), so what's gone ——— use of rhetorical question sets up rest of the article
wrong?

So, I thought I'd find out why he started the scheme and
whether he agreed with my analysis that it was a waste of
time? He told me, 'I needed to talk to someone when my cell—— good use of direct speech from imagined interview
phone was stolen by a gang last year and there was no one
to turn to. I strongly believe it was the right thing to do.'
Others back this up, like the the parent of a student who in—— excellent use of information from the letter, well linked in to argument
an anonymous letter welcomed the helpful and comforting
support their son received when there was illness in the
family, but – and here's the problem – when that same
student wanted further support, it just wasn't available
as the lines were closed. Family help was forthcoming, but
what if it hadn't been?

Furthermore, two decisions he made are baffling everyone I have spoken to at the school. Firstly, his decision was to have boys manning the phones. He believed that male voices offered greater comfort and security, but the lack of calls from girls suggests this isn't the case. Indeed, because the number of calls is quite low, perhaps he needs to think again? It may be the case that he's right – but I suggest he needs to do further research and find out who teens really want to answer their calls. We just can't have the situation where the same anonymous student who was bullied was advised by a volunteer to 'deal with it' by confronting their aggressors, rather than following tried and trusted approaches through the school system.

Paolo accepts that his system isn't perfect but tells me, 'It's better than nothing at all. Those 3 or 4 calls we get might be a lifeline for the students involved. I know how low and frightened I felt.'

Whatever the truth, Paolo needs to reconsider. Having five untrained boys, who are only available once school is finished, is surely a recipe for disaster? What happens if a real problem is missed? Or a student gets bad advice again? The service needs to be opened up to girls, made available all day and serious training in being a counsellor needs to be done. Then 'Call me!' might succeed.

linking word changes direction and signals writer's view

writer offers own suggestion to solve the problem

draws on further information from the letter to emphasise a key point

powerful short sentence neatly sums up the writer's evaluation of scheme

excellent set of questions raises issues

pattern of three hammers home and summarises key ideas

Feedback

This is a perceptive response that integrates key information from the letter and the interview notes and then uses it as a springboard for writing. The interview quotations from Paolo are also cleverly woven into the argument and rhetorical devices, especially towards the end, make the evaluation crystal clear.

Recommended Band: 1

Sound progress

- I can write in the correct form and for the correct purpose as directed by the question.
- I can generally use sentences fluently and put them in a logical order or sequence.
- I can structure my writing to reshape material from the passage.
- I can punctuate my writing correctly most of the time.
- I can generally spell correctly, with only minor errors.
- I can use material from the passage and develop it with some idea of 'voice' and/or viewpoint.

Sound progress

- I can write in the correct form and for the correct purpose as directed by the question.
- I can take material from the passage, but I do not lift it or copy it directly.
- I can write in a style that is different to the original, with some idea of 'voice' and/or viewpoint.
- I can write sentences that are generally fluent and well sequenced.
- I can generally punctuate and spell correctly, with only minor errors.

Excellent progress

- I can demonstrate a good range of ideas which are modified and developed to fit the purpose and form of the question.
- I can show a close and detailed reading of the passage, developing ideas intelligently and with understanding.
- I can structure my writing to reshape material from the passage in a way that is extremely appropriate to the form of writing used.
- I can use my own ideas, which are consistently well-related to the passage and include plenty of supporting detail.
- I can vary my language use, making it interesting and well structured for effect.
- I can write, spell and punctuate accurately throughout.

Composition questions

Composition questions give you the opportunity to write at length.

To answer this type of question you will only need to use your writing skills to:

- articulate experience and express what is thought, felt and imagined
- sequence facts, ideas and opinions
- use a range of appropriate vocabulary
- use register and/or voice appropriate to audience and context
- make accurate use of spelling, punctuation and grammar.

Composition questions require you to show your understanding of the conventional content and structure of either narrative writing or descriptive writing.

1 Understanding composition tasks C E

● To understand what is required for composition tasks.

Composition tasks require you to make quite a few choices. It is important you fully understand what those choices are and how these will affect the response you write.

There are normally two types of writing to choose from – descriptive or narrative – and for each of these there will be two possible tasks. So in total there is a choice of four writing tasks. However, remember that you must only choose **one** to produce a written answer of **350–450 words.**

Exploring skills

1 Here are two possible tasks. Link each one to the two types of writing mentioned above. Then discuss with a partner **why** they match.

> (a) *The sound of whispering attracts your attention to a room in your house. The door is partly open. Describe what you can see, as well as what you can hear, as you peep in.*
>
> (b) *'Although it was almost midnight, I heard the sound of footsteps approach our house. I opened the door...'. Use these two sentences to start a story.*

Building skills

You will realise from these examples that each type has its own **conventions**, which might be **structural** (how the information is sequenced or ordered) or **stylistic** (how language is used).

2 Copy and complete the chart below:

	Conventions of good narratives	Conventions of good descriptive writing
Structure	Structure to add interest Strong opening that hooks the reader Use of flashbacks? Surprising ending?	Ideas are very developed and detailed
Style	Vividly paints picture of setting and characters in reader's mind using imagery	

Developing skills

You can practise and develop your understanding of the conventions before the exam. But you will need to deal methodically with the questions themselves, like this:

1 Read the four questions (two under each heading).
2 Select the **one** task from the four for which you:
   - understand the conventions (the form/purpose and its style and structure)
   - have a good range of ideas (it's no good choosing a topic or theme which you know nothing about or cannot picture in your mind))
   - can write in a complex, sophisticated way (not just stating the obvious but providing detail and depth of language and ideas).
3 Quickly plan your answer.

(3) Reread the two questions on page 190. Which would you choose and why?

The next step is to make sure you understand **what** the question is asking you to do. Here is an example of how a student has highlighted the key words in one of the questions. The annotations show what the writer was thinking and understood.

a narrative is a story, so use what I know about good storytelling

Narrative writing

(c) *'Although it was almost midnight, I heard the sound of footsteps approach our house. I opened the door...' Use these two sentences to start a story.*

to be told in the first person ('I')

the content: a person hears someone coming to the house and opens the door

make sure I only write the beginning

Applying skills

(4) Now identify the key words in the following question.

Descriptive writing

'The unhappy customer'. Paying particular attention to the sights and sounds in the shop, describe the scene as a customer complains to the shop manager about something he or she has bought.

Sound progress

- You understand what each task is asking you and select a form you feel you can write competently.

Excellent progress

- You understand the range of tasks on offer and draw creatively on what you know of them to enhance the potential for a higher grade.

2 Planning and developing a composition Ⓒ Ⓔ

Learning objectives

● To understand how to plan and develop an answer from the question you have selected.

Exploring skills

Highlighting the key words and phrases in the question is important, but how does it help you to develop an answer to the question? Look again at the following question. The key words have already been highlighted.

> ### Descriptive writing
> *'The unhappy customer'. Paying particular attention to the sights and sounds in the shop, describe the scene as a customer complains to the shop manager about something he or she has bought.*

What does this mean for your answer? Think about the **content** and **structure**.

- Include the **right content**. If it says 'unhappy customer', do not make him/her happy! Make it an **interesting** faulty item.
- Keep to the **main elements** in the task. Don't try to tell a long complex story. Focus on the incident (the argument and what's going on at that time).
- Focus on the **descriptive possibilities**: for example, 'sights and sounds in the shop' could include what's on the shop's shelves, its lighting or colours.

(1) Follow the same process for the question below. Highlight the key words and then jot down:
- the main elements of the task (and what you should/should not include)
- the descriptive possibilities (for example, buildings, objects).

> ### Descriptive writing
> *Describe a place, real or imaginary, when you felt most relaxed and at ease. Concentrate on your surroundings and feelings at the time.*

Building skills

How do you take this even further? Look again at the 'shop complaint' task.

(2) What could you describe based on this task? Make your own quick list, for example:

> • the customer: appearance, reactions, gestures, clothing
> •
> •

Developing skills

The second key aspect to consider is the **style** you will use. For example, the 'shop complaint' task asks for **descriptive** writing. One stylistic feature of descriptive writing is an 'up-close' focus on details.

In this way, your plan for your answer could look like this:

> Facial features of customer: how his nose gets redder and redder!
> Reactions: how he screws his eyes up in anger

Key term

style: the vocabulary, sentence variety and literary techniques that relate closely to a form or type of writing

(3) Note down some other 'up-close' descriptive details about the customer (clothing, gestures, how he or she stands) or something else from the plan you made.

Applying skills

(4) Look at this final task. Go through the process, highlighting the key words and deciding how your response will cover each element.

Top tip

Try to choose a task that allows you to show some originality. Ask yourself: can I look at this situation in an unusual or different way? For example, what if the customer were a small child? Or perhaps someone you know (your brother, father or best friend)?

Narrative writing
'The lost umbrella on the bus'. Use this as the title of a narrative.

(5) Discuss the question with a partner. Then write your own notes in which you record:
- the form and focus of the question
- the possible content of your answer
- specific details you might include
- any stylistic conventions of language or structure you will use
- something that might make your answer different or original.

Sound progress	Excellent progress
• Your understanding and planning of the task shows that you know what the form is and have some ideas for your response.	• You don't just understand the task set, but are able to think creatively of detailed and original ideas before you start.

3 Descriptive writing: imagery and sensory detail Ⓒ Ⓔ

Learning objectives

● To understand two key features of good descriptive writing.
● To practise using these features in your own writing.

Imagery is the creative use of words to create visual pictures in the mind. **Similes**, when you compare one thing to another using 'like' or 'as', and **metaphors**, when you make a direct link between things, are both types of imagery. Images play a key role in bringing your descriptive writing to life, although it is important not to use too many or the reader can lose track of the place or person being described.

The **senses**, too, are very important to descriptive writing. Good descriptions often evoke sounds, smells, textures, sights and tastes.

Exploring skills

Here are two good examples of imagery in description:

> The man's hoarse voice was like a **broken brick on sandpaper**. *(simile)*
>
> The child's fingers on mine as I opened the door were **tiny splinters of ice**. *(metaphor)*

1 Discuss the following with a partner.
- What different senses does each description appeal to?
- What is particularly effective about each description?

Building skills

The best imagery is about choosing your ideas carefully. For example, the following is not a good simile. Why not?

> The man's hoarse voice **was like flowing honey**

2 Read the beginning of each description below. Then discuss with a partner which of the similes fits best with what is being described.

> Her angry words hit me like a **soggy towel/sharp whip/bowl of warm rice**.
>
> His powerful serve crossed the net like a **speeding missile/gentle butterfly/hovering helicopter**.

3 Now have a go yourself: can you complete these atmospheric images?

> The light burst through the wide gap onto the floor like...
>
> (*add your simile*) (think of a liquid)
>
> A narrow ... of light shone onto the floor. (*add your metaphor*)
>
> (think of something thin, nasty and sharp)

Developing skills

The best descriptive writing combines and links images to create an **overall effect**. For example, read the extract below:

> The midnight lake shone like a huge, silver brooch, and around it, in the swaying grasses, glow-worms glittered like miniature diamonds. The moon, which hung from the sky's dark neck, was an enormous locket which I felt I could reach out and touch. I was poor in terms of money but living in such a beautiful place, I was like the richest prince on earth.

(4) Write the **three similes** and **two metaphors** used in the text.
- What is the main sense these images appeal to?
- What links all these images together?

You will have noticed how all the images build up to the final sentence. They ensure the final sentence makes sense.

Here is another paragraph on a different topic.

> There was a wild rush to get to the front to see the band. Like bees racing towards their favourite lily, we sped towards the stage. From the sides of the arena, other people swarmed over the barriers like soldier ants or a tide of beetles swallowing up the space.

(5) Discuss these questions with a partner.
- What idea links all the images here?
- Look at these three possible final sentences below. Which fits best with the paragraph above? Why?

    A I was a tiny leaf swept up in a huge, unstoppable storm.
    B I felt like a leader of an army.
    C I felt free and in control.

Applying skills

(6) Write your own description of 75–125 words which includes at least three similes or metaphors. Try to link the images so they create an overall effect. Your description will be about a journey through a busy city. Use one these ideas to link your images:
- the city is like a jungle
- the journey is like a ride at a funfair
- the city is like a wonderful feast.

Include descriptions or images which refer to the senses – taste, touch, sound, sight and smell.

Top tip

Make your images original and unusual but ensure they are always suitable for the topic.

Sound progress	Excellent progress
• Your images and descriptions are well-chosen and fit the topic. • Some of your images are interesting and original.	• Your images create a range of sensory appeals using comparisons to powerful effect. • Your images are well-linked, varied and original, yet appropriate to the task.

4 Descriptive writing: structure and detail Ⓒ Ⓔ

Learning objectives

● To understand what makes a good piece of descriptive writing.
● To plan, develop and write an interesting descriptive piece.

Exploring skills

Checklist for success

Descriptive writing should:
✔ be well developed and include well-defined ideas and images (offering depth and detail)
✔ focus on creating atmosphere, setting and a vivid picture in the reader's mind
✔ not read like a story: it should focus on detail, not events.

So how can these things be achieved? Let us revisit this question:

(b) The sound of whispering attracts your attention to a room in your house. The door is partly open. Describe what you can see, as well as what you can hear, as you peep in.

First, let us look at how you can create a well-developed description. In your exam, you will not have much time to plan, so you need to think quickly around the task.

① Copy and complete this spider diagram, noting ideas. Remember, this task is about describing things and defining them clearly.

- Who is whispering? Who is listening?
- Whispering in room; door open
- How does whispering sound?
  - Angry, male voice?
  - Frightened child's voice?
  - Hoarse and unwell?
  - Excited, fast?

The best descriptions create a vivid picture and focus on detail. Look at this sample response to the example task on page 196:

> Through the door I could see a table with a box on it. The box was covered in wrapping paper and had a tag hanging down from it.

If the response continued in this way, it would be of Band 3 quality because it offers a description that is relevant and clear. The writer has shown us some objects in the room, but the description is quite basic and unimaginative.

To give this description life, the writer needs to focus in and develop the detail further. For example:

- What **sort** of table? (Rectangular, oval, dining, desk?)
- What **colour/material**?
- How **large/small**?
- Where is it **placed**? (Near a window? By a fireplace?)

(2) Copy and complete this more developed description, adding **adjectives** or **prepositions** in the spaces provided:

> Through the door, I could see a huge ... (adjective) table, positioned ... (preposition) a glittering ... (adjective) mirror.

(3) Complete the original paragraph, adding further details for the box and the tag. Think about shape, colour, appearance and texture.

(4) Compare your description with a partner's. Could you have added even more to the description? If so, what?

(5) With a partner, practise the skill of visualising what you are writing. Put yourself in the shoes of the narrator and describe out loud what you can see as you look into the room. Your partner can help by prompting you with questions.
For example:

> **You:** As I look into the room I can see broken glass on the wooden floor.
>
> **Partner:** Where's the glass from?

Key term

adjective: a word that describes a noun: *ugly, brown* rat
preposition: a word that shows the relationship between objects: *the pot beside the sink; the car in front of the house*

Developing skills

When you are writing descriptions, it is tempting to change the location and start relating events rather than focusing on creating atmosphere. For example:

> I peered through the door and then went in. There were two thieves by my father's desk, so I shouted at them and they jumped through the window. I chased them down the street...

To aim for higher grades, it is much better to focus on small movements and details. These details can, when combined, build the tension or suspense. For example:

> I gingerly placed my pale, shaking hand on the oak door to my father's study. I nudged it forward. Bit by bit, it moved. I hoped I could get a better look at the men inside the room. My hand brushed the rusty key and it creaked inside the lock... had they heard?

This example offers focused detail on three aspects (the writer's hand, the key rattling and the door) which combine to create suspense.

6 Plan your own paragraph in which you (the narrator) try to get closer to the partly open door to listen to what is being said. Use these suggestions to help you.

Structure (no big events, just small changes or movements)

- First sentence: describe how you change your position to be able to listen.
- Second sentence: describe how you put your ear to the door.
- Third sentence: describe what happens when you do.

Style (detail and variety)

- Use a variety of long and short sentences to create tension (perhaps a question too).
- Make sure you use adjectives and prepositions for detail but do not overdo them.

(For more on descriptive writing, see pages 98–103.)

> **Top tip**
>
> A longer sentence followed by a short, sharp one can mimic the movements or feelings of a character who is suddenly made aware of something frightening or unusual. For example: *The corridor was made of sandstone, with no windows, decorations or other defining features except for one facing me on the door at the end. A question mark – in blood.*

(7) Now write your paragraph. Try to make it as exciting and tense as possible. You could start:

> *I knelt down very slowly and carefully on the...*

Applying skills

(8) You have already seen how imagery and sensory detail are vital to good descriptive writing. So too are characterisation and voice. Whilst you must not slip into story-telling, a description without an emotional voice can be very dull. Look at these examples below:

> The house was now covered in ivy and the brickwork was crumbling.

> As I gazed at the house I grew up in, my heart sank at the sight of the ivy that smothered the walls and the brickwork which, like my memories, was crumbling away.

Key term

imagery: words that create a mental image. Similes and metaphors are both forms of imagery

simile: a vivid comparison of two things or ideas using 'like' or 'as'

metaphor: a powerful image in which two different things or ideas are compared directly

(9) Complete this description of someone looking through an old trunk they have discovered in a locked room. Decide in advance what emotions you will express – sadness, fear, joy, curiosity?

> Slowly, I lifted the rusty lid of the trunk, and pushed it back. I felt ...

Sound progress	Excellent progress
• Your description covers the main elements mentioned in the task and you make some attempt to create atmosphere. • You create a series of points, but they don't combine to create an overall atmosphere or feeling.	• Your description covers the main elements from the task and develops them in detail and depth. • You focus on small movements or details in one setting, creating a structure. • You use characterisation and voice, as well as imagery, a variety of sentences and a range of adjectives, verbs and prepositions to create a convincing overall atmosphere.

5 Narrative writing: structure and detail Ⓒ Ⓔ

- To understand what makes a good narrative.
- To plan, develop and write an engaging narrative.

Exploring skills

> ### Checklist for success
>
> Narrative writing needs:
> ✔ a strong opening to hook the reader
> ✔ a complex, interesting narrative (the events are told in an original way)
> ✔ a carefully managed ending (that fits with the story as a whole)
> ✔ detailed description and ambitious vocabulary used when appropriate.

So how can these things be achieved? Let us revisit this question:

> **(c) 'Although it was almost midnight, I heard the sound of footsteps approaching our house. I opened the door...'. Use these two sentences to start a story.**

How can you meet the key success criteria?

1 With a partner, think about creating an interesting narrative. This means writing a good story that will engage the reader. Add further ideas to the right-hand column of this table or ask questions for which you provide answers.

Who is approaching?	A stranger in the house? Another member or members of the family?
Who are 'you'?	Are you a teenager in a house like your own? Or are you someone else, older, an adult?
Why has the person come to the house?	To meet someone? To reveal a secret? To steal something?
What will happen next?	An argument? A chase? A mysterious event?
What might have happened earlier?	Other visitors? Someone watching the house for weeks?

2 You may have come up with lots of ideas, but now make your key decisions (for example, **who** the person is and **why** they are there). Bear in mind that the more original the idea is (without it being ridiculous), the better the story will be.

Building skills

A good narrative often:

- uses flashback (the writer recalls or goes back to an earlier time)
- includes a surprise and/or suspense (things are not as they first appear)
- withholds information (does not tell the reader everything at once).

The beginning of the narrative is a vital element. It will shape and form what follows, including the use of these techniques.

(3) Here are two potential openings to the story. Decide which one uses the techniques above.

> Although it was almost midnight, I heard the sound of footsteps approaching our house. I opened the door. In front of me stood my brother, Paulo. He had gone missing ten years earlier and although he had changed, I knew it was him.

> Although it was almost midnight, I heard the sound of footsteps approaching our house. I opened the door. For a moment I peered into the darkness. Was there someone there or not? I took a step forward and a hand grabbed my shirt.
>   'You?' I gasped.
>   Suddenly, I was five years old again, playing in the yard, making a mess, making our mother yell at me.

(4) Working on the second example, note down your own ideas for what happened to the brother.

- Did he run off and get lost?
- Did he go off to find work and not return?
- Did he get into trouble?
- How old was he?
- What sort of person was he?

(5) Continue the flashback from this point (writing about 100 words). For example:

> We were always close, even though he was much older than me, but that day in the yard was the last day I saw him – Paulo. My brother…

(6) Then compare your flashback with a partner's.

- Did you come up with similar ideas?
- Whose works best? Why?

7 Flashbacks only really work when they have some impact later in the story. Imagine that the person at the door is the brother who has disappeared. Note down some reasons for his return: for example, he is in trouble and needs help.

Developing skills

Good stories work towards a **climax**, when everything comes together in a dramatic moment, followed by an ending that resolves or completes what has occurred, for good or bad. For example:

> **Key term**
>
> **climax:** the most interesting or exciting point in a story

Stage 1: grab reader's attention	Mysterious stranger at the door turns out to be brother, Paulo.
Stage 2: development or complication	Flashback – why he left, has returned because he is penniless, living rough. Wants me to steal food for him from the cupboard. Makes me promise not to tell parents.
Stage 3: climax	Parents catch me and brother in the kitchen.
Stage 4: ending	They forgive him for running away – all is well.

This plan ends, 'all is well', but the best stories often contain twists – something surprising – in their conclusions. What could be the twist or unexpected ending here?

8 Read these two endings and complete one of them with a final twist, or come up with a completely new ending of your own.

> My parents hugged my brother, and we all sat down around our small wooden kitchen table. My father poured us all some water with lime juice. Then my brother sighed, 'I have something else to tell you.' He got up, went to the door and opened it...

> As we sat there drinking lime water, I looked at my brother again as he raised the glass to his lips. There was something wrong, something not right...

(For more on narrative writing techniques, see pages 104–107.)

Applying skills

A good story is not just about structure, however interesting the plot twists are. The style and language are just as important and will help you reach the higher grades.

Two very important aspects of style and language are sentence variety and vocabulary.

- **Sentence variety:** crafting short and longer sentence for effect. **(For more on sentences for effect, see pages 40–41.)** For example:

> By the old, wrinkled tree in the yard, a shadowy figure stood, looking intently at our door. Then it was gone. Or was it? No – the shadow had simply moved back. Suddenly a light went on in our kitchen window. The shadow disappeared.

- **Vocabulary:** choosing specific words that precisely describe the situation. **(For more on vocabulary choices, see pages 48–49.)** For example:

> By the old, wrinkled **oak** in the yard, a shadowy figure **loitered, staring** intently at our door. Then it was gone. Or was it? No – the shadow had simply **retreated**. Suddenly a light went on in our kitchen window. The shadow **evaporated**.

> **Key term**
>
> **imagery:** words that create a mental image: *evaporated* creates a picture of a ghostly mist

9 With a partner, discuss these questions.
- What is the effect of the varied sentence lengths? How does it help to keep your interest as a reader?
- What slightly different or more specific meanings are suggested by the second example's vocabulary? (For example, what happens when something 'evaporates'?)

10 Now return to the original task. Using either the ideas you have worked on or coming up with a new idea altogether, write your response to the task. It must be **350–450 words** long.

> *'Although it was almost midnight, I heard the sound of footsteps approaching our house. I opened the door...'. Use these two sentences to start a story.*

Sound progress	Excellent progress
• Your story contains the main structure of introduction, development, climax and ending. • You sequence your story clearly and generally use simple, clear sentence structures and vocabulary.	• Your story contains the main structure of introduction, development, climax and ending, but you experiment with it, using features such as flashback, twists and holding back information. • You manage elements such as the climax and ending well, fitting them to the story in a way that satisfies the reader. • You use complex, but appropriate and varied sentence structures and ambitious vocabulary for effect.

6 Narrative writing: characterisation and dialogue

You do not have much space in which to tell your story in so it is vital that you balance dialogue and description, and use language cleverly to reveal characters.

Exploring skills

It is important that you **show**, rather than **tell**, the reader about a character or situation. For example, your story may hinge on the actions of a bored child which lead to a dramatic event.

Don't write:

> Mina was bored. She spent all day in her room thinking about what to do.

Do write:

> Mina lay on her tiny bed staring at the ceiling. She had already counted the rows of dull, fading flowers on her wallpaper and had read her tatty school-book three times. She sighed heavily and listened as her bedside clock ticked slowly.

> **Top tip**
>
> When implying character and context, small details can reveal a lot: for example, 'tatty school-book' implies Mina is perhaps untidy and disorganised as well as bored!

(1) The second example not only implies something about Mina's character – that she is bored – but cleverly **shows** her being bored. How is this done? Discuss these questions with a partner.

- What is Mina doing?
- How is she acting? What details add to the overall tone of boredom?

Building skills

Do not spend too much time on just one part of your story. You must create a **balance** between the different elements. For example, if you spend too much time on Mina in her room, then that might not leave space for what this makes her do. A good plan might look like the one on the facing page.

(2) Complete the section about Mina in her room using 35–40 words.

Introduction:	Mina bored in her room	75 words
Development and complication:	Flashback: she's been sent there for not doing her homework. She climbs out of window, tries to find her friend's house but it is dark and she gets lost	150–175 words
Climax:	She is chased by someone or something and cornered; it turns out to be her father, desperate to find her.	100–125 words
Resolution:	Back at home, she now finds her room a comfort.	75 words

Developing skills

Dialogue can help bring your story and characters to life.

Checklist for success

For successful dialogue:
- ✔ keep the conversation simple, make it reveal something about the characters.
- ✔ don't overuse 'speaking verbs' such as 'whispered' or adverbs such as 'curiously'
- ✔ make sure the speech is broken up with action or description.

(3) Read these two dialogue extracts. Then complete the improved version.

First version

'Well, Mina, I have to say that I'm very disappointed in you because you haven't done your homework so I'm really, really cross,' said Mina's mother angrily.

'It's not my fault I haven't done it, you know. It's because I've been helping with Granddad. So I don't think that's fair,' replied Mina stubbornly.

Improved version

Mina knew she should have done her homework, but she sat down with a thump and ...

'I'm very disappointed, Mina,' said her mother, angrily turning her back and starting to wash the plates.

Applying skills

Complete the story about Mina. It is a narrative in response to this task:

'The Escape' – write a narrative with this as a title.

Or write your own narrative response to this title.

Sound progress	Excellent progress
• You include easily-understood characters and a recognisable setting. • You include all the main elements of a story with equal balance.	• Your characters are clearly-drawn, detailed and believable with the right balance of dialogue and action. • Your setting and descriptions are vivid and interesting.

Key skills

You will need to show the following skills when answering composition questions:

- articulate experience and express what is thought, felt and imagined
- sequence facts, ideas and opinions
- use a range of appropriate vocabulary
- use register appropriate to audience and context
- make accurate use of spelling, punctuation and grammar.

Exploring responses: composition tasks C E

1 Read the following exam-style composition task and the sample response that follows. Then write about 350–450 words.

> *Narrative writing: 2(a) Write a story which begins with you overhearing a phone call which is meant to be secret.*

Response 1

I was on the stairs in the middle of the night when I heard the phone call. It was a very hot night and I couldn't sleep and needed a drink. I was coming down the stairs, rubbing my eyes, when I saw my father by the phone. He was speaking quietly and he had his back to me so he couldn't see me. The hall is long and narrow so there was no way he could spot me.

    'He mustn't find out. Have you got that?' my father whispered.

    I could not tell if he was worried or angry, but I began to ask all sorts of questions to myself. Who was 'he'? I was the only boy in the house, so it must be me. My father and mother had been acting quite secretively, it was true. They seemed to be whispering to each other all the time.

Nice visual detail but much more needed

'I realise this is the best time to phone, but be careful. Don't call again. I'll call you,' my father said.

Be careful about what? Was my dad involved in something bad? Had he got into debt? But why hide it from me? — Good use of questions but we need to find out more about the narrator

The next day, I watched my parents carefully. But they didn't give anything away. I even followed my dad to the train station one morning before going to school, but nothing strange happened.

In any case, my mind began to think about other things. It was my birthday at the weekend. That was when it all made sense! Of course, my dad had been talking to someone about my present! He wanted to keep it secret from me. But why speak to someone in the middle of the night? That was still weird.

The day came. I opened my presents which were what I'd asked for – like a new bike but no real surprises. Then my dad said he needed to pop out to get something – and could I help him? I said yes of course.

Suddenly, we seemed to be going to the airport. What was going on? — Needs detail or imagery to create pictures in the mind

Our car pulled up at the short stay parking. I saw — More detail needed
someone walking towards us. No. It couldn't be! It was! It — Rather too much 'telling' rather than 'showing'
was my older sister who had emigrated to America five years ago. She had come back just for my birthday. So that was why my dad was talking in the middle of the night.

'Hello, little brother!' she said, hugging me. — Good, concise ending which shows us how close they are

Feedback

The structure of this response is clear, achieving a balance between dialogue and events, although it ends very suddenly. The characters are clearly drawn but they are not described in any detail. There is a lack of imagery and sense of location or setting, and rather too much 'telling' of information to the reader.

Recommended Band: 4

2 How could this response be improved to make it a Band 3? Work with a partner to decide, using the Sound progress box in Check your progress on page 213 as a guide.

Exam-style questions and sample responses: composition tasks

(3) Now read the second sample response.

Response 2

I heard my older brother Fabrice's hushed tones as I walked past his room. The door was slightly open and I could see him, in his tracksuit, sitting on the edge of his bed, speaking on his mobile. I stopped.

> **Good opening tells us how brother is speaking**

'No way, man. I can't do it! You got me?'

Fabrice sounded anxious, upset. What was going on?

> **Realistic speech and good characterisation**

Suddenly it went quiet. The call was over. I heard footsteps coming over to the door. I froze and couldn't move. My brother opened the door wide.

'What you doing? Have you been listening?' he said, angrily.

'No – I mean, well – I heard something, but I didn't understand,' I replied, worriedly.

> **A bit repetitive and not really a proper word**

'Keep it that way!' Fabrice said. Then he slammed the door.

That weekend was a big athletics meeting at Wood Park. My brother was a brilliant runner and he was the favourite for the 100 metres race. But just before the race began I saw him talking to a gang of older boys. One of these boys grabbed him by his white vest.

> **Good 'showing' rather than 'telling'**

Fabrice came towards me. He had tears running down his face, but walked straight past.

I followed the gang of boys as they went behind the stand. I was small so they couldn't see me.

They handed each other money. I understood what was happening. They were betting on the race and they had told my brother to lose because they could win more money that way.

I went over to my brother, convinced that I needed to tell him.

> **Vocabulary could be more varied, e.g. raced over'**

'I know what is happening. You must not lose the race. It's not right!' I told him, as forcefully as I dared.

'Just keep out of it!' he said.

Then the race began. At first my brother was a long way behind and I thought he was going to lose but in the last few metres he overtook all the others and crossed the line first! He had won!

> **This is the climax but it is over too quickly**

Later I saw him with a long red sash with a shiny medal on it round his neck. He came over to me.

'I'm sorry I yelled at you, bruv,' he said.

'It's alright,' I replied. 'What are you going to do?'

As I said that, I saw the gang of boys walking over. They did not look happy at all.

Fabrice put his arm around my shoulders.

'Guess we'll just have to face the music, won't we?' he said, gripping me tightly.

Good ending – resolves situation between brothers but leaves us wondering too

Feedback

This response demonstrates good characterisation by showing characters' individual actions and contrasting ways of speaking. There are also some nice pieces of descriptive detail, but more is needed. Elements of the plot are a bit unbalanced: there could be more suspense at the climax (for example, would Fabrice lose the race deliberately or not?).

Recommended Band: 3

Exam-style questions and sample responses: composition tasks

4 Read the following composition task and the sample response that follows. Then write about 350–450 words.

> *Descriptive writing 3 (a) 'The Secret Garden'. Imagine you found a hidden garden. Describe your emotions and feelings as you discover it, and what is remarkable about it.*

Response 1

The garden I enter is through a tall hedge. There is an oak door with a large, brass handle and when I pull it, the door opens slowly. Through the door, the garden opens up and I can see, feel, hear and smell so many things.

 — *clear opening sets the scene but with no sense of where the garden is or how the writer got there*

The first thing to attack my senses is the fragrance of the flowers. It is almost overpowering and hits me in a great wave. I am not sure I like it all that much, but the discovery of the garden is so amazing that I control myself and continue walking.

 — *use of the senses to convey feeling*

Now I see old trees bending down over me with curved branches like old men's arms which seek to grab me. I push them to one side and find I am standing on a stone bridge over a sparkling stream. Little fishes twinkle below the bridge.

 — *use of imagery, if a little unoriginal*

All around the garden is the tall hedge, like a box, and inside there are lots more hedges creating a maze-like effect. I feel like I am inside a game and don't know where to turn. Now I am not sure of the way out so I go back the way I came over the little bridge and past the old man trees. But I cannot find the door.

 — *interesting comparison, but not really developed*

I look up above and the sky is a brilliant blue. Birds from the garden, ones I don't recognise – they don't look very nice or friendly – swoop down and peck close to me. I think they are some sort of seabird, which seems strange because we are not near the sea. The grass by the path is like a green blanket, soft and inviting, so I sit down while I consider what to do next.

 — *rather weak description*

 — *more vivid imagery*

Now the smell of the flowers is really getting to me. They are almost sickly and suffocating. It is surely time for me to leave so I go to have another look for the door, which will let me escape. This time, miraculously, it is there.

I feel like Alice in Wonderland waking up but I haven't been asleep so this is not a dream. I will come back to this garden again if it is still here.

 — *intriguing idea that could have linked to the game concept, but not really fully explored*

Feedback

Whilst the response presents a clear and vivid picture, there is something lacking here. There is little sentence variety and the descriptions, though easy to visualise, are sometimes a little dull given the possibilities. Ideas are suggested but not fully developed. There is evidence of original thought, but it never quite gets going. Having said that, this is a more than competent response that does have imagery, control and a fluent structure.

Recommended Band: 2

5 How could this sample response be improved to make it a Band 1? Work with a partner to decide, using the Excellent progress box in Check your progress on page 213 as a guide.

6 Now read the second sample response.

Response 2

At the top of my parents' dull, grey apartment block is a set of iron stairs that lead onto the roof – or so I thought. —— **gets the reader thinking**
The metal sign warns, 'No entry – danger,' so I can't tell you what gets into me that afternoon when I decided to climb them. —— **change of tense correct?**

Forcing open the heavy trap door, I stepped into another world. For there, facing me was the most lush, luxuriant —— **good variety of adjectives**
garden I have ever seen. An arch, twisted round with the delicate fingers of fragrant pink roses confronted me, and —— **imaginative use of metaphor**
beyond was a matted walkway, sprinkled with sand, like —— **effective simile, if not the best comparison**
golden paper.

As I took my first tentative steps, the tinkling sound of tiny fountains at either side rose up, like a thousand mini- —— **excellent, original simile**
orchestras tuning up. They glimmered as water spouted from sculptures. Below, the sound of the brutal city streets continued. Cars snarling like wild cats. People chattering like monkeys. I am at peace. Away from it all. —— **short sentences provide effective contrast**

Yet there was more. Off the main pathway were further —— **new topic sentence and connective links to new description**
routes. I explored each in turn, each revealing a new delight.
Down one, a hammock swung between bamboo trees, as if its owner had just disappeared. Down another, were rows of tiny flowers I didn't recognise, which seemed newly-planted. I had no idea what was watering them but despite the intense tropical heat they were thriving.

How could I have missed this place? Who created it? — questions engage directly with the reader

Whoever it was must have realised that we all need an escape from the speed of everyday life. This was a real oasis, not a mirage. It felt like mine, as if I was the first explorer.

My dreams were broken by a melody interfering near my — ambitious vocabulary, but perhaps not quite appropriate – would something pleasant 'interfere'?

side. I glanced down at the pathway railing. On it, a row of tiny bluebirds, six or seven, I can't recall exactly, sat like a little choir, chirping out their song – just for me! I reached down and one hopped onto my hand and tilted its head as if — attention to physical movement adds to atmosphere

checking me out. Then, in a flash of blue it was gone and so were the others. Perhaps they'd heard something.

I suddenly felt like an intruder. Time to leave. Will I tell my — feelings of the writer

parents? I felt like I wanted to keep the place to myself, like a dream which you think you will ruin if you reveal it.

I closed the door behind me. Immediately it was as if the garden had never existed. Below I could hear the sounds — excellent list of details for contrast

of couples arguing in their apartments, pots bubbling in kitchens, televisions blaring out.

I was back in the real world. — effective short final sentence emphasises what was special about the garden

Feedback

This is an excellent piece that really conveys the setting and atmosphere of the garden. The description is built up very well, with each paragraph developing what has gone before or taking the reader down new pathways (literally). There is a real variety of vocabulary and imagery, although for the very highest marks it would need to be inventive and perfectly matched to the desired atmosphere. We also get a real sense of the 'interior voice' of the writer and his or her feelings. Occasionally it felt as if the description was going to spill over into storytelling but fortunately that didn't occur. Very occasionally, too, tenses were a little insecure, although overall the account was consistent in this respect. The use of sentences was excellent with shorter sentences used for effect. All in all, a very impressive piece.

Recommended Band: 1

Sound progress

Content and structure

Descriptive	Narrative
• I can select effective ideas and images that are relevant to the topic and task. • I can attempt to create atmosphere and provide some details. • I can provide a series of points rather than a sense of their being combined to make an overall picture. • I can develop some ideas successfully, but they are rather straightforward and simple. • I can sequence sentences in a satisfactory way.	• I can create a straightforward story (or part of a story) with satisfactory features such as character and setting. • I can structure my overall story competently, with features of a developed narrative. • I can sometimes miss opportunities for appropriate development of ideas. • I can sequence sentences to narrate events.

Style and accuracy

- I can show occasional fluency, with correctly constructed sentences of some variety and complexity.
- I can use appropriate and accurate vocabulary, occasionally choosing words to communicate precise meaning or to add interest.
- I can use simple grammatical devices correctly; my sentence separation is mostly correct.
- I can use other forms of punctuation but perhaps inconsistently.
- I make some spelling mistakes but my errors do not prevent me communicating my meaning.

Excellent progress

Content and structure

Descriptive	Narrative
• I can include well-defined, well-developed ideas and images, describing complex atmospheres with a range of details. • I can provide an overall structure through a range of devices such as the creation of a short time span, atmosphere or tension. • I do not confuse description with writing a story. • I can avoid repetition, using a sequence of sentences that makes the picture clear to the reader.	• I can create a complex and sophisticated narrative which may contain devices such as sub-texts, flashbacks and time lapses. • I can provide cogent details where necessary or appropriate. • I can carefully balance and manage different sections of the story, such as the climax. • I can sequence sentences to produce effects such as the building of tension or to provide a sudden turn of events.

Style and accuracy

- I can use a variety of fluent sentences, including sophisticated, complex ones, to achieve particular effects.
- I can use a wide, consistently effective range of vocabulary with appropriately used ambitious words.
- I can use some grammatical devices, an assured range of punctuation and accurate spelling.

Section 3 Applying Key Skills in Written Coursework

In Section 1, you learnt a range of key reading and writing skills:

skimming and scanning	summarising
selecting information	writing in a range of forms and genre
understanding explicit meanings	writing for a range of purposes
inferring and deducing implicit meanings	

These can be applied in a number of contexts, both in everyday life and in your examinations.

	Everyday life	Assessment situations
Skimming and scanning Selecting information	When you need to find specific information: for example, looking up the address of a restaurant.	Tasks where you need to read a text and be able to select key ideas and the evidence used to support them.
Understanding explicit meanings	When you need to work out the obvious, immediate meaning: for example, reading a news article describing a local event.	Tasks where you need to read a text and be able to explore the key ideas stated and formulate your view of them.
Inferring and deducing implicit meanings	When you need to 'read between the lines': for example, reading a piece of fiction and forming an impression of a character.	Tasks where you need to read a text and be able to explore the key ideas and attitudes and formulate your view of them.
Summarising	When you need to take information from a number of sources and present it succinctly: for example, reading a number of film reviews and then pulling the key points together to persuade someone else to go and see it with you.	Tasks where you need to select and reproduce succinctly the key ideas from a text before adding your own opinion.
Writing in a range of forms	Personal situations where you may need to write: for example, a blog journal post or a letter.	All coursework tasks, as you are free to choose the form that you use and variety is encouraged. You are also required to write across three genres.
Writing for a range of purposes	Personal situations where you may need to write for a particular purpose: for example, to advertise a room for rent.	All coursework tasks, as you are required to write for three different purposes.

Chapter 8

Approaching written coursework

For the coursework option included in the Cambridge IGCSE, you will complete a portfolio of three pieces of writing. These give you the opportunity to explore ideas at length and to select unusual or original ways of responding, giving your own views on your experience of the world about you. One assignment will be written in response to a non-fiction text.

This is a real chance to impress! You will have time to experiment with different viewpoints, structures and time sequences, to try out unusual forms and to develop characters in detail.

The chapter takes you through the different assignment possibilities, allowing you to develop your skills before you start on your real coursework assignments. It also offers a range of extended extracts on the theme of 'Danger in the wild' to help you think about forms, structures and techniques you could use in your own writing.

You will have to write **three** assignments:

- informative, analytical and/or argumentative
- descriptive and/or narrative
- a response to a text or texts chosen by your teacher. The text(s) should contain facts, opinions and arguments. You will engage with the text(s) in your response by selecting, analysing and evaluating points from the material. You can write in any appropriate form you choose.

You will need to focus on these writing skills:

Writing:
- articulate experience and express what is thought, felt and imagined
- sequence facts, ideas and opinions
- use a range of appropriate vocabulary
- use register appropriate to audience and context
- make accurate use of spelling, punctuation and grammar.

For the third assignment you will also need to use your reading skills:

Reading:
- demonstrate understanding of the explicit meanings included in the passage
- demonstrate understanding of implicit meanings and attitudes in the passage
- analyse, evaluate and develop facts, ideas and opinions.

Understanding the form, purpose and style of different texts Ⓒ Ⓔ

Learning objectives

● To explore a range of different texts, drawing out what makes them distinctive and effective.

Exploring skills

Good writers are good readers. Thinking consciously about the techniques used by other writers and analysing what makes other texts work will help you to become a better writer, able to make deliberate choices of your own.

The next pages offer four exciting – and very different – texts on a similar theme: 'Danger in the wild'.

Purpose, form, structure and style

What is it that makes us choose particular texts to read? Essentially, it is four elements.

● **Purpose**: What do we want from the text? Is it information? An exciting story? A vivid picture of a place, person or situation?

● **Form**: Does the shape and layout suit our needs or provide the information in the way we want? Is it in the form of newspaper report? A webpage? A diary?

● **Structure**: Is the order of the information or story organised in such a way that it draws us in? Does it make us want to read on?

● **Style**: Does the language make an impact on us? How well does it paint a picture in our heads? Are the facts, events or information conveyed clearly? Do we understand the voice or viewpoint of the writer?

You will need to consider each element carefully in your own writing.

Read the following text. In 1987, the businessman and adventurer, Sir Richard Branson attempted to cross the Atlantic from the US to Ireland by hot-air balloon with his partner, Per Lindstrand. After a disastrous attempt to land, Per has leapt into the sea to save himself but Branson remains in the balloon.

Alone in the balloon

Whatever I did in the next ten minutes would lead to my death or survival. I was on my own. We had broken the record but I was almost certainly going to die. Per, with no survival suit, was either dead or trying to swim on. I had to get somebody to find him. I had to survive. I cleared my mind and concentrated on the options in front of me. I hadn't slept for over 24 hours and my mind felt fuzzy. I decided to take the balloon up high enough so I could parachute off the capsule. I blasted the burners and then found my notebook and scrawled across the open page, 'Joan, Holly, Sam, I love you.' I waited until the altimeter showed 8,000 feet and then climbed outside.

I was alone in the cloud. I crouched by the railings and looked down. I was still wheeling through the possibilities. If I jumped, I would be likely to have only two minutes to live. If I managed to open my parachute, I would still end up in the sea, where I would probably drown. I felt for the parachute release tag, and wondered whether it was the right one. Perhaps due to my dyslexia, I have a mental block about which is right and which is left, especially with parachutes. The last time I had free-fallen I pulled the wrong release tag and jettisoned my parachute. At the time, I had several skydivers around me, so they activated my reserve parachute. But now I was by myself at 8,000 feet. I slapped myself hard across the face to concentrate. There had to be a better way.

'Give yourself more time,' I said out loud. 'Come on.'

As I crouched on top of the capsule, I looked up at the vast balloon above me. The realisation dawned that I was standing beneath the world's largest parachute. If I could bring the balloon down, then perhaps I could jump off into the sea at the last moment before we crashed. I now knew I had enough fuel for another thirty minutes. It must be better to live for thirty minutes than jump off with my parachute and perhaps live for only two minutes.

'While I am alive I can still do something,' I said. 'Something must turn up.'

I climbed back inside and took off my parachute. I made up my mind. I would do anything for those extra minutes. I grabbed some chocolate, zipped it into my jacket pocket, and checked that my torch was still there.

Peering out of the capsule into the fog below me, I tried to work out when I should stop burning, when I should open the vent, and when I should leave the controls and climb out on top of the capsule for my final jump. I knew I had to judge the last burn exactly so that the balloon would hit the sea as slowly as possible. Despite losing all our fuel tanks, the balloon was still carrying a weight of around three tonnes.

As I came out through the bottom of the clouds, I saw the grey sea below me. I also saw an RAF helicopter. I gave a last burn to slow my descent, and then left the balloon to come down of its own accord. I grabbed a red rag and climbed out through the hatch. I squatted on top of the capsule and waved the rag at the helicopter pilot. He waved back rather casually, seemingly oblivious to my panic.

I peered over the edge and saw the sea coming up. I shuffled round the capsule trying to work out where the wind was coming from. It was difficult to be sure since it seemed to be gusting from all directions. I finally chose the upwind side and looked down. I was fifty feet away, the height of a house, and the sea was rushing up to hit me. I checked my life jacket and held on to the railing. Without my weight, I hoped the balloon would rise up again rather than crashing on top of me. I waited until I was just above the sea before pulling my life-jacket ripcord and hurling myself away from the capsule.

The sea was icy. I spun deep into it and felt my scalp freeze with the water. Then the life jacket bobbed me straight back up to the surface. It was heaven: I was alive. I turned and watched the balloon. Without my weight, it quietly soared back up through the cloud like a magnificent alien spaceship, vanishing from sight.

1 Working in a group, use each bullet on page 216 to discuss how effectively the text works to engage the reader and create a vivid picture of what is happening to the narrator.

2 Discuss the text in your group.
  - What **form of text** is this? (An advertisement for hot-air balloons?) How do you know?
  - What do you think the **writer's purpose** is? (To provide instructions on how to fly a balloon?)
  - **What specific aspects of style, structure and language** make the text effective? (For example, how does Branson convey a vivid picture of what is happening?)

> **Top tip**
>
> Considering how the writers create an impact on the reader will help you when you come to write your own pieces.

Building skills

Now read this second extract from the novel *My Ántonia* by Willa Cather, which is set in Nebraska in the early 20th century. Jim is living with his grandparents and has made friends with a Bohemian girl, 'Tony', who is four years older than him. In this extract, they are exploring a prairie-dog hunting ground while on a trip.

The snake and Ántonia

I was walking backward, in a crouching position, when I heard Ántonia scream. She was standing opposite me, pointing behind me and shouting something in Bohemian. I whirled round, and there, on one of those dry gravel beds, was the biggest snake I had ever seen. He was sunning himself, after the cold night, and he must have been asleep when Ántonia screamed. When I turned, he was lying in long loose waves, like a letter 'W.' He twitched and began to coil slowly. He was not merely a big snake, I thought – he was a circus monstrosity. His abominable muscularity, his loathsome, fluid motion, somehow made me sick. He was as thick as my leg, and looked as if millstones couldn't crush the disgusting vitality out of him. He lifted his hideous little head, and rattled. I didn't run because I didn't think of it – if my back had been against a stone wall I couldn't have felt more cornered. I saw his coils tighten – now he would spring, spring his length, I remembered. I ran up and drove at his head with my spade, struck him fairly across the neck, and in a minute he was all about my feet in wavy loops. I struck now from hate. Ántonia, barefooted as she was, ran up behind me. Even after I had pounded his ugly head flat, his body kept on coiling and winding, doubling and falling back on itself. I walked away and turned my back. I felt seasick.

Ántonia came after me, crying, 'O Jimmy, he not bite you? You sure? Why you not run when I say?'

'What did you jabber Bohunk for? You might have told me there was a snake behind me!' I said petulantly.

'I know I am just awful, Jim, I was so scared.' She took my handkerchief from my pocket and tried to wipe my face with it, but I snatched it away from her. I suppose I looked as sick as I felt. 'I never know you was so brave, Jim,' she went on comfortingly. 'You is just like big mans; you wait for him lift his head and then you go for him. Ain't you feel scared a bit? Now we take that snake home and show everybody. Nobody ain't seen in this kawntree so big snake like you kill.'

She went on in this strain until I began to think that I had longed for this opportunity, and had hailed it with joy. Cautiously we went back to the snake; he was still groping with his tail, turning up his ugly belly in the light. A faint, fetid smell came from him, and a thread of green liquid oozed from his crushed head.

'Look, Tony, that's his poison,' I said. I took a long piece of string from my pocket, and she lifted his head with the spade while I tied a noose around it. We pulled him out straight and measured him by my **riding-quirt**; he was about five and a half feet long. He had twelve rattles, but they were broken off before they began to taper, so I insisted that he must once have had twenty-four. I explained to Ántonia how this meant that he was twenty-four years old, that he must have been there when white men first came, left on from buffalo and Indian times. As I turned him over, I began to feel proud of him, to have a kind of respect for his age and size. He seemed like the ancient, eldest Evil. Certainly his kind have left horrible unconscious memories in all warm-blooded life. When we dragged him down into the draw, **Dude** sprang off to the end of his tether and shivered all over – wouldn't let us come near him.

We decided that Ántonia should ride Dude home, and I would walk. As she rode along slowly, her bare legs swinging against the pony's sides, she kept shouting back to me about how astonished everybody would be. I followed with the spade over my shoulder, dragging my snake. Her exultation was contagious. The great land had never looked to me so big and free. If the red grass were full of rattlers, I was equal to them all. Nevertheless, I stole furtive glances behind me now and then to see that no avenging mate, older and bigger than my quarry, was racing up from the rear.

Both 'Alone in a balloon' and 'The snake and Ántonia' deal with narrators facing dangers, although very different ones. In each case, you can learn how the narrator's viewpoint is conveyed by reading carefully.

3 How does Willa Cather convey Jim's feelings and perceptions about what happens? Make notes on:
- Jim's description of the snake before and after he kills it
- how the incident makes him feel
- the impression we get of Ántonia through the events and dialogue
- the impression we get of Jim's feelings towards Ántonia
- the impression we get of Jim's character from his behaviour and from his narration.

4 Now consider how both writers convey the excitement and fear of each situation. Write **100–150 words** on the two passages. Consider in particular:
- the use of verbs of action and movement
- the length and variety of sentences
- any use of dialogue
- any other devices or techniques the writers use to keep us interested and to create fear or tension.

Developing skills

In your own writing, remember that you can approach a single theme or story idea in a huge range of different ways.

The following extract from a poem by D.H. Lawrence also deals with an encounter with a snake. But it is different from 'The snake and Ántonia' in a number of ways, including its form, structure and style.

Snake

A snake came to my water-trough
On a hot, hot day, and I in pyjamas for the
   heat,
To drink there.

In the deep, strange-scented shade of the
   great dark carob tree
I came down the steps with my pitcher
And must wait, must stand and wait, for
   there he was at the trough before me.

He reached down from a fissure in the
   earth-wall in the gloom
And trailed his yellow-brown slackness soft-
   bellied down, over the edge of the stone
   trough
And rested his throat upon the stone
   bottom,
And where the water had dripped from the
   tap, in a small clearness,
He sipped with his straight mouth,

Softly drank through his straight gums, into
   his slack long body,
Silently.

Someone was before me at my water-
   trough,
And I, like a second-comer, waiting.

He lifted his head from his drinking, as
   cattle do,
And looked at me vaguely, as drinking
   cattle do,
And flickered his two-forked tongue from
   his lips, and mused a moment,
And stooped and drank a little more,
Being earth-brown, earth-golden from the
   burning bowels of the earth
On the day of Sicilian July, with Etna
   smoking.

The voice of my education said to me
He must be killed,
For in Sicily the black, black snakes are
   innocent, the gold are venomous.

And voices in me said, If you were a man
You would take a stick and break him now,
   and finish him off.

But must I confess how I liked him,
How glad I was he had come like a guest in
   quiet, to drink at my water-trough
And depart peaceful, pacified, and
   thankless,
Into the burning bowels of this earth?

Was it cowardice, that I dared not kill him?
Was it perversity, that I longed to talk to
   him?
Was it humility, to feel so honoured?
I felt so honoured.

And yet those voices:
If you were not afraid, you would kill him!

5 We get a strong sense of Jim and the snake in 'The snake and Ántonia'. What picture do we get of the poet and snake here?

- Read the poem again and note down any specific descriptions of the snake's appearance and behaviour: for example, 'He reached down from a fissure in the earth wall'.
- With a partner, discuss briefly how the description is both similar and different from that of the snake in Willa Cather's account. For example, think about:
  - **Form**: how the length and shape of the lines convey a different atmosphere (Fast-paced? Slow?)
  - **Style**: contrast the similes and metaphors used to describe the snake in both texts.

Key terms

voice: the specific persona or style of speech used by a narrator

viewpoint: the particular attitude, perspective or opinion of the narrator (or others)

One of the keys to gaining higher marks in your written coursework is to establish a convincing **voice** or **viewpoint** in your text.

6 With a partner, discuss **how** Lawrence conveys his emotions and feelings during the encounter. For example:

> 'I, like a second comer, waiting' suggests the poet respects the snake's right to be there first, drinking.

Although the poem is not exciting and full of action like Willa Cather's story, it does have suspense and tension. Will Lawrence kill the snake or leave it?

7 Discuss with a partner what you think happens next. Then read the whole poem.

Of course, all three pieces you have read so far **could** have been written in different forms and with different purposes. For example:

- a factual report of the balloon landing written by the helicopter pilot
- a diary of what happened written by Ántonia
- a speech or poem about D.H. Lawrence written by the snake!

Look at this possible beginning for the last suggestion:

> The man was watching me as I drank
> Slowly, as if this was his water not the whole world's...

8 Choose one of the tasks above and complete an opening paragraph or verse in the voice or style that you think fits the speaker or narrator.

Applying skills

The final text in this themed section is in a different form and has a different style and purpose, but still focuses on an element of 'Danger in the wild'. Here the narrator (a news reporter) is not so personally involved in the story or information being conveyed.

Adventures of a high-rise window cleaner

After cycling from Toronto to the West Coast and back, then sailing from Scarborough to Iceland, K.C. Maple was having trouble adjusting to the confined life within the tall towers of Toronto.

That was until he found a job that let him climb to the top and dangle off of them.

For the past two and a half years, the 24-year-old with long, blond hair pulled back in a ponytail has washed the windows of Toronto's highrise buildings. It was on the way to a native sun dance ceremony that the part-Swede, part-aboriginal met a man who cleaned windows for a living.

'That was the pivotal point that brought me into the joy of this business,' he says. He is sometimes afraid, but mostly he enjoys the thrill of being up so high. And the money is good. He tells me a beginner who works fast can usually make around $50,000 a year.

'It's great to be paid to go out there, have a little danger and have some fun,' he says. 'I've always wanted adventure, excitement, physical danger.'

Maple spends his days speeding up elevators with 250 feet of ropes draped over his shoulders, then lowering the rope down the side of buildings and repelling on a small plywood seat, holding a couple of squeegees, a suction cup to help him keep close to the windows and a five-gallon bucket filled with water and dish soap.

It's great exercise, especially pulling the ropes up at the end of the day – 'From a fitness standpoint, you've got a lot of reps,' he explains.

Instead of feeling trapped within the walls of a crowded city, he feels liberated in scaling them.

'I love the peace out there – on the outside of the building. You're not inside the fishbowl.'

And what he finds on the high-rise windows, besides layers of dust, bird faeces and grease from unburned fuel, is an urban ecosystem. There are spiders, birds of all types and far too many midges for his liking – a midge can leave a long streak on a window if it gets caught between the squeegee and the glass. Even the peregrine falcon at Yonge and Eglinton has warmed up to him. 'He used to scream when I'd come up,' he says. 'But over the last year and a half he doesn't make noise.'

Then, of course, there's the life on the other side of the glass. Maple tells me that despite what people might imagine, he isn't usually looking through the glass, but at it. Sometimes, though, he will be distracted by a stunning condo interior, or a cluttered one. Other times, people will wave to get his attention.

'I have people showing me their babies a lot,' he says. But really, he admits, they're probably showing their babies the window cleaner.

I ask him how long he thinks he will do this job.

'Until I can come down,' he says, referring to his passion for the work. 'I can't see myself doing anything else.'

Metro Toronto

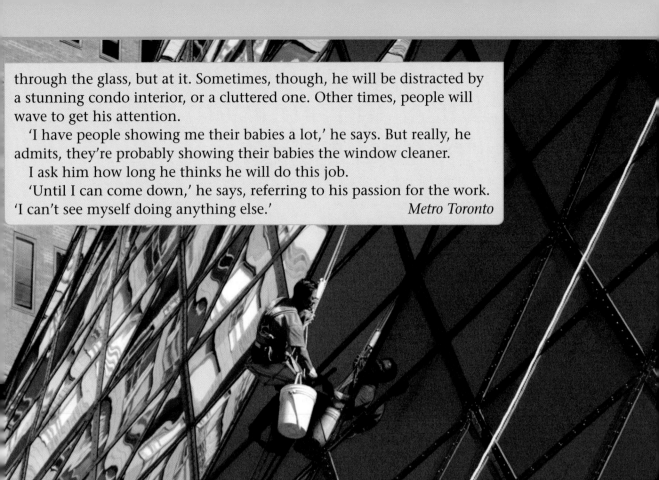

9 Make brief notes on the conventions of the report.
- What key 'newsworthy' facts do we learn from the opening two paragraphs?
- How does direct speech play a part?
- What opinion or viewpoint – if any – comes through from the writer of the report?

10 Think about how the report would have been different if written from a different perspective. For example:
- by someone living inside one of the tower blocks that K.C. Maple cleans
- by the spider building its web on the window Maple is about to wash.

What would need to be changed or added?

11 Have you seen or read about the films, *127 Hours* and *Sanctum*, which tell real-life stories of adventurous people who find themselves trapped by nature? How might any of the texts you have read here inspire you to write a similar story or account? Jot down four or five ideas, which you might use later: for example, 'Trapped in a cave of snakes'.

Top tip

When you write your coursework texts, approaching a theme, story or idea from a different angle or perspective can lead to higher marks.
Using what you know about the conventions of particular texts can make your writing effective and your voice and viewpoint convincing.

2 How to approach informative, analytical and argumentative assignments Ⓒ Ⓔ

Learning objectives

- To plan ideas for informative, analytical and argumentative assignments.
- To draft an appropriate response.

Exploring skills

One of your coursework assignments will require you to write in one of these broad types of writing:

- **informative writing**: to inform, explain or describe
- **analytical writing**: to analyse, review or comment
- **argumentative writing**: to argue, persuade or advise.

Your writing could be in the form of a letter, article, diary, report, for example, and should be written in continuous prose. It should include:

- evidence, such as facts and statistics, expert opinion, anecdotes
- logical, linked arguments or ideas, which may be quite complex
- clear expression and language, using a variety of sentence types
- relevant, precise and specific vocabulary.

So, how do you decide what to write about? Think about what interests you. Remember, writing from your own experience will make your assignment more original. Are there local or national issues that concern you? What do you feel strongly about? For example, look at this set of initial notes:

My interests
- the local environment
- endangered species
- dangerous creatures from my part of the world

Possible ideas
- Komodo dragon - why write about it?
- very rare, fearsome beast, but under threat
- have kept lizards since I was little

1 The next step is to consider the form you will use. Can you add further ideas under the headings for Form 3 and Form 4?

Form 1: letter to a friend
Describe visit to local wildlife sanctuary and seeing a Komodo dragon for first time
Form 2: article for school magazine
Why we should care about saving Komodo dragons
Form 3: diary entry

Form 4: Save the Komodo dragon leaflet

Building skills

Your initial ideas can also lead to wider possibilities, still linked to your interests. For example:

- Why animals deserve our respect but also our fear (analyse and persuade)
- Lion-taming – the best job in the world? (analyse and persuade)
- A diary of my trip into the Australian outback (inform)
- *127 Hours, Touching the Void* and *Sanctum* – Why are we fascinated by films about real-life dangers? (review and comment)
- Why I believe zoos should be closed (argue).

Top tip

Remember: each writing purpose has its own conventions and features. See Chapter 3 to remind yourself of the main conventions of **writing to persuade and argue (pages 88–93), analyse (pages 80–83), inform (pages 94–95), review (pages 96–97) and describe (pages 98–103).**

2 Note down three ideas of your own for assignments based on your interests or concerns (one each for informative, analytical or argumentative writing).

You now have a range of possible titles. Follow this plan to help you build your assignment.

Stage 1

Note down your chosen title. For the higher grades, it will need to be an assignment that is challenging enough for you to demonstrate original thinking, constructing subtle and complex arguments and ideas. Generally, argumentative or analytical tasks will offer more challenge than informative tasks.

How to approach informative, analytical and argumentative assignments

Stage 2

Generate ideas using a spider diagram like the one below. Each 'leg' could be one paragraph or two.

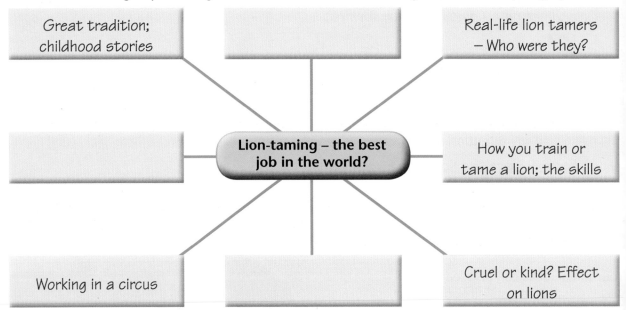

Developing skills

Stage 3

Develop your plan so that each area is expanded with more detail. Make sure you select the details that will most interest the reader and best support your larger points. For example:

> Paragraph 3: real-life lion tamers/why they fascinate me
> • Rose Flanders Bascom, 1900s, killed by lion
> • Clyde Beatty, 1920s
> • Gunther Gebel-Williams, modern, uses different techniques

3 You will need to decide the sequence and structure of your assignment. Consider the following questions.
- Do I want to begin with a surprising fact or quotation?
- Is it best to start with information and then move on to personal reflections?
- Will each paragraph build towards a conclusion where I tell the reader my future career plans?

The way you begin your assignment will depend on your purpose and will establish the tone.

4 Look at these example beginnings and decide:
- what the writer's purpose is
- how they engage their audience
- what tone they establish.

> **Top tip**
>
> Expanding your points and grouping them into paragraphs will also help you to move logically from one area to another.

> **Top tip**
>
> Remember: analysis, arguments and informative writing all need strong conclusions that weigh up evidence or evaluate the different options discussed.

Beginning 1

I will always remember my first encounter with a lion. I was six years old and my father had taken me to the local zoo. Through the bars I watched this sleepy, rather shabby old beast. I was a little disappointed.

But then, just as we were about to move on, the lion let out this tremendous roar. From that moment, I was hooked.

Beginning 2

Sometime in 1915, female lion-tamer Rose Flanders Bascom climbed into the ring with one of her lions. No one knows exactly what happened to this fearless 35-year-old, but she was badly clawed and later died, leaving her husband and young daughter Agnes behind. Reading this story caught my attention and I realised what I wanted to do. If Rose could do it, so could I.

Beginning 3

'Taming' a lion should not be confused with the domestication of a species such as pet dogs or cats. The truth is you can never truly 'tame' a lion. After all, how can you expect a creature bred for the African plains and hills to forget his heritage?

Applying skills

Stage 4

5 Write your draft. Then edit it by checking you have a clear set of well-linked sentences and paragraphs. Check the spelling and grammar, and change any words or phrases that are not appropriate or do not create the effect you intended.

Checklist for success

✔ Your assignment must be **500–800** words long.
✔ Your plan should allow you enough scope to write but not be so crammed with points that you do not explore anything in detail.
✔ You need to link paragraphs fluently by using connectives such as *however*, *furthermore* to guide the reader through your ideas.

Sound progress	Excellent progress
• Your choice of content is engaging with some interesting facts and details.	• Your content clearly arises from personal interest and absorbs the reader throughout.
• Your structure is clear and can be followed.	• Your structure is planned for effect.
• Your style matches the main conventions of the chosen text type.	• Your style is well-matched to the text type and has a clear sense of audience.
• Your spelling, sentences and punctuation are largely accurate.	• Your writing is accurate throughout and sentences and punctuation are used well for effect.

3 How to approach descriptive and narrative assignments (C) (E)

Learning objectives

- To identify the differences between descriptive and narrative writing.
- To plan and draft ideas for descriptive and narrative pieces.

Exploring skills

One of your coursework assignments will require **descriptive and/or narrative writing**. In order to make an impact on the reader, you will need to **explore**, **imagine** and **entertain**.

- **Explore**: you look deeply into an idea, situation or storyline and come up with a range of possible directions you could pursue.
- **Imagine**: you do not simply imitate texts you have read or things you have seen, but come up with original and creative ways of conveying ideas or stories to the reader.
- **Entertain**: you create conscious effects: for example, making the reader feel shock or surprise, sympathy or anger, sadness or joy.

You might write in the form of a short story, a description or even poetry (although you would need to add a commentary to the poems explaining your work). One student listed some ideas around the theme of 'Danger in the Wild'.

> growing-up, fear, showing-off, excitement, danger, children, killing, death, exploring, friendship, kindness, respect, friends, confusion, the earth, thirst, hot country, conscience, water, sea, tides, dogs

Any one of these words could lead to a story idea. For example: 'Two school friends exploring a cave by the sea get trapped by the tide and are rescued by fisherman.'

1 Note your own story idea on the theme 'Danger in the wild'.

You may find it helpful when refining your ideas to answer these questions:

> *Is there an old story or single event you know of which could form the basis of a longer narrative? What would you need to change or develop?*

> *Can you think of a location or setting that made a powerful impression on you? Who could you 'put' in that setting?*

> *What might that character be doing, or have done?*

Top tip

The best ideas are the ones **you** want to write about. They can spring from anywhere: from your head, from ideas in texts you have read, from something you have seen or heard, from an interest of yours.

Building skills

Remember to use the five-part story structure. For example:

Introduction: two friends are exploring some caves by the sea

Development: they decide to go further into the caves and forget the time

Complication: the tide begins rushing in; they are cut off from the entrance

Climax: the water is rising and they are trapped; their only choice is to try to swim out underwater

Resolution: they manage to swim out and flag down a passing fishing boat; they are rushed to hospital

Top tip

Remember that your narrative or story must 'go somewhere'. It must be more than just a series of observations and have an effective beginning and ending. **(See pages 100–103 and 200–204 for help with this.)**

2 Use the advice above to note your story ideas. Then describe your best story idea to a partner, making sure you follow the checklist above. Are there any aspects you could change to make it particularly original or interesting? Think about the following questions.

- **Who** tells the story? (Someone unusual or an animal? Perhaps an object, such as a mirror?)
- How is the story told? (In the first or third person? Perhaps by two narrators each with contrasting views?)
- Could you change the **gender**, **age**, **characteristics** or **occupation** of a character (for example, one character is blind and unable to swim)?
- Could you use a **flashback?** (Perhaps the story begins with its dramatic climax and then the main character looks back to how he/she reached that point.)

Developing skills

How would your assignment differ if you chose to write a descriptive piece rather than a narrative?

Descriptive writing needs:

- well-developed and well-defined ideas (offering depth and detail to the description)
- a clear focus on establishing a setting and atmosphere to evoke a vivid picture
- well-chosen use of imagery, sensory language and sentence variety to bring the description to life
- a clear structure: this could be chronological, or to do with a change of mood or a shifting perspective
- details that 'show' rather than 'tell' the reader about the scene or a character's feelings.

Narrative writing needs:

- a strong opening to hook the reader right from the start
- an interesting plot (where events are told in an original way)
- carefully developed main characters – one or two preferably
- a well-managed ending that fits the story as a whole
- where appropriate, detailed description using amibitious but well-chosen vocabulary.

By choosing a title carefully and avoiding writing about a series of events, you can make sure that a description doesn't become a story. For example:

The dog that remembered me (story)	Stray dog in the village (description)
It was just last week that I had to go into the village to the market. My husband had gone to find work in the city a year ago and hadn't come back so I had to scrimp and save for every penny. It was a lonely life and so I immediately empathised with the poor, thin wreck of a dog I saw sheltering from the midday sun under a market stall.	He sits or lies on his battered side all day long near the market stalls. Trying to find shelter from the oppressive heat, he shuffles from stall to stall, puffs of dust kicked up wherever he goes. His eyes are pale and have lost their shine, like cheap jewels, and his tongue hangs out like a scrap of tatty cloth. Around him, life continues, unaware of his existence.

3 With a partner, discuss the most noticeable differences between the two texts. Think about: character, events, detail and viewpoint.

4 How could you make these texts more interesting and original? You could perhaps:

add a flashback
- the story could begin with the writer cradling the dog before flashing back to how she found it

use a dual narrative
- there could be two voices telling the story or describing – it could be the dog and the new owner.

Note down a further idea for how the story or the description could:
- flashback to an earlier time
- be told by a different voice – someone watching the scene.

5 Now write two paragraphs from either the story or description using one of your ideas from activity 4 for either two voices or a flashback.

Applying skills

Before you start to draft a narrative or description piece, check the advice on page 230 about the key conventions.

Also refer to **pages 98–103** and **196–199** for more on **description** and **pages 104–107** and **200–205** for more on **narrative**.

Ideas can come from anywhere: from real-life experience or occasionally from other texts you have read.

6 Look back over all the texts you read at the start of this chapter. Decide on an idea from one of them and develop it as a story or a descriptive piece. For example:

- Tales from a high window cleaner: story about the cleaner getting stuck while doing his job or falling and being in a dangerous situation without help at hand
- The City from the sky: descriptions of a city from various perspectives, from creatures or people living there.

> **Top tip**
>
> For **developing narratives**, the 'complication' is key; imagine your main character in his/her everyday life (however unusual) then consider adding: bad news, an unexpected arrival/ disappearance, accident or a secret revealed.

> **Top tip**
>
> For **developing description**, 'zoom in' and focus on objects or people as if you had a camera, or 'pan' around to reveal the rest of the scene.

Sound progress

- Your description covers a variety of features, which fit the task but are not always sufficiently detailed or vivid, and slips into storytelling.
- Your narrative is clear and logical, but not particularly interesting or varied in style or plot.

Excellent progress

- Your well-structured description mixes observation with personal interpretation and feeling; language chosen creates a vivid picture.
- Your narrative conveys original ideas and characters in an effective plot. You use structures such as flashbacks or dual narrative to tell the story.

4 How to approach assignments engaging with ideas and arguments from other texts C E

Learning objectives

● To understand and respond to the views expressed in a non-fiction text.
● To identify counter-arguments.
● To plan and draft a response to one of these assignments.

Exploring skills

In one of your coursework assignments you may have to:

● read and respond to a non-fiction text on a particular issue
● show you understand the key arguments and views expressed
● produce your own text responding to these arguments, views or ideas.

In this text, Chris Packham, a BBC presenter and wildlife expert, expresses some very strong views.

Pandas – worth saving?

I don't want the panda to die out. I want species to stay alive – that's why I get up in the morning. I don't even kill mosquitoes or flies. So if pandas can survive, that would be great. But let's face it: conservation, both nationally and globally, has a limited amount of resources, and I think we're going to have to make some hard, pragmatic choices.

The truth is, pandas are extraordinarily expensive to keep going. We spend millions and millions of pounds on pretty much this one species, and a few others, when we know that the best thing we could do would be to look after the world's biodiversity hotspots with greater care. Without habitat, you've got nothing. So maybe if we took all the cash we spend on pandas and just bought rainforest with it, we might be doing a better job.

Of course, it's easier to raise money for something fluffy. Charismatic megafauna like the panda do appeal to people's emotional side, and attract a lot of public attention. They are emblematic of what I would call single-species conservation: ie a focus on one animal. This approach began in the 1970s with Save the Tiger, Save the Panda, Save the Whale, and so on, and

it is now out of date. I think pandas have had a valuable role in raising the profile of conservation, but perhaps 'had' is the right word.

Panda conservationists may stand up and say, 'It's a flagship species. We're also conserving Chinese forest, where there is a whole plethora of other things.' And when that works, I'm not against it. But we have to accept that some species are stronger than others. The panda is a species of bear that has gone herbivorous and eats a type of food that isn't all that nutritious, and that dies out sporadically. It is susceptible to various diseases, and, up until recently, it has been almost impossible to breed in captivity. They've also got a very restricted range, which is ever decreasing, due to encroachment on their habitat by the Chinese population. Perhaps the panda was already destined to run out of time.

Extinction is very much a part of life on earth. And we are going to have to get used to it in the next few years because climate change is going to result in all sorts of disappearances. The last large mammal extinction was another animal in China – the Yangtze river dolphin, which looked like a worn-out piece of pink soap with piggy eyes and was never going to make it on to anyone's T-shirt. If that had appeared beautiful to us, then I doubt very much that it would be extinct. But it vanished, because it was pig-ugly and swam around in a river where no one saw it. And now, sadly, it has gone for ever.

[...] I'm saying we won't be able to save it all, so let's do the best we can. And at the moment I don't think our strategies are best placed to do that. We should be focusing our conservation endeavours on biodiversity hotspots, spreading our net more widely and looking at good-quality habitat maintenance to preserve as much of the life as we possibly can, using hard science to make educated decisions as to which species are essential to a community's maintenance. It may well be that we can lose the cherries from the cake. But you don't want to lose the substance. Save the Rainforest, or Save the Kalahari: that would be better.

http://www.guardian.co.uk/environment/2009/sep/23/panda-extinction-chris-packham

---

1 Go through the text and note down:
- what each paragraph of the text covers
- at least **three** reasons Chris Packham gives for not saving the panda.

Building skills

2 Share your ideas with the rest of your group. Make a group list of all Chris Packham's arguments.

3 In your group, discuss what Chris Packham says. Do you think he is right? Why/why not?

Now list the arguments and counter-arguments in a table like the one below:
- what message would be sent to children (and people in general) if the panda is allowed to die out
- why focusing on bigger creatures to save could help habitat
- the pleasure pandas give
- dangers in a wildlife expert saying what Packham does.

For	Against

4 Chris Packham is clever in other ways in trying to persuade us. Note down any examples of him:
- giving the other point of view so he can 'knock it down'
- making personal references to show he loves animals
- showing his knowledge of wildlife through technical subject-specific vocabulary.
- using more informal turns of phrase to make what he says seem like common sense.

Developing skills

You are now going to plan a response to Chris Packham. The task will be:

> *Write a letter to Chris Packham in which you try to persuade him to change his views and to take back his comments about letting pandas become extinct.*

In your letter, you will need to:
- make reference to his arguments to show you understand what he says and whether or not you agree with it
- add your own arguments against his views
- use a range of persuasive techniques to get your views across.

Content

Your argument can be based on the ones your group came up with. But the ecological arguments alone will not be enough. You will also need to include:

- your own **personal opinion** about **each of the points** Packham makes
- your own **feelings** about pandas and what they mean to you (perhaps you saw them at a zoo as a child)
- **persuasive language**: rhetorical questions (*Surely you don't believe that...?*); powerful, emotive language (*incredibly beautiful; fragile ecosystem*); repetition or lists (*no pandas, no polar bears, no eagles*) (**For more on persuasive techniques, see pages 88–89.**)
- other **ideas** or **facts** drawn from other texts or sources you have read (for example, you could consider D.H. Lawrence's idea about snakes and the traditional view of snakes as evil or sly).

5 Decide on a suitable beginning and ending for your letter. There are many different ways to do this. Here are some ideas.

Beginnings	Endings
Begin straight away with your point of view: *Dear Mr Packham,* *I fundamentally disagree with your...*	End with a forceful final summary of your main point or points: *To sum up, letting pandas die will mean that...*
Start with something more subtle, such as a visual description of a happy panda: *Imagine the wonderful sight of a panda, chewing on bamboo...*	Use an emotional final image: *Just imagine a world in which the forests of China no longer feature the...*
	Use a rhetorical question: *Do you really want to be responsible for...?*

Applying skills

6 Write a full and detailed bulleted plan to draft your letter and cover all the key points. Remember, it needs to be **500–800 words** long. Make sure each point can be expanded into a fluent and persuasive paragraph in your actual response. For example:

> *Saying we should let pandas die is irresponsible for someone like you.*
> - *As a conservationist no one will listen to what you say in future.*
> - *You are influential and people might hunt pandas if they think it's ok.*
> - *You have a job because you want to save wildlife; it's hypocritical.*

Top tip

Use **topic sentences** (often the first sentence in a paragraph) to direct what you are going to say, as the example below shows.

Sound progress

- Your plan shows basic understanding of the main arguments and you include the opposing viewpoint, making some relevant points.

Excellent progress

- Your plan is detailed and explains the views presented in the original text in depth, developing each point and arguing clearly and persuasively.

5 Ways of developing your own views C E

- To engage with ideas, facts and opinions in other texts.
- To choose an idea for a response and a form in which to present it.

Exploring skills

When you respond to a non-fiction text as part of your work for a coursework assignment, it can be useful to collect other facts, statistics or expert opinion to inform what you write. Of course, you must not copy this information directly from another text.

Look at the web page opposite. It is from the World Wide Fund for Nature website.

Here are some sample notes for an assignment in response to Chris Packham's article.

> Only about 1600 giant pandas still in wild
>
> WWF has created over 60 protected nature reserves
>
> Funding needed will help local communities recover from earthquake
>
> Funding promotes green reconstruction in local communities

1 Write 2–3 points of your own about how pandas are presented *visually* on the site, or how they are *described* (for example, the toy panda).

Building skills

How would this help you in a response to Chris Packham's article? First, look at how one writer began her own analysis of the article using some of the information from the website.

2 Copy and complete the table using information from the WWF site or your own ideas.

Original point in article	Agree?	Disagree?
Should just buy 'rainforest' with charity money not panda habitat.		Disagree: funding pandas also helps support local communities in rebuilding rather than destroying 'green' (i.e. natural) areas.
Pandas useful for promoting conservation, but they don't have much use otherwise.		
Pandas are only supported because they are seen as 'fluffy'		
(Your own ideas)		

It's shocking to think that there are only about 1600 giant pandas remaining in the wild. Today they can only be found in the forest areas high in the mountains of south-western China.

If pandas are unable to roam freely through the forest to find mating partners - and females are only in season for two or three days each spring - the chances of breeding are even more limited.

Make a real difference.

Adopt a panda.

You can adopt Zhu Xiong, a female wild panda. Zhu Xiong represents all the pandas we help.

Without cubs...
...what hope is there for pandas

We will send you

 A cuddly toy panda + A fact book about pandas + And loads more fun stuff!

Choose a monthly amount

○ £3 ⊙ £5 ○ £10 ○ £ [   ] (Min £3)

This adoption is ⊙ for me ○ for someone else

(Prefer a one-off payment?)

Cu... **Adopt Now**

Last minute gift?

No problem! If you are worried the adoption pack might not arrive in time, you will be able to print or email a gift certificate to give on the day.

How you can make a real difference

WWF was the first international conservation organisation to work in China - and has been instrumental in implementing a very successful panda project since 1980 which has led to the creation of over 60 protected nature reserves where the panda can safely roam.

We still need to do much more, and last year's tragic earthquake makes the need ever more pressing. We are now working with the Chinese government on a reconstruction plan which will:

✓ help restore damaged nature reserves and field stations

✓ restore panda monitoring and patrolling routes

✓ help local communities to recover from the earthquake

✓ promote green reconstruction in local communities

✓ Your support will also help fund other essential WWF conservation work around the world.

 Recommend

You recommend **Adopt a** Panda - WWF-

Contact us | Sitemap | Terms & Conditions | Data protection | Copyright

5 Ways of developing your own views

Here is an example of how this analysis was turned into a counter-point in the response to the article.

3 With a partner, discuss how the writer has woven information into their argument to counter Chris Packham's argument.

> Packham's argument that panda money should be — nicely paraphrased in own words
> used to buy rainforest rather than panda habitat — viewpoint expressed
> is very limited. In fact, funding pandas, as the World — linking phrase introduces counter-argument
> Wide Fund for Nature's own website suggests, can
> also help communities on the spot and encourage — good synonym for 'local'
> them to invest in natural resources rather than
> simply build over forest and field. — good synonym for 'green reconstruction'

Developing skills

4 Now write a paragraph of your own. Respond to Packham's idea that pandas are promoted because they are 'fluffy' and how this distracts from the real issues.

Try to include your own views on this point as well. You could include a personal anecdote that would add more weight to your argument – for example, about a visit to a zoo or a documentary you may have watched about pandas.

Applying skills

Of course, as with the other assignments, choosing an appropriate – and even original – form for your final piece is important. Here is part of a **transcript** from an interview from a television programme called *Issues*.

> **Studio 1: 7 p.m., Channel One programme: Issues, Series 1, Episode 2**
>
> (*Titles over montage of images of wild animals: polar bears, tigers, pandas, a whale.*)
>
> **Presenter**: (*to studio camera*) Conservation – a force for good, or a huge and expensive waste of time? Chris Packham's recent comments about the unnecessary focus on pandas have created a passionate response and here I have two key players in the debate: Professor Ruth Ahmed from Imperial College and Steve Unwin, Chair of Endangered Species

Key terms

transcript: a written version of a conversation, talk or interview as it actually occurred

Glossary

montage: a compilation or collage of overlapping images

Watch. So, let's start with you, Professor Ahmed. You have argued for many years that conservation is a waste of time…

Professor: Er… I wouldn't put it quite like that. I simply feel that conservation must be targeted. We do not have a bottomless pit of resources, and the money big businesses and nations have outweighs the tiny funds charities can manage…

Unwin: That is very defeatist. Charities have shown, time and time again that action does make a difference…

Presenter: But species are disappearing, aren't they? …

5 Make brief notes on how this transcript shows:
  - what the **topic** or **theme** is (What does the presenter say at the start? What information is given about images and shots?)
  - the **different views and roles** of the people in the programme.

6 Having read Packham's article and the WWF website, and seen how the same issues can be explored in a different form, in this case a television discussion programme, what approach would you take in your own response? Consider these options or think of your own. Which would work best for you?
  - A proposal for a new television series about nature conservation and whether it is worthwhile.
  - An analytical article for a newspaper weighing up the facts, arguments and viewpoints.
  - The script of a conversation between you and your parents, which starts with you asking them to pay your membership to a wildlife conservation organisation. They refuse, saying it's a waste of money.

Key skills

You will need to show the following writing skills in all your coursework responses:

- articulate experience and express what is thought, felt and imagined
- sequence facts, ideas and opinions
- use a range of appropriate vocabulary
- use register appropriate to audience and context
- make accurate use of spelling, punctuation and grammar.

You will need to show the following reading skills in one of your coursework responses:

- demonstrate understanding of explicit meanings
- demonstrate understanding of implicit meanings and attitudes
- analyse, evaluate and develop facts, ideas and opinions.

Exploring sample responses: informative, analytical and argumentative assignments

1 Read this extract from a sample response to inform, explain, describe. The response considers working life and a possible career based on personal interests or experiences.

Response 1

The work of a park ranger

'Park ranger' is an old word it comes from 13th century ——— *missing punctuation*
England and means people who ranged (which means walked
a long way) across the countryside, usually to help prevent
poaching or stealing of cattle and that sort of thing. ——— *rather casual*
Nowadays of course it may still mean that but more
normally I think it refers to the job of people who look after
or protect national forests, parks, etc. In some countries
the same job might be called 'Game warden' or 'Park warden'. ——— *interesting but not developed*

   It is a fascinating job and a job that lots of people want ——— *hints at personal interest but doesn't expand*
to do. It is your responsibility to help and care for the
natural enviroment, especially as there are also lots of ——— *incorrect spelling*
people who want to ruin it. People don't always think when
they are on holiday or visiting parks or forests how much
damage they can do.

   The sorts of responsibilities and duties of a park ranger ——— *clear new point*
are these. They might have to make sure the rules and laws
of the park are kept. For example, even simple things like
lighting fires near dry, wooded areas when they shouldn't
and getting people out if a fire happens. Or parking in places
that might disturb wildlife. Even things like litter or trash,
which can effect the enjoyment for other visitors. ——— *incorrect spelling*

   Another important part of their job is to provide
emergency help. It is natural when you have lots of tourists
and visitors, especially in large national parks like the ——— *good examples, but need to say where these are*
Kruger or Yellowstone, that accidents happen. These could
be medical or things like cars or RVs breaking down. That is
when the Park Ranger will be really needed as they will know
the park like the back of their hand. ——— *bit of a cliché – find a better expression*

Feedback

A reasonably clear explanation of the role of a ranger, but no real purpose
is given for writing and there is no sense of personal involvement or
feelings. Some errors of punctuation and spelling are evident. Vocabulary,
while reasonable, is occasionally repetitive or unimaginative: for example,
'evacuate' could have been used instead of 'getting people out'.

Recommended Band: 4

2 How could the sample response on page 241 be improved to make it a Band 3? In pairs, decide, using the Sound progress box in Check your progress on page 255 as a guide.

3 Now read this extract from another sample response to inform, explain, describe. This response also considers working life and possible careers based on personal interests or experiences.

Response 2

Why I'm more suited to office life than outdoor work

I have been thinking about my future career and wondering
what job would suit me best. At the moment I don't know — **gives clear personal reason for writing**
exactly the sort of work I want but I do know that I would
rather work indoors than outside. Why is this? Well, there
are several reasons. — **clear structure – sets up rest of assignment**

   First, I am just not an outdoor type. Even as a young boy — **useful sequence word**
when my brothers wanted to play football or climb trees
I preferred to stay in with a good book. Sometimes they
would come in with a bruise or something and I would say, 'I
told you so.'

   Another reason is that I'm not very keen on fresh air. I
know that sounds kinda funny but it's true. Fresh air to me — **too informal**
means getting freezing cold or very very hot. No one wants
to feel that. So that's why an office job would suit me best. — **limited vocabulary**
I am sure I will be very happy sitting at a desk with a computer. — **surely there is more to say here**

   Besides, office jobs are very friendly as you get to mix and
chat with lots of people. Outdoors you might be on your
own. I need to have people around me so I can gossip and
share jokes and news. In fact it almost sounds like it's not a
job but meeting with friends which is always enjoyable. — **good, but there is probably a better way to introduce it. Also, is this the only research? Many more examples could have been included**

   I have done some research too into outdoor jobs and some
of them are just too dangerous! I read about this guy who
cleans windows in high-rise offices – like hundreds of levels.
His name is K.C. Maple and he lives in Toronto and even he — **it would have been good to have a direct quotation from the article**
says that he likes adventure and danger. That is not for me.

Feedback

A clear and structured response to the task, with evidence of personal response and some detail and examples supplied. Vocabulary is appropriate if a little unadventurous, whilst punctuation and grammar are generally competent. Further development of points and a wider range of sentence structures would help to push up the mark.

Recommended Band: 3

Exploring sample responses: informative, analytical and argumentative assignments (C) (E)

1 Read this extract from a sample response to analyse, review, comment. It is related to reviewing television programmes and followed class debates on how wildlife is presented in the media.

Response 1

SHARKS IN THE LIVING ROOM
How we all love nature programmes — **headline and by-line make the form (newspaper article) clear**

What is it about television nature programmes that is so — **more specific question provides focus for the article**
appealing? A quick glance at my pocket-size TV guide
reveals no less than six nature programmes on Channel One
yesterday, starting with <u>Swimming with Dolphins</u> at 10 a.m.
through to <u>Human Planet</u> at 9 p.m. Pretty amazing. And — **effective minor sentence**
that doesn't even take into account the news items about
animals. It seems that nowadays we are all animal fans,
especially if they are on the television.

What interests me, though, is why. After all, we can't — **further refines analysis**
touch, feel, smell or chat with animals on television, even
in 3-D or high-definition. Surely seeing and hearing them — **good use of rhetorical question to connect with reader**
in the wild would be better? But I guess that's just too
expensive, too far away or too difficult. After all, lots of
these programmes now show how the films were made, like
<u>Human Planet</u>, and you find out it was incredibly hard and
took loads of time to get the shots they wanted. — **more appropriate phrase for a news report needed here**

Maybe though, watching animals on TV is a dangerous
trend. Does it mean that we can't be bothered to see
what's in our backyard? If I get off my backside and look — **interesting new point and well-expressed**
out into my yard I know that if I wait long enough, lizards
start to crawl out of cracks in the wall. Also, there are — **good personal engagement in topic**
these strange-looking birds that I really ought to know the
name of. I could even make my own programme using a video
camera! Not very likely – I'm definitely a watcher not a doer!

My own favourite nature programmes are not about the
obvious creatures, but the ones we would never know about
if it wasn't for the programme makers. Like that one which — **a bit lazy – more specific factual information here would make it more like an article**
showed those dancing sea-horses/dragon things (can't
remember the names). You'd never see those in a million
years would you, probably not even in a zoo?

Feedback

A good reflection and analysis of the topic with, in some places, well-developed and interesting points of view. Ideas are well-ordered and there is some variety of vocabulary and sentences in places. The latter part of the extract is less successful as ideas trail off a bit and lack of detail is apparent, but the personal engagement, if a little clumsy, is interesting and appealing.

Recommended Band 2

2 How could the sample response on page 243 be improved to make it a Band 1? Work with a partner to decide, using the Excellent progress box in Check your progress on page 255 as a guide.

3 Now read this extract from another sample response to analyse, review, comment. It results from the same class debates on how wildlife is presented in the media.

Response 2

WATCH OUT! GREAT WHITE IDIOT NEARBY

SHARK WATCHER (9p.m. Discovery channel)

Animal documentaries are, unlike sharks, not dying out. There are huge numbers on television and it seems that, if you want to guarantee viewers, the television companies think all you have to do is take a camera to some exotic location and stick a celebrity in front of it where they will moan about how much they will miss the Lesser Spotted Green Horny-backed Toad.

    Shark Watcher is a new documentary presented by Dominic Doran, who we all know as a comedy actor in brainless sit-coms. The first time we see him in this new documentary, he is sitting on a lovely boat in sunny weather; the next moment he is telling us how dangerous it is watching sharks. Yes, Dominic, very dangerous when you are sitting on a huge boat with a camera crew. Next, he tells us, 'The Great White Shark is under threat from mankind'. Really? You're kidding!

    The programme then proceeds to follow Dominic as he fails to actually see any sharks at all. Instead we get long shots of Dominic looking thoughtful as the sun goes down. Or we get close-ups of him going to sleep with sad music playing. It drives me mad!

    The programme is also irritating because it uses the same old ideas: Dominic interviewing a conservationist but clearly not understanding a word he is saying; Dominic phoning home and telling his girlfriend he misses her (does he think he's on I'm a Celebrity Get Me out of Here?) and Dominic pretending to read a difficult book all about sharks.

Annotations (margin notes):

- clever, funny heading establishes viewpoint
- tongue-in-cheek first sentence continues mocking tone
- further humour for effect
- basic factual information included first
- semi-colon shows grammatical structure for shades of meaning
- normally too informal, but fits style here
- short sentence doesn't add anything
- new point shows writer's understanding of media conventions
- good vocabulary

Feedback

The analysis and argument in this review is developed here in an engaging, often humorous way but with specific reference and detail from the programme included. There is variety in sentences – from the headline onwards – and appropriate vocabulary too, with reference to 'location', 'long shot', etc. The piece stops just short of being over-expressive and suits the tone of a mocking television review.

Recommended Band: 1

Exploring sample responses: descriptive and narrative assignments C E

1 Read this extract from a narrative writing response. It comes from the end of the narrative.

Response 1

Stranded by the sea

So we were stuck and it was all Carla's fault.

'I didn't want to come to this stupid cave in the first place,' I said.

Carla didn't say anything. We both felt so cold and I could see the water levels creeping up. We huddled on a ledge but it was very narrow and we weren't sure if it would be high enough. —— **good detail but more description would help**

Then something stirred in the surface of the water. —— **good use of suspense**

'What's that?' Carla screamed.

'I don't know.' I replied. —— **speech punctuation error**

There was another movement, and then a sort of hand reached up for our ledge. It looked like a young woman's hand as it has slim long —— **too vague / should be past tense**
fingers. Then slowly the rest of the person emerged from the grey-looking water. It was a beautiful lady with long, flowing hair, like a doll.

I had no idea how she got there, because the water was so cold no one would survive for long. The huge waves were now crashing into the —— **good further detail**
cave's entrance and I knew we didn't have long.

'Come,' the woman said, holding out her hand.

'I'm not jumping into that!' Carla stated.

'If you do not follow me, you will die, it is your choice.' Said the woman. —— **punctuation needs correcting**
Then she added. 'I know a tunnel under water, but you must trust me, you need to hold your breath for a few seconds.' —— **good attempt at imagery**

I took one look at Carla and jumped. Then the water hit me like a slap in the face from an ice-block. Then I was underwater and to my shock I saw what the woman looked like. She had a tail of a fish which was —— **narrative twist, but perhaps more could be made of writer's shock**
shimmering green and blue. Perhaps the cold water was blinding me and I couldn't see properly that would explain it.

Next I heard Carla splosh into the water too. —— **better verb choice needed**

Feedback

The structure for the story on page 245 seems pretty clear and easy to follow. However, there are too many errors of punctuation, tense and grammar. In places there are odd moments of original description, but these are never fully developed and sentences and plot are rather too predictable ('next', 'then', etc).

Recommended Band: 4

2 How could this sample response be improved to make it a Band 3? Work with a partner to decide, using the Sound progress box in Check your progress on page 255 as a guide.

3 Now read this extract from another narrative writing sample response. This time it is the opening to the story.

Response 2

The shrinking land

Now the sand had shrunk to a tiny area of about two metres square around me. The cold easterly wind howled and in the dark I could no longer see my fellow fishermen. — **excellent first line plunges the reader right into the action**

They say that when your life is under threat then your past flashes before your eyes. In my case, all I could remember was my wife's face that morning when I left to look for work. — **use of flashback to set scene**

'You don't have to go out on the sands. Everyone says it's dangerous,' she told me.

We were standing in our one room hut, the baby was crying. — **incorrect use of comma – full stop or joining word needed**

'I do,' I told her. 'We have no money.'

She was right of course and perhaps now I wouldn't see her again. I thought of my fellow fishermen and women and wondered if they knew the sands and tides better than me. Perhaps they were safe at home now with their families. — **needs more detail on these people, when they met, etc.**

I looked for a light or any sign of life. Where was the beach? There was no moon or stars to guide me, but I had to move or I'd be dead. I plunged waist up into the swirling water and headed in a straight line. — **good, dramatic visual details**

The water then rose to my chest. Then I just dropped my baskets of — **repetitive**
the fish so that I could swim. I felt miserable. Even if I survived I would lose my job. I didn't like the gang boss but I needed this job. But if I came back with no catch they would get rid of me. — **needs more detail on why**

I imagined my wife and baby. I had to make it for them. — **good short sentences**

Suddenly I saw a light and now felt some hope – surely I could survive now? Well we would see in the next few horrible minutes.

Feedback

This starts very effectively indeed and the use of flashback to fill in detail is quite sophisticated. There is real feeling too and this part is very believable. However, after that, there is a lack of detail about other characters – the other fishermen, the 'gang boss' – and some rather repetitive sentences spoil what could be a much higher level of writing. There are sparks of originality here, nevertheless.

Recommended Band: 3

Exploring sample responses: descriptive and narrative assignments Ⓒ Ⓔ

1 Read this extract from a descriptive writing sample response.

Response 1

Two cities — good choice as it opens up the possibilities of description

Voice 1: From the roof of my city I see a tangled network of dusty streets and sand-coloured buildings topped with red or brown roofs. — excellent, vivid details and vocabulary

I hear a symphony of sounds, like the clatter of cattle and the distant horns of cars and trucks which weave between the crowded inhabitants. — good metaphor, which is developed in the following images

There are cyclists and motorbikes too, dodging in and out of the crowds, stopping, then going again. No one waits for the traffic lights, although all take notice of the police officer in white gloves waving people past.

Voice 2: In my city as I look down, the rain smashes the puddles of the — well-chosen, powerful verb

pavements and glistens in the lamplight. Taxis move in straight lines up and down the Royal Mile and deposit late-night shoppers or tourists. The buildings are iron-grey in the evening rain and look as solid as stone robots. — interesting simile – Does it work? Why 'robots'?

I am pleased to be here to escape my parents and watch the world go by. They don't usually allow me on the roof of the apartment — slipping into telling a story?

but they have tonight.

Voice 1: The evening fades and the baking sun slowly slides down over the edge of the city. But nothing stops and the city never sleeps. Just new people appear. New cars and workers going to night-time work.

Everything seems jumbled up like whoever built the city just threw all — clever idea, but a bit clumsily expressed

the buildings up in the air and let them fall on the ground like playing a game. — short sentence adds variety

Voice 2: Office workers are trudging home, umbrellas up. They look like — again slips into storytelling and rather weak expression

flowers from above. The street lamps are necklaces along the streets. I hear my mother calling me to come down and I must be needed but I will come up here again soon. It's so relaxing.

Feedback

In many places this would deserve a higher mark especially in Voice 1's account, which feels authentic. However the slip into storytelling for Voice 2 takes away from the simple contrasts that worked so well – perhaps the writer was running out of ideas. But overall there is some excellent imagery and vivid detail.

Recommended Band: 2

2 How could this sample response be improved to make it a Band 1? Work with a partner to decide, using the Excellent progress box in Check your progress on page 255 as a guide.

3 Now read this extract from another descriptive writing sample response.

Response 2

THE CITY IS AN OCEAN

Like a huge, silver eel the highway curls around the coral buildings, suffocating the little roads and paths, like tiny minnows. It growls and snarls and swallows onrushing vehicles and throws them out again, forever hungry and never satisfied.

In offices, sharks prowl the corridors in business suits, their jagged words cutting down their enemies. Smaller fish – little frightened crabs, scuttle into rooms to avoid their bosses and cower behind doors or under desks, afraid they'll be netted. The shark's narrow eyes settle on a useless bloater, a slow moving salesman who failed to hide. He's not been selling much so the shark snaps him up and sends him home never to return.

    Above the city
    The sky is another ocean
    Serene, still and deep blue
    It reminds all fish of other peaceful worlds
    Where no nets come and food is free.

On the streets, married couples and friends cling to each other like sea-urchins, wrapping their fronds and spines around each other's bodies. They sway along the pavement in the breeze, fearful of being swept up by the tide of time. It's only six hours till work begins again.

    In the city
    The waves sleep and the eel settles.
    It eats but now more slowly
    Half-watching, waiting, ready
    For the rush.

Annotations:
- very expressive and original opening metaphor/image
- present tense suits description
- inappropriate word choice – sharks can't 'prowl'?
- clever link
- metaphor cleverly extended and developed
- perhaps too literal – him being sacked?
- using a poem allows student to change tone and focus
- excellent simile and vocabulary choices

Feedback

This is an outstanding response, which is both original and appropriate. The idea for the extended metaphor of city/ocean opens up lots of possibilities to look at the city in a new way. Occasionally the description is a bit forced – the shark/bloater idea – but the inclusion of poetry makes this especially unusual and engaging.

Recommended Band: 1

Exploring responses: assignments engaging with ideas and arguments from other texts Ⓒ Ⓔ

1 Read the coursework-style assignment and then the extract from a sample response to analyse and evaluate.

Text(s): a range of articles and transcripts (see pages 232–239) about conservation of the panda
Assignment: Analyse and evaluate the information and views expressed in Chris Packham's article and write a letter to him based on them. Your own views should be based on the content of the article.

Response 1

viewpoint expressed clearly at the start

Dear Chris

I think you are completely right about the panda issue. Just because —— *some understanding of the issue, but bit basic*
they are cuddly and lovely to look at does not make them worth saving.
From my point of view, spending all that money on pandas is just not
sensible. There is not enough money around so spending it on them is
a waste which is what you say. Well I agree with you because just think
what we could spend the thousands on! —— *not very close reading (Chris says 'millions') needs to expand the point with own examples*

You make the point that it is easy to raise money for fluffy animals
and that is correct too. It is definately easier. But that does not make *spelling error*
it right. Just because children and adults like cuddly-looking creatures
doesn't mean we should encourage them.

Another point you make is that the panda may not be a very strong —— *clearly stated new point in this paragraph*
species as it did not have a big habitat and it fed off quite rare
vegetation and stuff. So this means I think that you think perhaps the
panda was going to die anyway whatever humans did. And you say too —— *verb tense is incorrect – should be present*
that it's very difficult to breed them in zoos and parks. This all makes
it seem a bit of an effort for just one tiny species, so I think I agree
with you on that point.

sums up idea quite well

The other point you make is that people haven't bothered to save ugly animals like the Yangtze river dolphin. Personally I would have liked to see that creature – I have always liked weird looking animals and it's part of the wonder of nature that they exist.

> beginning to get a personal response but more needed

That's it really. I just want to say that I totally support what you wrote and I will not be giving money to panda conservation. Instead I will give money to animals that are not as well-known or as attractive.

> slightly misses the point of what Packham's main argument was

Feedback

Information is used reasonably well from the Packham text: the response shows some good understanding of Packham's points to begin with, but later seems to miss some of the main ideas. The writing begins with quite well-structured paragraphs, but they are rather repetitive and tend not to add anything to the original points. When they do so, as in paragraph 5, the point isn't really explored in any depth. Small grammatical and spelling errors could have been avoided by careful checking.

Recommended Band: 4

2 How could this sample response be improved to make it a Band 3? Work with a partner to decide, using the Sound progress box in Check your progress on page 255 as a guide.

3 Now read this extract from another response to analyse and evaluate. Note that the assignment is different to the one above, although the stimulus is the same. The extract is from the beginning of the article.

> *Text(s): a range of articles and transcripts (see pages 232–239) about conservation of the panda.*
>
> *Assignment: Analyse and evaluate the information and views you have read and write an article based on them for a wildlife magazine. Your own views should be based on the contents of the different texts you have read.*

Response 2

Strong feelings over pandas ——————— — relevant title for an article

There have been some recent arguments in the press over the need to preserve the panda. These have provoked lots of debate amongst —— first paragraph introduces issues in appropriate way for a wildlife magazine

wildlife conservationists, experts and members of the public. Last night, the Channel One broadcast, Issues, saw a big argument between Professor Ahmed from Imperial College London and Steve Unwin, showing just what people feel.

At the heart of the argument has been Chris Packham's statement that we can 'lose the cherries from the cake', by which he means —— evidence of careful reading of Packham's words, if not very deep

pandas, in order to keep the 'substance', by which he means animal habitats in general. I'm not sure about this because even if we agree with him that we shouldn't give all our efforts to preserving 'cuddly' or 'fluffy' creatures, this is not quite the same as saying we should let them die out altogether.

He also makes the point that single-species conservation was vital in raising awareness of conservation issues in the past decades but—— needs to say what the 'new approach' is – missed opportunity to develop an idea

now we need a new approach.

It might seem easy to agree with Packham when you see the way some charities and conservation campaigns approach saving the panda. The Pandas International website has a children's page which doesn't say much about conservation at all. All it does is —— further understanding of the second text

simply present cute photos and these activities in which children write 'save the panda' in Chinese. But, does any of this do any harm? If it raises interest levels with young people, then that's —— rhetorical question engages with readers

great, I think.

Packham may be being deliberately controversial so that we all sit up and take notice, but surely none of us want to see the disappearance of <u>any</u> species? If we can preserve pandas and save —— paragraph is clear and viewpoint expressed well

habitats then great. None of us want to see such lovable animals disappear. I want my children to enjoy them like I have.

Feedback

This extract presents some of the ideas clearly and shows some understanding of the texts. Some opportunities are missed to engage more deeply with the ideas and despite the fluency it lacks original ideas or much of a personal voice.

Recommended Band: 3

Exploring sample responses: assignments engaging with ideas and arguments from other texts Ⓒ Ⓔ

1 Read the following coursework-style assignment assignment and the extract from an analytical sample response.

> **Text(s):** *the poem 'Snake' and a range of texts about panda conservation*
>
> **Assignment:** *Write an essay in which you respond to the ideas expressed by different writers in two of the texts you have studied about the natural world, and how this influences your own viewpoint. Make sure you analyse and evaluate each text carefully.*

Response 1

In 'Snake', D.H. Lawrence describes how he comes to get some water in the morning and notices a snake at the 'water trough' drinking. He is in 'pyjamas' because of the heat, creating quite a comic personal scene. I can just imagine myself doing the same, feeling sort of embarrassed! — *makes a point about what is conveyed, but is it correct?*

The snake has come from a hole in the wall and the writer is fascinated to watch him there just drinking and taking no notice of anything. He describes carefully his 'yellow brown slackness soft bellied down' which doesn't sound particularly pleasant – and this is added to by the mention of his 'two-forked tongue' The man must be really afraid because if the snake turns on him he could be bitten, and as he is only wearing pyjamas, just think what would happen! — *shows the poet's description and uses quotations*

But then as the poem progresses it becomes less clear what it is the poet actually feels. For a start, he now refers to him as a 'guest', a form of personification that shows the poet's respect, and this is backed up by when he says he felt 'honoured' that the snake had visited him. So it must be something else that makes him feel he needs to kill the snake. Something about snakes' history and what we think of them. — *good – starts to see nuances* — *language device and effect* — *throwaway comment, but this is a key point to develop*

This is all very different from the Panda website we looked at. There is no choice here – you are just expected to love and save the panda. I thought the language was very direct, too – using imperatives such as 'Throw a panda party' – and really not very personal. But the personification does make a big impact in both of the texts. Whilst the website images make the panda cuddly, like a baby or toy, and not really like a real animal at all, the poem makes the snake on an equal level of respect, something I can really relate to. — *introduces the new text well* — *language focus* — *point not fully developed, and doesn't say how or why they relate to the poet's perspective*

2 How could this sample response be improved to make it a Band 1? Work with a partner to decide, using the Excellent progress box in Check your progress on page 255 as a guide.

3 Now read this extract from another analytical response to the same texts and assignment. This extract deals mostly with the poem.

Response 2

In the D.H. Lawrence's poem, the mythic and cultural power of the snake is humanised as the poet grapples with his feelings on seeing it appear at his water-trough. In a similar way, but with different results, websites such as Pandas International also humanise animals and create their own myths, something I find understandable, if somewhat disturbing.

— a powerful and compelling opening – but does the student explore this sufficiently?

When the snake first appears to the poet, I really share Lawrence's admiration of him and I get a strong picture of his 'straight mouth', 'straight gums' and 'slack long body', with these 's' sounds seeming to accentuate the soft hissing 's' s. I also feel I can picture the snake as he 'flickered his two-forked tongue' and 'stooped'. How could anyone kill something so noble?

— excellent focus on the effects of the poet's techniques on the reader

— good rhetorical question makes student's view clear

This theme of respect for an ancient being is developed further as the snake seems to be almost part of the earth itself – as if coming from the 'burning bowels of the earth', like a mother with a stomach.

— interesting, original point – could more be said?

However, I understand the poet's ambivalence at this point, when he says how his 'education' tells him he should kill the snake as it is dangerous. It is as if his natural feelings are to protect and worship it, but our society has made us think snakes should be destroyed. There are voices in his head arguing with each other, but he continues to feel 'honoured' by the 'guest' who has dropped by.

— clear understanding, but perhaps the idea could be further explored

— further supporting quotations woven into the sentence

This all makes me wonder about my own perspective on — fluently moves into own perspective and responses to the panda site
the natural world. Are there some creatures I value over others? Why? And how influential has my education and the stories I have been told been on how I see certain creatures? For example, on the Panda website I feel I am being manipulated by the soft and 'cuddly' language, encouraged to see the panda less as a wild creature and more as a furry toy I might keep in my bedroom.

Feedback

From the extract we can see an in-depth and mostly fluent response to the poem, with language devices and their effects analysed throughout. Occasionally the response jumps around a little and some ideas are undeveloped, such as the idea of the snake as coming from the earth's 'stomach'. It would be interesting to see how the writer developed his or her own views on nature, but this suggests it would be done at a high level, given the final paragraph.

Recommended Band: 1

Sound progress

Content and structure

- I can write in the correct form and purpose for my chosen assignment.
- I can write in a style that has some idea of 'voice' and/or viewpoint, and in at least one assignment, a sense of audience, too.
- I can write sentences and paragraphs that are generally fluent and sequenced or linked in an orderly way.
- I can generally punctuate and spell correctly, with only minor errors.

Competent writing with some development of ideas

- I can express feelings and ideas clearly and supply some detail, explanation and examples to help the reader.
- I can make a clear attempt to present facts, ideas and opinions in an orderly way or argue a point of view using a series of points, some of which are developed.
- I can use appropriate if sometimes unadventurous vocabulary and write sentences that mostly link ideas successfully.
- I can make a clear attempt in at least one assignment to write with a sense of audience and show some evidence of adapting style to context.
- I can use punctuation and grammar reasonably well, although without much variation and with some minor errors in my weaker work.

Excellent progress

Content and structure

- I can describe ideas and feelings about experiences in a thoughtful and mature way.
- I can structure my writing for effect, making creative use of a variety of sentences, vocabulary and paragraphs.
- I can vary my style confidently to suit the audience or context, as required.
- I can use punctuation and grammar accurately, but also vary structures to express different meanings.
- I can spell simple, complex and technical words accurately throughout.

Confident and stylistic completion of challenging tasks throughout your Portfolio

- I can describe and reflect effectively upon ideas, feelings and experiences, give detail and analyse thoughtfully. I can argue using mature and thoughtful ideas.
- My arguments and narratives are ordered logically, with facts, ideas and opinions carefully linked to the next. My paragraphs are used for effect and I am confident enough to experiment, where appropriate, in the structure of my expressive writing.
- I can use a wide range of effective vocabulary and varied, well-constructed sentences.
- I can vary my style with assurance to suit audience and context in all three assignments.
- I can write accurately throughout and use punctuation and grammatical structures to express shades of meaning. I spell simple, complex and technical words with precision.

Section 4 Speaking and Listening

This table shows the key speaking and listening skills you will use in your IGCSE course:

understanding, ordering and presenting facts, ideas and opinions	using language and register appropriate to audience and context
articulating experiences and expressing what you have thought, felt and imagined	listening and responding appropriately to the contributions of others
communicating clearly and fluently	

	Everyday life	Assessment situations
Understanding, ordering and presenting facts, ideas and opinions	When you are asked to give directions or recommend a game or a movie.	Individual tasks where you are asked to give a talk or speech on a specific topic.
Articulating experiences and expressing what you have thought, felt and imagined	Informal situations when you are asked to describe experiences such as a holiday or day trip. Semi-formal situations such as a job interview where you might be asked to reflect on your experience or skills.	Individual tasks where you are asked to give a talk or speech on a specific topic. Discussions where you are asked to enlarge upon or explain your ideas.
Communicating clearly and fluently	Clarity is vital in most situations, especially when giving instructions or making a request. Fluency is a higher level skill but it makes it far more likely that people will listen to you: for instance, when telling a story or persuading someone to accept your point of view.	All formal assessment opportunities value this quality highly.
Using language and register appropriate to audience and context	Everyday life presents us with a range of situations in which we need to communicate with different individuals. The ability to match the level of formality and the style of your speech to what others expect and are able to cope with makes you an effective communicator.	All formal assessment opportunities take this into consideration. It is particularly important when giving a talk the listener is required to focus for some time and they may be put off if they cannot understand or if their needs are not met by your style.
Listening and responding appropriately to the contributions of others	This ability is fundamental in any successful conversation or discussion. It makes the difference between an exchange of statements or opinions and a genuine exploration of ideas which may build to an agreement or conclusion.	This is vital in any discussion especially one that follows a presentation as your audience will have questions to ask which will allow you to show a developed understanding of your topic. It is also the key to any group task where examiners will look to see how you interact and what role your contributions play in building a successful discussion.

Approaching speaking and listening

Your school can choose to assess your speaking and listening skills through an exam or through a series of coursework tasks. This chapter will help you to plan, prepare and deliver each of the types of assessment you could be asked to prepare.

There are four types of speaking and listening assessment included in the Cambridge IGCSE.

A: Presentation

Part 1: Individual task For example, you will give a presentation, a talk, a speech or a monologue. (You might talk about your reactions to meeting a famous person or about a recent film you have seen and suggest why others would also like it.) Your talk should last 3–4 minutes.

Part 2: Discussion

Your talk leads into a conversation with the teacher/examiner about your chosen topic. This discussion should last 6–7 minutes.

B: An individual activity

You will give a presentation, a talk, a speech or a monologue: for example, you might talk about your favourite hobby or describe an interesting place that you have visited.

C: A pair-based activity

For example, you might role-play an argument between two neighbours or your teacher might interview you and another student about how something at school could be improved.

D: A group activity

For example, in a group, you might discuss who to invite (and why) to open the new local shopping centre or, in a parole board scenario, your teacher might present cases for prisoners and the group then discusses whether or not each case merits early release.

The same skills will be tested or assessed, whichever option you take:

- articulate experience and express what is thought, felt and imagined
- present facts, ideas and opinions in a sustained, cohesive order
- communicate clearly, fluently and purposefully as an individual and in dialogue with other speakers
- use register appropriate to audience and context
- listen to and respond appropriately to the contributions of others.

1 Using the right language for your audience C E

Learning objectives

- To understand what language and tones are appropriate to different audiences.
- To use language and tone appropriate to the audience.

Your **audience** is a vital consideration in any speaking and listening task. You might be making a formal presentation, talking to your teacher or another student in a paired discussion, or talking to other students and your teacher within a group.

You also need to use an appropriate **speaking style**. Remember that you are being assessed, so you should speak using accurate English, rather than in the casual way in which you might talk to friends.

Checklist for success

✔ Focus on using formal standard English.
✔ Use a suitable style and include suitable content to engage your audience.

Exploring skills

1 You are going to deliver a presentation on how your school's rules should be changed. With a partner, decide how you would vary your content and style for:
- the head teacher
- your classmates
- a meeting of interested parents.

In each case, ask yourself:
- What will they already know?
- What do I need to tell them?
- How can I put across my views most persuasively?

2 This sample is part of an unsuccessful presentation made by one student to a parents' meeting. Decide what needs to be improved.

> *Thing is, nobody likes any rules. They ain't cool. And the ones we have in this school are brainless. You've gotta be here to know we suffer. Man, do we suffer! Parents? They don't know nothing about stuff happening to us every day. We was stopped from eating our lunch outside on the field yesterday. Maybe they thought the grass was, like, upset. As if!*

To do well in speaking and listening, you will need to be able to use **standard English** in your tasks. That means:

- avoiding slang or language that is too informal
- speaking in full sentences, using correct grammar
- using vocabulary that will be widely understood.

(3) Deliver the speech above to a partner, changing it to standard English that would be more suitable for an audience of parents. Alter words and sentence structures where necessary.

Key terms

standard English: the most widely-used form of English that is not specific to a particular location or region. For example, in standard English, you would say *we **were** going* not *we **was** going* and you would use the word *argument* rather than *tiff* or *barney*.

Building skills

The tone you use is always important. This is a Band 1 student talking with her teacher about healthy diets.

Sara: … So, really, healthy eating is something we should all be aware of.

Teacher: I'm sure we would all agree with that.

Sara: We would, sir, but agreeing is not necessarily the same as acting, is it? After all, it is easy to say, 'Yes, let's eat more vegetables and consume less sugar', but it's much harder to apply that philosophy when we arrive at the supermarket.

Teacher: Well… aren't we all very aware that our diet is crucial if we are going to live a long and healthy life?

Sara: I guess… So… are you suggesting that fundamentally affects the products we choose?

Teacher: Maybe… Does it?

Sara: Perhaps… But probably not often enough. You need to consider clear examples… Like my family… or even your family… I mean… How often do you weigh yourself? Do you think your diet is healthy enough, sir…? Do you get to the shop and think… 'Mm, I'd better buy less chocolate and more oranges.' Or is it easy for all of us to accept being a few kilos heavier…

Written English is considered and can be reworked; spoken English is formulated moment by moment and demands an instant response. So, here, we find Sara working out her ideas as she speaks ('I guess… So…') and using part-sentences.

However, she still uses appropriate English and her **tone** is perfect for her audience. She is thoughtful and makes points without becoming too casual or offending her teacher.

Key terms

tone: the way you vary your voice and language to suit your audience and get your meaning across, for example to express a certain emotion or create a particular mood

4 How does Sara make her conversation effective and engaging? Consider her use of the following features:

- **rhetorical questions**
- quotations
- sensitive challenges to her teacher
- vocabulary.

Key terms

rhetorical questions: questions used for effect to make the audience think, but which do not require an answer

Developing skills

Read this sample in which Band 4 students, Majid and Lennie, talk with Carlos, a Band 1 student, about transport problems. Notice how Majid and Lennie struggle at times to use effective English, which would clarify their ideas for their audience, and fail to include enough detail for Carlos.

Majid:	I get sick of traffic jams. Boring traffic jams.
Carlos:	It's a problem we all face, isn't it? Have you had particular problems?
Lennie:	I've been stuck for hours sometimes. Ages.
Majid:	Take last week. Hardly moving at all. You were there, weren't you, Lennie? We need better roads making.
Carlos:	So, I guess you were stranded for a while? Where was that…? Was there something actually wrong with the road?
Majid:	Yes! And it's not enough to say 'ride bikes'. We need to get to places quickly. You can't cycle across the country, can you? And the trains are rubbish.
Carlos:	I can see you don't like those either…
Majid:	They're rubbish. We need someone new in charge, if you ask me… Someone who knows what's wrong.
Lennie:	And puts it right…

5 Rewrite this conversation, trying to improve:

- the variety of sentence lengths and types
- the style, making the speech of Majid and Lennie less chatty, though still natural
- details, so that the ideas are developed.

In assessments, you are expected to speak in effective standard English whether you are in role or simply talking in a discussion. In the next extract, two students are in role as a customer complaining about a delayed train and an official at the railway station.

Customer: ... I'm afraid the way you have tried to justify what happened is not making me feel any better at all. I am still here and I should be at my meeting already. Is there nothing you can do to sort out the situation?

Official: I can only apologise again, madam. If the engine breaks down, the track is blocked and no other train can pass. Thankfully, it happens only rarely, but I fear it is beyond my power to move the train. We have a team on its way out there and I'm hoping to have some news quite soon now.

Customer: In the meantime, do we all have to stand here in this heat? It's appalling. This is the 21st century, you know, not the 19th...

6 How do these students craft their language to meet the purpose of the role play and to satisfy the audience. Consider:
- the variety of sentence length and construction
- appropriate vocabulary
- the tone used by both speakers to fulfil their roles.

7 Now read this sample opening to a presentation, in which a student talks to her class about her favourite country. Then consider these points.
- What makes this opening engaging?
- How does she show she has thought about her audience?
- Again, think about the vocabulary, sentences and the tone of the speaker.

Greece is a place that attracts people from all over the world nowadays: in fact, some resorts are just too popular. However, if you don't want that kind of holiday, there are still secluded spots, hidden from the main tourist traffic, which remind you of what the whole of Greece once was like and even today offer an experience that will prove unforgettable. There are wonderful attractions: for example, in the tumbling town of Hora, on the island of Serifos, you can stand by the church, hundreds of feet above the port, look out across the sea and dream, just the way the philosophers must have done all those years ago...

Applying skills

8 Prepare the opening of a presentation to your class, describing your favourite place and explaining why you like it. Use an appropriate style to engage your audience, and varied vocabulary and sentences. You might include:
- a precise description of what it is like
- why it is special for you or your earliest memories of it
- a story about it that would be suitable for your audience.

Sound progress	Excellent progress
• You use varied vocabulary. • You communicate clearly and engage the interest of the listener or audience.	• You use an appropriate style consistently, with varied sentences, vocabulary and expression. • You speak confidently for a given purpose and audience.

2 Choosing and researching a presentation topic Ⓒ Ⓔ

Learning objectives

- To understand how choosing the right topic can lead to higher marks.
- To understand the importance of selecting and using content wisely.

Checklist for success

✔ Choose your topic and approach carefully; think about how to make it interesting for your audience.

✔ Know or research your topic in detail, so you will be confident to talk and answer questions about it.

Top tip

When asked to give a presentation, make sure the topic allows you to do your best. If not, negotiate a change of topic or emphasis, if possible.

Exploring skills

1 Which of these topics could you talk about most successfully? Why?

- ○ Argue that problems caused by teenagers are sensationalised in the press.
- ○ Advise the parents of primary school students to send them to your school.
- ○ Explain why teenagers prefer technology to real life.

Building skills

Some speaking tasks are more challenging than others. Once you've chosen your topic, think about what angle you could take on it. For example, it is harder to persuade someone that your football team is the best than to describe what happened during a match. You gain more credit for completing a more complex task.

2 Look at the following sample extracts from presentations, showing different responses to the same topic. With a partner, identify what is good about the Band 3 response and the more advanced skills shown in the Band 1 response.

Band 3 sample response

The trip was a huge success. We met at 6:45, which was really early for most of us, then the bus arrived at about seven. I rushed straight to the back, to sit with Jenny and Asma, and a whole gang of us were on the back seat. Mind you, we didn't feel like singing that early in the morning. I swear Lucy was still chewing her breakfast when she got on...

— a clear topic sentence

— sets the scene

— adds humour

Band 1 sample response

I know what the reaction from most of you will be when I ask this, but... how can anybody justify a trip to a theme park in school time? And before you start, yes, I know everyone enjoys it – but what in the world does it have to do with education? Wouldn't it be better to sit in lessons during the week and go to an amusement park at the weekend? It's lovely to see the teachers having fun and running around, of course, but weekdays should be for learning...

— direct address to audience/ rhetorical question

— an engaging approach

— challenging

— light humour

Developing skills

If your **content** is not relevant, you will lose the attention of your audience.

Researching your topic carefully to find the most interesting material is vital. This means being selective and finding information from different sources that suits your purpose. Avoid copying material from any source.

This extract is from a sample Band 1 presentation. The speaker chose her topic, then her approach: to explain what made Muhammad Ali 'the greatest'. She is comfortable with her topic because she has researched it thoroughly. It is **full of detail** and uses a **rich vocabulary** and **varied sentence structures**.

> *Most boxing experts agree that Muhammad Ali should be considered the greatest boxer of all time. As Cassius Clay, he won the gold medal at the Rome Olympics in 1960, then turned professional and became world heavyweight champion in 1964, defeating Sonny Liston, the monster everyone else feared. Clay was handsome, 'floated like a butterfly and stung like a bee', and the world loved him. However, he courted controversy. After his conversion to Islam, Ali refused to fight for the USA in the Vietnam War. He had his title taken from him...*

> **Top tip**
>
> Each point you make needs to be clear and precise. If the audience misses a point, they have no second chance to hear it.

3 With a partner, discuss the questions.
- How many facts does the student include?
- How does she use the facts?
- What is her main point?
- How does she try to make us interested in Muhammad Ali?

The talk on Muhammad Ali:
- offers facts which give a clear picture of what was happening
- indicates what was special about him
- gives an impression of why he was such a great boxer
- only includes facts relevant to the main topic – Ali and why he was outstanding.

> **Top tip**
>
> When planning a presentation, remember each detail needs to support your overall purpose. Finding the facts is just the start. What counts is how you use and develop your ideas around them.

Even a fairly everyday topic like school rules can be made more interesting by including:

- **statistics**: how many rules are broken
- **survey results**: how students feel about particular rules
- **comparisons**: with other schools.

Applying skills

4 Prepare a talk for your class on your favourite hobby. Complete a table like the one below, which is about running.

Points you would select	Why you would choose them	How you would develop them to show their effects or go into more detail
Running is healthy	Health issues important at any age	How much weight I lost / How my life changed as I became healthier
15 million British people run	Pleasure / competition / feeling of well-being	Age no barrier: Constantina Dita became world marathon champion at 38; Buster Martin ran in the London marathon aged 101

3 Structuring your presentation

Learning objectives

- To organise ideas for maximum effect.
- To develop the skills to plan effective openings and endings.

In a **well-structured** presentation, the speaker knows what they are going to say and in what order. In particular, you will need to think about the different ways to begin, develop and end your presentation.

Exploring skills

(1) Imagine you have been asked to give a presentation about your favourite school subject.

- List the points you might make.
- Put them into a logical order.
- How would you begin your presentation?
- How might it end?

Plan your ideas in detail. Then summarise them so they fit on a cue card you can use in the exam. Remember that you will only be talking for about 4 minutes.

(2) Complete a table like this to develop your ideas. Add more detailed information to the right-hand column. Then, using your plan, run through what you would say.

Main idea	Points to be included
Teachers	Miss Spivey (teaches top sets and brings cakes to school)
	Mr Jenkin (simply adores volcanoes)
Lessons	Lots of videos
	Drama improvisations about other countries
Trips	Include field trips, camping

> **Top tip**
>
> Planning a presentation is similar to planning an essay. However, when you are talking, you can develop ideas on the spot and interact with your audience using different tones of voice and gestures.

Building skills

Your **opening** sets the tone for what follows. It should make it clear what you intend to talk about. It should also immediately engage your audience, so they listen.

Some possible techniques to use in an opening include:

- **rhetorical questions:** *Have you ever had the wrong tooth extracted?*
- **relevant humour:** *Have you heard the one about the dentist, the missing tooth and the court action for damages?*
- **powerful facts:** *Last year in Britain, 57% of children under the age of 10 had at least one tooth extracted.*

(3) Use these techniques to write three interesting openings for the presentation about your favourite school subject.

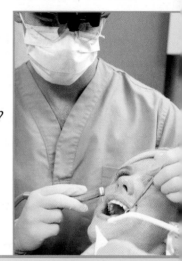

Developing skills

Your choice of ending will depend on your topic, purpose and audience. Try to leave a powerful impression upon your audience, using one of these techniques:

- a summary of your argument
- one final, convincing point
- a joke
- a **rhetorical question**.

4 Read this sample Band 1 ending and then, in pairs, decide what the purpose of the talk is and how the speaker hopes to impress the audience at the end.

> *The actions of careless governments across the world have led us to this state. We all know it's not too late to save the world but it's going to have to be last-minute stuff, because midnight is approaching. And if you think you can party through the night and all will be well tomorrow, you're wrong. There won't be a tomorrow… We must fight to make things better, petition parliament… If we all use our grey matter, there might still be hope.*

Now read this sample Band 3 conclusion to a presentation about a favourite subject.

> *Anyone coming to our school should look forward to doing Maths. We really do have the best teachers. The equipment and books are all new. What is more, the way they present the subject makes it fun from the start to the finish. And they manage to find things to do outside the school, so we get away from our desks for a while. The Maths department really could not be any better. It's my favourite subject, and I bet it will be yours.*

5 Produce a better conclusion to the presentation by:
- organising the material more effectively so that the ideas develop more logically
- adding more detail and commenting appropriately
- rephrasing or rewriting where necessary to leave the audience with a memorable idea.

Applying skills

6 Plan a presentation to persuade your local community to donate to a charity supported by your school.
- Make a plan in bullet points.
- Add details to each of the bullet points.
- Prepare what you are going to say to open and close the presentation.

Sound progress
- You structure your presentation to communicate clearly.
- You engage the interest of the listener.

Excellent progress
- You use appropriate spoken styles for the audience.
- You organise your content well for the given purpose.

4 Using imagery, rhetorical techniques and humour for effect C E

Learning objectives

● To understand how imagery and repetition can improve a presentation.
● To learn how to use rhetorical questions, humour and exaggeration to engage the audience.

Including **imagery** and **repeating** key words or phrases will help you to emphasise important points. Careful use of **humour**, **rhetorical questions** and **exaggeration** will appeal to listeners.

> ### Checklist for success
>
> ✔ Use imagery and repetition in your presentation to create more of an impact.
> ✔ Use rhetorical questions, humour and exaggeration sparingly and only when suited to a topic or an audience.
> ✔ Plan in advance which of these techniques you will use.

Top tip

If you choose a presentation where you must speak in role, you will need to adapt your tone to suit that role.

Key terms

imagery: imaginative comparisons, such as similes and metaphors
rhetorical questions: questions asked of an audience to involve them, without expecting a reply

Exploring skills

This extract is from a sample Band 1 presentation. Although it is spoken as Caliban from Shakespeare's *The Tempest*, the response is in standard English. It has been enriched with imagery and repetition.

> *I curse that man – Prospero! – and everything about him. He demands and he demands. Always craving more. He holds himself like a god and wields his power as if he even ruled the world. As if he would be worthy to bow and crawl at my mother's feet; as if he would be worthy to sit at her table; as if, were it not for the sprite who does his bidding, he could look down on me today. He is mendacious. He is truly the serpent on this island…*

Top tip

In general, avoid repeating yourself. However, using repetition skilfully to hammer home a point will earn you marks.

1. Identify the imagery and repetition in the extract. Then:
   ● comment on each example and its effect
   ● explain the effect of 'Always craving more.' This is not a conventional sentence. Why is it used?

2. With a partner, discuss why each example you have found is appropriate for the purpose.

Building skills

3 Read this extract from a sample Band 3 presentation spoken in role as Miranda from *The Tempest*. Rewrite it, adding imagery and repetition.

> *My father is a wonderful man. He does everything in his power to keep everything under control and he has led a very difficult life. He has so much trouble with Caliban, because he behaves so badly, and my father simply has to discipline him. It seems that punishment is all Caliban understands…*

Developing skills

Rhetorical questions can be used to challenge the audience to think more actively about an issue. For example:

- Can this ever be acceptable? (The desired reaction is *Probably not!*)
- Why, then, have these changes been introduced? (The desired reaction is *Tell me more.*)

4 Add two rhetorical questions to this extract to add interest.

Top tip

Exaggeration can also make a considerable impact: for example, *Her make-up was so thick her nose was only just poking out of it.* But use exaggeration sparingly.

> *When we look across the world, there is no reason why we should not all work together, towards a common future. Someone from Asia is really no different from someone in Canada. We have lives that may vary and we may have different beliefs, but we are all human beings, who love, laugh and cry.*

Adding **humour** and witty touches can encourage the audience to warm to you. Try:

- a funny **anecdote** (short story) to support your point: for example, *I caught measles on holiday. Well, actually, measles caught me. What happened was…*
- an **aside** (a quick throw-away comment): for example, *Who'd be interested in this train photograph? My dad said I'd do better with a picture of Shakira…*

5 Add a funny follow-on to each of these sentences.
- Anyone can dress well if they know where to shop.
- I try to help my cousin.

Applying skills

6 Produce a presentation opening about the job you would like when you are older. Use the following techniques, underlining each example:
- imagery and at least one example of repetition for effect
- rhetorical questions, humour and exaggeration.

Sound progress	Excellent progress
• You use varied vocabulary when speaking.	• You select and use a wide range of language devices.
• You engage the interest of the audience with some language devices.	• You vary expression confidently.

5 Delivering your presentation and answering questions C E

Learning objectives

- To understand how to deliver a presentation effectively.
- To develop the skills to respond appropriately to questions.

To deliver a presentation effectively, you must present the material with style. If you are not prepared, you could underperform.

Checklist for success

✔ Organise your presentation so that you know what to say and in what order.
✔ Know how to handle your audience: this is crucial for success.
✔ Make sure you anticipate at least six questions you might be asked and have extra information and ideas to discuss.

Exploring skills

(1) In a group of four, improvise two scenes where young people attend job interviews at a local food store. One interviewee knows about the job and is prepared and enthusiastic. The other knows nothing about the job and shows no interest. Afterwards, talk about the different impressions created.

Building skills

First impressions count. If you appear calm and prepared, you will impress your audience. People notice body language, so try not to look nervous.

Having created a good impression, you need to maintain your confidence throughout. Remember these points:

- a strong opening is wasted if it is followed by a muddle of points
- move through your well-planned material towards a clear ending
- listeners can get bored quickly, so to sustain their interest vary your pace, pause for effect and use a suitable tone of voice.

(2) Use these techniques to deliver the following section of a speech:
- to amuse the audience
- to make the event seem sad.

> *I was only four years old when I locked myself in a cupboard. What a way to spend an afternoon. I had no toys. No chocolate. And no toilet. It was a tragedy of major proportions.*

> **Top tip**
>
> Making regular eye contact with the audience shows confidence. A smile helps too.

> **Top tip**
>
> Never read from a screen or from notes. You get no marks for reading from a script. You can only use your postcard-sized cue card.

3 With a partner, discuss which of the following will make the worst impression on your audience. Then decide what you could do to remedy each of them.

- Losing track of where you are in your notes.
- Messing up a funny line.
- Speaking in a monotone and not making eye contact.

Developing skills

You will have to answer questions at the end of your presentation. Try to foresee questions you might be asked and have the information ready. For example, if you were talking about 'My life outside school' and what makes it interesting, you might have prepared information on:

- your particular hobbies or interests
- a job you have
- how you spend the rest of your time.

4 With a partner, decide what other details you would need to know in case a range of questions were asked.

5 Look at these sample answers to the question: What more can we do to help old people?

With a partner, discuss why the Band 1 sample answer is better.

Band 1 answer

> *Obviously, it's never easy. Charities like Age Concern give out leaflets like this one, with advice, but we can't just wave a magic wand to transform the lives of old people. Nevertheless, to just give up on them isn't an option. And even little things matter. Last week, for instance, the paper boy knew my grandma was unwell and asked if she would like an extra magazine the next day…*

Band 3 answer

> *I have a friend who suggests we should all think about what it will be like when we get older. If we all thought about that, I am sure we would treat old people much more kindly. It is not just about raising money for charities; it's important to be nice to old people every day.*

Applying skills

6 Imagine you will deliver a presentation on 'My favourite kind of movie'. It could be about rom-coms, action movies or horror movies. You will talk about why you enjoy this kind of movie. You will also be asked some questions so, in note form, prepare answers to the following.

- Aren't these movies just a form of escapism?
- Shouldn't we spend our time in more meaningful ways than watching this sort of movie?
- Making movies costs a huge amount of money. Can you justify making movies like this?

7 Think of further questions you could be asked and prepare for those too.

Sound progress	Excellent progress
• You use varied vocabulary and communicate clearly. • You respond to questions effectively.	• You express yourself confidently. • You sustain and direct discussion, responding to questions fully.

6 Preparing for discussion

Learning objectives

- To understand how preparation can improve different types of discussion.
- To learn how to prepare for a discussion.

The type of preparation needed for discussion will depend on the topic. For example, if you are discussing teenage crime, you could **research facts, figures and opinions**. If you are asked for ideas to improve your local community, you might **assess a range of options** and then **adopt a point of view**.

So what sort of discussion might there be? For the exam option, you will make a presentation and then answer questions from an examiner. For coursework, you might take part in:

- a paired discussion, with your teacher or another student asking questions
- a group discussion with your teacher and other students.

> ### Checklist for success
>
> ✔ Know what you will be discussing and, if appropriate, what your role in the discussion will be.
> ✔ Prepare ideas and information, and note them down.

> ### Top tip
> Brief notes are fine, but you should never read directly from them.

Exploring skills

1 What would you need to decide and find out in advance to allow you to contribute successfully to this discussion?

> *In a group, come to an agreement about who are or were the five greatest individuals the world has ever known.*

Building skills

You might be asked to **chair a group discussion**. As chair, you need to have questions ready to ask and information ready to keep the discussion going. You will also need to be able to direct the discussion, but be prepared to adapt to what others say.

2 Imagine you have been asked to chair a discussion about how a large sum of money should be spent to improve your school. Draw up notes you might use.
- How will you start? For example, you could offer a range of ideas to be discussed.
- Will each person speak in turn?
- Will there be summaries?
- How might you draw the group towards making a conclusion?
- How you might lead the group to an acceptable conclusion?

You may be asked to **adopt a particular point of view**. If so, you need to be clear about what view you represent and prepare how you are going to support that viewpoint.

3 Imagine you are to be involved in the discussion about spending this large sum of money. Prepare notes supporting the view that:
   - half the money be spent on new sports facilities and half on new teachers
   - or, the money should be spent on a new resource centre, including brand new computers.

4 In a group of three, discuss the topic, with one person chairing and the others arguing the two different points of view. Then, change roles and try again.

> **Top tip**
> Make sure your notes are brief. They can be put into a possible running order, but should not be developed into any form of script.

Developing skills

Preparation can help with paired as well as group discussion and you need to be equally ready to face questions from your teacher, following your presentation.

5 With a partner, imagine you have given a presentation supporting the view that teachers are the most valuable resource in a school. Your partner asks you questions about why you hold that view and challenges your opinions.

6 With your partner, discuss:
   - how well you coped
   - which questions were the most difficult to answer
   - whether detailed preparation would have helped you respond more convincingly
   - what precise information you needed in order to answer with confidence.

Applying skills

7 Working in a group of three, discuss the following statement: 'Poor people don't want charity; they want jobs and a decent wage.' One person will chair the discussion; one will support the statement; and one will represent the view that not all people can have jobs right now, so they must be helped in the meantime.

Prepare for the task and then hold the discussion. The chair is responsible for bringing it to a conclusion that can be accepted by all three.

Sound progress	Excellent progress
• You prepare for discussion so that significant contributions can be made.	• You prepare for discussion, so that discussion can be sustained.
• You prepare to answer questions and respond appropriately.	• You prepare for discussion, so that it is possible to take the initiative when answering.

Developing and supporting ideas with confidence ©E

Learning objectives

● To understand how to appear more confident in discussion.
● To learn how to develop ideas and argue effectively in discussion.

You will feel more confident in your speaking and listening assignments if you are well prepared and can develop your ideas in detail with evidence and examples. You will need to engage with what others say, making sensible responses to stay in the discussion.

Exploring skills

1 Imagine you are going to discuss this topic: 'There should be a ban on competitive sport.' List the points you make in favour and those that might be made against you. Make a note on how you would counter each one.

2 In this extract from a sample Band 1 discussion, the students are analysing advertisements. They have clearly prepared their ideas. What impression do you get of Jenny and Abi as speakers and listeners? Give your reasons.

Abi:	So, this magazine cover balances the idea of men ruling the world – that's why he's standing on all that money – with the figure of the intelligent woman over here. It's a neat concept. But does it work for readers of this magazine?[1]
Jenny:	I think so. The woman holds a book and looks like a head teacher. That works for me.
Abi:	Yes. Good point. Anything else?[2]
Jenny:	Strong colours for both of them. That makes them sort of impressive. Also, there's the lovely contrast between the money and the book. Different symbols of power... And what do you think about the boat in the background?[3]
Abi:	Maybe it's a symbol of power. Are we meant to think they both own it; or either could own it; or they are both on a wave of success?[4]
Jenny:	Clever. But is that too clever...?[5]
Abi:	I don't think so...

Both speakers here are working positively and intelligently. They support each other, asking relevant questions, encouraging the other's responses and praising interpretations.

Questions can be used to make discussions more effective, for example, by:

- requesting extra information: *So, if you think Pythagoras was the greatest mathematician ever – what did he do that has improved my life?*

- encouraging someone to extend an idea: *Excellent, James – can you develop that point?*

- challenging someone else's idea: *Surely not! Have you forgotten Van Gogh?*

3 Use a table like the one below to record how questions 1–5, labelled in the discussion between Abi and Jenny, match the different types of question listed above.

Question	Type of question and use
1	Abi is encouraging Jenny to provide more information
2	
3	
4	
5	

Building skills

Developing someone's idea is an important part of a successful discussion.

4 If the points below were made in a discussion, how could you develop them and argue against them?

Statement	Development	Counter argument
Football is a total waste of time.		
Nothing in life is more important than love.		
The whole world is obsessed with America. There are other countries, you know.		

Developing skills

Discussions are better if you make your own ideas more detailed and encourage others to clarify their ideas.

> Checklist for success
>
> ✔ **Extend your own ideas** by adding **supporting evidence**: for example, facts or statistics, examples, anecdotes or others' opinions.
> ✔ **Encourage others to extend their ideas**, by using phrases like: *True! What else?; And can you take that idea one stage further?*
> ✔ Develop an idea yourself, by using phrases like: *Yes. And that reminds me of…; Not only that, but…*

5 Write down what would you say in response to these statements from a group discussion. How would you counter each point successfully? (If it is easier, choose a different country.)

There is only one good place to live: Australia. Australia has everything anyone could ever want. Only a fool would choose to live anywhere else.

Remember to **argue your point** in a controlled way or **counter a different view** by:

- supporting a viewpoint
- challenging an alternative viewpoint
- trying tactfully to to change other people's minds.

Applying skills

(6) In a group of three or four prepare and then discuss the topic: 'You don't need to travel to enjoy life.' Use the skills you have practised in this lesson.

Sound progress	Excellent progress
• You make significant contributions. • You show a readiness to listen to others and respond appropriately.	• You sustain and direct the discussion through the use of a variety of contributions. • You vary what you say, speaking confidently.

8

Responding to talk, seeing implications and summarising

Learning objectives

- To understand why it is important to listen closely and how to show that you are listening.
- To recognise implications in what people say.
- To develop the skills to summarise what others say.

You are assessed on your ability to **talk** and **listen**, so you will need to demonstrate both these skills.

Checklist for success

✔ Focus on listening carefully because what you hear affects how well you respond.
✔ Offer a clear summary of what has been said to show that you have listened well.

Exploring skills

Effective listening allows you to absorb other peoples' ideas and develop new ones of your own.

1 Read this extract from a group discussion about people we respect. With a partner, discuss:
- how Lucy's listening skills are limiting the discussion
- how the others show they are better at listening.

> **Shabnam:** OK. So we're putting these people into order of importance. Lucy, you start.
>
> **Lucy:** Princess Diana.
>
> **Kamal:** I think she was overrated. No one talks about her now. When did she die?
>
> **Lucy:** There's Martin Luther King, too. He was good.
>
> **Kamal:** They all were, weren't they?
>
> **Shabnam:** One my dad never liked was Margaret Thatcher. What was she like?
>
> **Kamal:** First woman Prime Minister…
>
> **Lucy:** President Kennedy… I don't know anything about him…
>
> **Shabnam:** He changed America, didn't he? He fought Russia or something and got shot.
>
> **Lucy:** Mahatma Gandhi…

Top tip

To gain higher marks, make sure you respond directly to what others say, counter their ideas, ask them for more detail or develop what they have said.

Building skills

Responding sensitively means not only engaging with what people **say directly** but with what they **imply**. People regularly say things that imply something else, for example: *I love your new dress. It's so ... different*. A good listener picks out what is implied and comments on it.

Top tip

Look out for what other speakers are implying and for when they are inconsistent. Challenge them if necessary.

(**2**) Look at this discussion extract and then answer these questions.
- Which responses could be challenged by a perceptive listener?
- What is implied in each response you have identified?

Dan:	Geography's like RE: a total waste of time.
Tejinder:	I agree. I've always hated it. I've had Mrs Bates every year and she's always been horrible to me.
Dan:	Too right. And I've had Mrs Cowen. How can she teach? She's too old to even know what's going on.
Syra:	She said, 'An understanding of geography is vital if we are to understand the world around us.' You don't have to have a degree to know that's rubbish.
Dan:	And she said, 'You've got to work hard to achieve anything.' That's like something my grandma would say.

Developing skills

Summarising briefly what is said during a discussion proves that you listen and understand well. It also helps to round off the discussion.

Making brief notes means nothing is missed. Notes are useful to:
- group members, for weighing up different opinions
- the chair, for maintaining the balance between different views
- the summariser, for commenting at the end.

Top tip

To summarise effectively, use phrases like: *On one hand...*, *Whereas on the other hand...* This shows you are considering both views in a balanced way.

(**3**) In groups of four, prepare a discussion entitled: 'Space exploration is a waste of time. The money could be spent on more worthwhile things.' Two of you should take up each viewpoint.
- Note down the points made by each speaker taking the opposite view.
- Summarise what each speaker thinks.

Applying skills

(**4**) In a group of three, discuss this: 'Out of school, most teenagers waste most of their time.'
- Look out for implications and challenge them.
- Afterwards, each member of the group should summarise the discussion.

Sound progress	Excellent progress
• You make significant contributions, mostly as directed by other speakers.	• You sustain discussion through the use of a variety of contributions.
• You show a readiness to listen to others and to respond appropriately.	• You listen carefully and take the initiative.

9 Leading a group discussion

Learning objectives

● To develop the skills to manage a discussion successfully.

In group discussion assignments, high-achieving students will show they can support others in the group, responding to and showing understanding for their ideas, and can lead the group through a discussion to its conclusion.

Exploring skills

1 Notice the leadership qualities here:
- **initiating:** *Right, to kick things off, why don't we like this story?*
- **prompting and supporting others:** *Are you sure, Satish? Let's just look at…*
- **directing:** *Well, that's a totally different point. For now, can we get back to…?*
- **summarising:** *That's agreed, then. We think…*

Building skills

This sample extract shows the difference in performance between Sheri and Abdul, students working in Band 3, and Jessica, the Band 1 student, who leads the discussion.

Jessica:	So, are we in favour of nuclear power or against it? Abdul?
Abdul:	It's the only way forward. The world is running out of energy but nuclear power is endless…
Jessica:	Sheri?
Sheri:	The problem is that it's dangerous. Look at what happened in Japan, and there have been other nuclear disasters in the past. Chernobyl, for example.
Abdul:	That's a silly line to take. We learn from what happens so it will all be safer in the future. Things improve all the time, you know.
Jessica:	OK. So, you don't seem to agree at all. Is there any 'middle road'? Do we have to be totally 'for' it or 'against' it?
Abdul:	Look, it's simple: we need it…
Sheri:	But in some parts of the world it has caused so much suffering… They build nuclear stations all over the world and some are just too risky.
Jessica:	Are we saying, then, that the nuclear industry just has to be more closely regulated? Could we agree that nuclear power is something that can help the world move forward, but we have to supervise the industry much more closely?

2 With a partner, discuss these questions.

- What skills are being demonstrated by Jessica?
- How does she prompt and negotiate with Sheri and Abdul?
- How does she summarise?
- How might the others react to her suggestion at the end? Explain why.

3 Here, a group is discussing where they would like to live. What might a leader in the group have said to make this discussion more positive or move the discussion forward?

Wayne:	This is the worst place to live.
Jane:	It's better than the middle of a slum.
Wayne:	This is a slum.
Jane:	It's not. Have you ever been to places with rubbish lying around and broken windows everywhere?
Wayne:	It's like that round here...

Developing skills

4 Your local government has decided to spend a large sum of money on your local area. A meeting is called to discuss how the money should be spent. With a group of three friends, improvise a formal meeting between various interested parties, including:

- the leader of the local youth group
- a representative of the elderly residents' association
- the person who leads the local traders' association.

The final member of the group is a local politician who will chair the meeting.

- Discuss what should be done. The task of the politician is to bring all parties to an agreement.
- Following the discussion, decide how effective the politician was, and why.

Applying skills

5 In a group of three, have a discussion in which two take directly opposed viewpoints and the third is responsible for leading them to an amicable conclusion. You could use this topic:

- Exams should be banned.

The important thing is that it must be a topic on which there is strong disagreement. Repeat with a different topic and different roles of your choosing.

> **Top tip**
>
> Leading a discussion doesn't stop you agreeing with one point of view. However, you must make sure that all viewpoints can be discussed and that all participants feel comfortable.

Sound progress

- You make significant contributions, mostly in response to the directions of other speakers.
- You show a readiness to listen to others and to respond appropriately.

Excellent progress

- You sustain discussion through the use of a variety of contributions.
- You listen with sensitivity and take the initiative.

10 Getting into role C E

- To develop the skills to improvise a role.
- To explore different ways of improving a performance.

In Speaking and Listening assignments, you may be asked to **improvise a role** using drama techniques. You might have to play someone from real life, such as a person in local government or a neighbour, or you might have to represent a viewpoint in a discussion – supporting a new leisure complex, for example.
You may even choose to make your individual presentation in character.

You need to prepare in advance to create and develop a **convincing character**.

Checklist for success

In order to portray someone convincingly, you need to consider the following:
- ✔ **their history:** what has happened to them
- ✔ **their attitudes:** what they think about different issues and people
- ✔ **their behaviour:** how they speak to and treat others
- ✔ **their relationships:** with people around them
- ✔ **their motivations:** why they behave as they do.

Exploring skills

1. Choose one of the following roles. Then make notes about the character for each of the areas listed in the checklist above.
   - an older relative
   - a famous painter
   - a prison guard
   - a movie star

2. In a groups of three, each choose a character from the list above. Introduce your character, describing your life and what has happened to you.

Glossary

monologue: a speech, in role, by one character without interruption

Building skills

Next, you are going to deliver a **monologue**.

3. Imagine you are a distressed old person who has witnessed a daring bank raid and a television reporter asks you to tell the viewers what happened. Plan, so that you can:
   - give details of the incident
   - deliver your story, without interruptions, in role.

   You will need to appear upset, perhaps confused and frightened. When you are ready, improvise your monologue.

Top tip

As you prepare, think about how you will use tone of voice, pauses, unfinished sentences and repeated details. Also plan how to show your emotion through body language and facial expression.

Developing skills

How well you perform can often depend on how well you work with others. In most cases, shared preparation and positive criticism will improve performances.

4 In this example improvisation a head teacher is meeting an angry parent. What is each character like and what do you think has happened?

> **Lisa:** *(Sitting at her desk)* Hello, Mrs Choi, please come in.
> **Katie:** Yes, well, I had to come. *(She sits down)*
> **Lisa:** I think I know why you're here.
> **Katie:** I'm not happy about what's happened to Jiao.
> **Lisa:** No, I thought that would be what has brought you in. Would you like some tea?
> **Katie:** Er... No, I don't think so. I'm here to talk about my daughter, not drink tea.
> **Lisa:** OK. So, what exactly would you like to happen? *(Sipping a cup of tea)*
> **Katie:** That's obvious, isn't it? I want Jiao back in school. She didn't do anything wrong. We're tired of her being held responsible for everything that happens in this place. She's a good girl.
> **Lisa:** Well, let's not get over-excited, Mrs Choi...

5 With a partner, discuss what advice you would give these performers to help them improve their marks. Consider:
- what they say
- their movements
- who controls the situation.

6 Improvise the situation, bearing in mind the improvements you have suggested.

Applying skills

7 With a partner, act out your own head teacher/parent interview. Choose your own topic. Make notes to help you play your role. Make your character distinctive through gesture, movement or ways of speaking. Think about the sort of person you are playing: are you shy, aggressive or worried? Also, decide what event or situation has provoked the interview.

> **Top tip**
>
> Avoid exaggerating your character as your performance could turn into a caricature.

8 After the interview, ask yourselves which were the most successful parts of your performance, and why. How could you improve? Then adjust any details and repeat the role play.
- Do you need to establish more background for the characters or the situation?
- Can you structure how the conversation will start, develop and finish, perhaps to build to a climax?

Sound progress	Excellent progress
• You choose your vocabulary to suit your role.	• You select and use appropriate spoken styles and registers for your role.

Speaking in role C E

Learning objectives

● To develop a role through what you say and how you say it.

When speaking in role, sometimes characters appear two-dimensional and unconvincing to the audience. Establishing your character's background will help your performance to be convincing. You also need to pay attention to **how** your character speaks and what they say, so you reveal **what** they are thinking and feeling.

Checklist for success

Before you practise your performance, ask yourself:
✔ Have I prepared properly?
✔ Have I thought through what will happen and what I need to do at every stage?
After a practice run-through, ask yourself:
✔ Have I worked effectively as part of the pair or group?
✔ What can I do to improve my performance?
Before the final performance, ask yourself:
✔ Do I know roughly what I will be saying at each stage?
✔ Am I secure in my character? How will I react?

Top tip

You need to plan what will happen as a group before you begin so that no one in the group is surprised by events. Beyond that, you should feel free to improvise what you do and say.

Exploring skills

In these sample extracts, two mothers are talking about their sons, who have been having problems with other children. Both students are convincing in this role, but the Band 1 speaker has developed his part by adding more emotion.

Band 3 response

> *I find it hard to decide what to do sometimes. I think he should stay away from the children who are causing trouble, but he likes them and says they are his best friends. It is a difficult situation for any parent.*

Band 1 response

> *This is all so difficult to deal with. Like you, I love him and only want what is best for him, and I know he needs to break away from the rest of the group, because they will lead him into real trouble. I hardly sleep at night. I imagine you have nightmares too. In many ways, he is too young for all this...*

1 Write down what creates the emotional appeal of each sentence in the Band 1 sample response.

Building skills

When performing in role, you need to use language that is appropriate for your character. For example, politicians will speak differently from people who work in a burger bar.

2 Work with a partner. You are talking about whether space exploration is a waste of time and money. Talk as if:

- one of you is a government minister who supports space research
- the other is a shop worker who recognises the minister from television.

Before you begin, write down some appropriate words or phrases for your character.

Developing skills

When you are in role, you need to speak clearly, but you also need to speak in the way your character would.

Look at this sample Band 1 improvisation in role as a television reporter. Notice how she speaks, giving the audience a vivid feeling of what happened at the end of a marathon, how people reacted and an impression of the sort of person she is.

> *Only rarely in my life have I felt so many people united in joy: when Alexandro crossed the finish line, there was an outpouring of emotion the like of which many here today will never have witnessed. He had run the entire race in absolute agony, but was not prepared to give in, and 42 kilometres is a long, long way to suffer. As he finished, the whole crowd was cheering and many were crying. I cried too…*

3 With a partner, discuss what features of her speech make it successful.

4 Continue the report, making up any details, but maintaining the tone of the reporter's speech.

Applying skills

Choose a character from the media or real life. It could be the character you chose in the 'Exploring skills' activity on page 284. Other possibilities include:

- a leading politician
- someone in your favourite television show
- a singer
- a sports star.

5 Demonstrating clearly how they speak, make a three-minute speech as your character about significant event: perhaps you have lost your job, won a medal or fallen in love.

Sound progress	Excellent progress
• You use varied vocabulary when speaking.	• You select and use appropriate spoken styles and registers.
• You communicate clearly and engage the interest of the listener.	• You vary use of sentences, vocabulary, language devices and expression confidently for a range of purposes.

12 Interviews C E

Learning objectives

● To develop the skills to act as an interviewer or interviewee.

Interviews only work effectively if both interviewer and interviewee know what is expected of them.

Checklist for success

✔ Be effective as an interviewer by asking probing open questions.
✔ Be effective as an interviewee by giving detailed answers.

Exploring skills

1 Watch two different interviews on television, one involving a TV personality and one a politician. Compare the two styles of interviewing.

- How and why do the interviewers ask questions differently?
- How and why is the style of answers different?
- What is the purpose of each interview?
- What are your impressions of the interviewers and interviewees?
- What are the differences in language, facial expressions and body language?

Top tip

As the interviewer, it is fine to have a list of questions but only as a guide. You need to listen to the answers, ask for clarification, comment on what is said and alter your next question if necessary.

Building skills

In any interview, good questioning and responsive answers are the secret to success.

2 In this interview, a teacher is interviewing two speakers. What does he do well?

Teacher:	Right, if you're ready, please tell us anything you can remember about your early life.
Beata:	I was brought up in Warsaw, then we moved to England.
Teacher:	How old were you? And how did you feel at the time?
Beata:	I was only five. But I was frightened…
Teacher:	About?
Beata:	Almost everything…
Moswen:	I felt like that when we came from Africa when I was ten. A new country is really scary.
Teacher:	But you could speak English?
Moswen:	A little, yes…
Beata:	I couldn't speak any at all.
Teacher:	That must have felt very strange. So, can you both tell us about the early days? I bet they were very similar, in many ways. Can you remember your first day in a new school, with new friends…? Beata first…

Developing skills

As interviewee, you should prepare fully for the interview, ensuring that you know your subject well.

Always try to extend answers with **relevant details** and **opinions**. An extended answer might even become a short monologue. For example, in this sample opening to a Band 1 performance, Sanjay is being interviewed in role as a mountaineer who was recently rescued from the top of Mount Kilimanjaro.

Interviewer: Did you ever give up hope?

Sanjay: There were times when, I must admit, all seemed lost. At night it was freezing. I wore all my clothes inside my sleeping bag, but it was too cold to sleep. You begin to think you will never see anyone again, and when the frostbite started, I was certain I was doomed. But it's odd. One night I must have fallen asleep and my mother seemed to be with me. She was stroking my head and telling me not to worry: I had to be strong and I could survive and I would survive. I knew it was just a dream, but it lifted my spirits…

(3) How are details, **anecdote**, vocabulary and a variety of sentences used convincingly here?

(4) Imagine you are an Olympic champion. You are asked: 'What was it that made you think you could become the best in the world?' Decide how you would answer. Include an anecdote to support what you say.

Applying skills

(5) Imagine you are a famous person of your choice. Prepare to answer these questions in role, inventing any necessary details.
- What are your earliest memories?
- What was your time at school like?
- How has fame affected your life?

Sound progress	Excellent progress
• You use varied vocabulary when speaking.	• You select and use appropriate spoken styles and registers.
• You communicate clearly and sometimes change the course of discussion.	• You confidently and enthusiastically develop discussion.

13 Exam-style tasks and sample responses C E

For the examination option included in the Cambridge IGCSE, you have to give an individual presentation, which will be assessed by an examiner. You will then discuss the topic with the examiner (or your teacher).

Part 1: individual task

You will give a presentation, a talk, a speech or a monologue that is **3–4 minutes** long. For example, you might talk about your reaction to meeting a famous person or about a recent film you have seen, suggesting why others might also like it. You may use a dictionary to prepare for the task, but may not take one into the exam.

It always helps if the individual presentation is on a topic you know in some depth. For instance, although it is possible to talk about a film you have seen, without a genuine initial knowledge or interest in film, your talk is likely to turn into an unimpressive account of what happened and the follow-up discussion could reveal a lack of understanding and knowledge. For example:

Examiner:

> *So, how was the story told? Did it simply move from beginning to end or were there flashbacks? In fact, for you, what is the best technique that directors employ to interest the audience?*

Student:

> *Erm… Those are difficult questions. I like a movie that has a car chase and fighting. I don't really care whether it ends happily or not.*

Clearly, the student is not impressing here. He or she does not respond directly to the questions asked and seems to be struggling to find any sort of appropriate answer.

Key skills

You will need to show the following speaking skills for the individual task:

- articulate experience and express what is thought, felt and imagined
- present facts, ideas and opinions in a sustained, cohesive order
- communicate clearly, fluently and purposefully as an individual and in dialogue with other speakers
- use register appropriate to audience and context.

Part 2: discussion

The Individual Task leads into a 6–7 minute conversation with the teacher or examiner about your chosen topic. So, for example, you could develop an account of meeting a famous person into a discussion of wider issues such as the nature and role of 'celebrity' and media intrusion into celebrities' lives. You could develop a talk about a film into discussion of wider issues such as censorship, popular culture and the film industry.

Key skills

You will need to show the following speaking and listening skills for the discussion task:

- articulate experience and express what is thought, felt and imagined
- present facts, ideas and opinions in a sustained, cohesive order
- communicate clearly, fluently and purposefully as an individual and in dialogue with other speakers
- use register appropriate to audience and context.
- listen to and respond appropriately to the contributions of others.

Exploring sample responses: individual task and discussion

1 Noor has already delivered a presentation on the fundraising she carried out for victims of the 2011 earthquake and tsunami in Japan. She talked about her sponsored silence, baking cakes for sale and a 20km sponsored walk she undertook with her friends. Read this sample extract from her discussion with her teacher.

Teacher: That was all very impressive, Noor. Tell me: did you reach your target for the funds you hoped to raise?

Noor: Yes, I did. In fact, I collected more than I was expecting, because people were so generous. And they were worried about the people who were suffering, obviously. — *clear and appropriate answer, offering a reason*

Teacher: Yes, we all were. So, do you think it's right that we should have to try to raise money like this?

Noor: We try to give money to the people who need it so badly. — *possibly doesn't quite understand the intention of the question*

Teacher: Of course – but might it not be better if all the money needed came straight from governments? After all, you raised a good deal, but they could give so much more, because they have so much more, haven't they?

Noor: I suppose so. The governments do send money to help, don't they? — *responds to new idea*

Teacher: Yes, indeed. But do you think it's enough? — *challenging and encouraging response*

Noor: I haven't really ever thought about that – but I suppose they give as much as they can, just like everybody else, because they have other things they need to spend money on too. I know what you mean, though. It would be good if they gave some more. — *honest answer, recognising a good new idea*

Teacher: Do you think rich countries give enough in foreign aid generally?

Noor: It would always be better if they gave some more, especially when there has been a volcano or an earthquake or floods. People living in villages can't help themselves if they have no homes and no jobs and they've lost everything. I think governments should give more. — *develops the idea, which shows she is listening well*

shows she has taken idea on board

makes significant, relevant points

Feedback

The student makes significant points throughout, listens carefully and responds to what is obviously an idea she had not thought of before. She mostly responds to what is asked, but does also challenge the teacher in an appropriate way. She speaks in formal English and presents her ideas in sentences.

Recommended Band: 3

2 Now read this extract from another sample discussion. In this case, Shane is talking with his teacher about the football World Cup, following his individual presentation about recent tournaments.

—sensitive response

Teacher: World Cups make a lot of money. Isn't it true, though, that the host countries make relatively little? Doesn't the organisation, FIFA, make an absolute fortune?

Shane: I'm afraid you're right. They even demand that they are not taxed on the profits they make, so they can just walk away with the proceeds. Countries like South Africa, who hosted the competition in 2010, got publicity and built new stadiums, but that was all: it's so bad that the people who had to build the grounds were only paid a fraction of what they deserved every day. It's shocking.

—adding vital and relevant details, using well-chosen vocabulary

Teacher: Yet you still think the World Cup is wonderful..?

Shane: Yes. You have to split the football and the excitement away from the corruption behind it...

—intelligent response, expressed with balance

Teacher: Can you do that? Should we do that?

—mature interchange with teacher

Shane: I see what you are saying – but if you love football, what's the alternative?

—takes initiative with a challenge

Teacher: Watch tennis?

Shane: Well... you could only watch your favourites on television most of the time, not live; and, frankly, tennis doesn't have the passion. At football, you can sing and shout and even be tribal again if you want. It's a release from the problems of the world, just for 90 minutes each week. Unfortunately, tennis doesn't offer you that. Have you ever been to a live football match?

—new idea, expressed with conviction

—rule of three used for effect

Teacher: No, though we all see it on television...

Shane: ...Where it is a different game. People can say what they like about players being over-paid and behaving like huge babies – which we all know they do – but the excitement generated is amazing. I took my mother to a match and she goes regularly now. I still cannot believe it, but she is swept away by the drama of it all. There are many things wrong with football finance and there is corruption too, but that cannot really detract from all that it represents to hundreds of millions of people around the world...

—sense of conversation, rather than just responding to teacher

—student finishes teacher's sentence, to support own idea

—excellent use of formal standard English

uses a cliché, but still emotive language

concludes with intelligent summary of his thoughts

Feedback

The student interacts with the teacher in a mature fashion, listens sensitively, uses formal standard English and offers a range of ideas that move the conversation on as he presents and expresses his ideas and arguments clearly. He has knowledge of the subject and sustains the conversation intelligently.

Recommended Band: 1

14 Coursework-style tasks and sample responses Ⓒ Ⓔ

You will be assessed during the course on three different speaking and listening tasks. You may use a dictionary to **prepare** for the tasks, but may not use one **during** the assessment.

An individual activity

For example, you will talk about a favourite hobby or an interesting place that you have visited.

A pair-based activity

You will do this task with another student. Your teacher may also be involved. For example, you will role-play an argument between two neighbours or your teacher will interview you and a partner about how something at school could be improved.

A group activity

For example, your group will discuss who to invite (and why) to open the new local shopping centre or, in a parole board scenario, your teacher might present cases for prisoners and your group will discuss whether or not each case merits early release.

Key skills

You will need to show the following speaking skills in response to all three coursework tasks:

- articulate experience and express what is thought, felt and imagined
- present facts, ideas and opinions in a sustained, cohesive order
- communicate clearly, fluently and purposefully as an individual and in dialogue with other speakers
- use register appropriate to audience and context.

You will need to show the following listening skills in response to tasks 2 and 3:

- listen to and respond appropriately to the contributions of others.

Exploring sample responses: individual activity

1 Read this sample extract from an individual presentation entitled 'My week in Italy'.

My holiday was with my brother, my mother and father. We decided to do something different this year, so we flew to Rome. Then we rented a car and drove down to the bay of Naples. That was quite an experience, because some of the drivers were crazy. When my mother was driving, my father kept covering up his eyes but in fact she was much safer than him.

When we arrived at the accommodation, it was great. It was miles from anywhere on a hillside in a converted farm. The people who ran it had a pack of Alsatian dogs who seemed to fight with each other all the time but never bit us. They lay next to us when we were next to the pool and they were waiting outside the door every morning. My favourite was Nero. He followed me everywhere. They said that he adopted someone every week, from the people renting the property. I wonder if he liked me because I get up much earlier than my brother so there was more time to throw balls. Also, I don't grunt as much as my brother does!

We went off to see things some days, like Pompeii and Herculaneum. Both of those towns were buried when Vesuvius exploded back in Roman times and you can see just what life was like back then. They had central heating and wall paintings and you can walk in the buildings themselves. It's very hot though, so you have to take water with you, to stop dehydration…

- appropriate but unoriginal opening
- offers some relevant detail
- journey is touched upon but lacks development
- rather casual expression
- engaging details about dogs
- repeats 'next to': lack of variety in phrasing
- lack of variety in sentence types; both simple sentences
- good use of humour to engage the listener
- sensible organisation of material into sections
- including place names adds interest
- emotive vocabulary although 'erupted' would be more precise
- appropriate use of details
- offers quality of 'being there' but ideas put together without firm sense of structure

Feedback

The speaker uses some varied vocabulary (including names) and has organised the presentation logically. There are some engaging touches. The language is suitably formal most of the time and there is some sentence variety. The response lacks more imaginative touches, such as the use of anecdote or extension of ideas, and sentences and vocabulary are accurate but do not exhibit flair or great variety. However, it is clear (without ever being exciting).

Recommended Band: 3

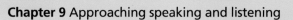

(2) Now read the following sample extract from a presentation, in which the speaker talks about looking after a grandmother with Alzheimer's disease.

I imagine most of you will have some idea of what Alzheimer's disease is: it progressively takes away the memory, so that sufferers lose touch with reality more and more, until they eventually can't even recognise their wife, their husband, or their children. They jumble the past and present. Until there is no past or present for them. They can't even recognise night or day. And my grandmother has Alzheimer's.

We noticed it starting when her memory suddenly got worse. She struggled to cook our special meal on Friday night, which had always been her treat for us at the end of the week. Then she wasn't sure what day it was. She didn't know what she had done earlier in the day. People's names were forgotten even more easily than they had been before. She needed – help.

We actually thought that we needed help too, but as time goes on, you discover that the early stages were nothing. It is a degenerative disease, which can only get worse. She takes tablets and somehow manages to still live alone, but now it is as if she is in a different kind of world altogether. Conversations are always the same:

'What day is it?'
'Wednesday.'
'Do I have meals on wheels tomorrow?'
'Yes, they'll be here.'
'Do I have to pay for them?'
'No, they are all paid for.'
'What day is it?'
'Wednesday.'
'Do I have meals on wheels tomorrow…'

Annotations:
- precise vocabulary
- complex sentence introduces the subject
- broken sentences, making it seem disturbing and emphasising 'Until'
- sense of climax for the paragraph
- examples to shock and emphasise the seriousness
- short sentences, hammering like nails
- possible pause before this word for effect
- personalised
- sophisticated vocabulary
- reality of conversation makes situation clear and tragic

Feedback

This speaker engages the audience and offers a variety of information, presented in interesting ways. Sentences are varied, there is some excellent vocabulary and the grandmother's situation is brought to life with the examples and conversation. Standard English with great confidence.

Recommended Band: 1

Exploring sample responses: pair-based activity

1 Read this sample extract from a role play where students are discussing, in role, a problem that has arisen at an airport. A business person (BP) is at the airline desk, complaining that her luggage has not arrived. The airline employee (AE) is attempting to calm her down.

BP: I keep telling you that I need my luggage. — convincing tone and phrase

AE: And I can only apologise, madam. If it hasn't arrived, I'm guessing that it has gone missing on the way. Perhaps it was never even loaded on the plane. — begins apologetically and offers explanations

BP: Could that happen? That's terrible! What can I do now?

AE: It won't be too bad if you have got insurance. You will be able to make a claim. We will be able to help you with that.

BP: But I don't want to make a claim. Isn't there anything you — uses direct appeal
can do? All my clothes are in the suitcase, and a special photograph of my dear husband, and my make-up. I can't do anything without my make-up. I have an important meeting tomorrow and I have simply nothing to wear. — extends the detail of the situation

AE: If the suitcase was never put on the plane, it might well arrive on the next one, madam. That will be landing at — tries to find a solution – a realistic portrayal
lunchtime tomorrow. Then your problems could all be over.

BP: I can't believe what you are saying. I'm supposed to be in the most important meeting of my life at nine o'clock in the morning: my career depends on it. What do I say? 'I'm — sarcasm indicates the passenger's frustration well
sorry I'm a mess but my clean dress is somewhere over the Atlantic?' That picture of my husband is so important to me. He died last year and I even sleep with it at night. — sudden switch in emphasis is less convincing

AE: What can I say, madam? I will do everything I can to help you get everything back. So, we should get down some — tries to relieve tension and diffuse the situation
details. What is your name, to begin with? — keeps in role, trying to sort out the problem practically

Feedback

Both speakers maintain their roles and create a scene that is credible. The business person gives some detail and sounds upset; the airline employee stays calm and professional, trying to do what she can to help. Both use appropriate standard English, though without any great variety of sentences or any imaginative vocabulary.

Recommended Band: 3

(2) Now read the following sample extract. The two students are in role as a prime minister and television interviewer.

Interviewer: Could I begin, Prime Minister, by asking you about your policy on the treatment of minor criminals? You stated in parliament that it's time to take a more rigorous — **sophisticated vocabulary** approach to sentencing and that you would be asking the judges to impose longer sentences and take a much less lenient approach. Do you think this will have any effect at all on the crime rate?

PM: We cannot say for certain that fewer people will offend, — **impressive, confident ministerial tone** but I am responding to what I feel is the mood of the country. Across the land, everyone is tired of criminals offending, then re-offending and only receiving a mild slap on the wrist before — **complex sentence used to show sequence of related events** they are sent back out to steal again. As a government, we have a duty to protect the public; and that is what I intend to do.

Interviewer: Yet, we are told by the experts that this will — **firm, authoritative tone** not change the criminals' behaviour. All you will be doing is — **signals different view, sharply focused** filling the prisons and adding an extra burden on the taxpayer, because it costs so much to keep a man – or woman – in prison…

PM: Punishment is what they deserve. And if they are in — **short, decisive and memorable sentence** prison, they are not terrifying old ladies in their own homes — **emotive language** or robbing the corner shop and taking the profits from decent hard-working people. It is my responsibility to defend the weak and our country will be better for the actions.

Interviewer: Because …? — **sensitive listening: demands reasons – developing the response**

PM: Because we are doing what is necessary. Right-minded citizens will applaud our actions. — **specific vocabulary for effect**

Interviewer: Or wonder why you are taking the easy way out, instead of looking at the real problem: why they offend in the first place… — **offers effective and challenging alternative interpretation**

Feedback

This is a convincing discussion. The role of the prime minister is portrayed with conviction and the language used is totally appropriate for the character. Vocabulary is wide and imaginative and there is the authority that might be expected from such a figure. The interviewer listens carefully and puts the prime minister 'on the spot' by refusing to accept the initial explanations offered. She prompts sensitively, always using language that is totally suited to her role.

Recommended Band: 1

Exploring sample responses: group activity

(1) Read this extract where, because a new head teacher has arrived at the school, the students have been asked to discuss the school rules and which ones should be changed.

Dhaljit: School uniform! Let's start with school uniform. It's about time that was changed. — *focused but emotional statement, lacking balance*

Ravi: I'm afraid we won't get far with that subject. — *offers a more mature sense of perspective*
I'm certain the school leadership team will be adamant we must retain what we've got. I don't think they will even be prepared to negotiate — *use of sophisticated vocabulary*
on ties…

Samira: I think the ties should go. They are uncomfortable and cause more problems than they solve. They say it's to make everyone look smart, but how — *clear, detailed point and extends ideas*
many students have them fastened loosely? That's not smart… and the teachers waste half their lives getting students to tie them properly.

Dhaljit: I hate mine. I might have to spend the rest of my working life wearing one, but I don't want to wear — *still on task, emotive, makes valid points but without genuine development*
one at school. They should listen to the students. No more ties, I say.

Ravi: If we stay on that topic, I fear we will just be — *diplomatic style*
wasting our time. Couldn't we broaden out the — *uses question for effect*
discussion? There are a host of school rules that — *impressive vocabulary*
we might not want to remove but we would like to amend and improve, so more of the school — *uses a good variety of sentences including complex sentences*
population accepts them without moaning…

Samira: Are you thinking about things like the school hours? I'd like to say that we should do something — *responds appropriately*
about the lunch break, because it would be good to have more time to do some activities, rather than just eating at a hundred kilometres an hour then rushing back into lessons…

Dhaljit: Yeah. Right. I agree with that too. And what about homework?

Ravi: We can get back to that in a moment, but perhaps we should consider the lunchtime situation properly first? Let's begin by clarifying what everyone thinks. Samira, how could we make life more pleasant for everyone? Would we have to change the whole school day, because that is asking a lot...

gives immediate agreement but doesn't add or extend ideas: shown in short sentences

managing the discussion

seeks detail, encouraging others to contribute

uses questions to move the discussion on

shows clear thinking by forseeing pitfalls

Feedback

Ravi is clearly in charge of this discussion, using effective standard English and confident expression.

Recommended Band: 1

Samira makes significant contributions, listens to what the others say and always responds appropriately.

Recommended Band: 3

Dhaljit listens to what is said and contributes relevant ideas to the discussion, though he fails to develop his ideas.

Recommended Band: 4

Sound progress

- I can use varied vocabulary when speaking.
- I can use language appropriately.

In an individual task

- I can organise my material so I communicate clearly.
- I can engage the interest of a listener and use some language devices.

In a discussion

- I can make significant contributions.
- I can listen to others and understand their ideas.
- I can respond sensibly to what is said.

Excellent progress

- I can select and use appropriate spoken styles, registers and language devices.
- I can vary my sentence structure, vocabulary and expression confidently for a range of purposes.

In an individual task

- I can organise my material so I deliver a full, lively and interesting presentation.
- I can use a wide range of language devices to maintain the engagement of the listener.

In a discussion

- I can sustain others' involvement through the use of a variety of contributions.
- I can listen with sensitivity, and sometimes take the initiative.
- I can respond fully and confidently to questions and changes of direction.

Section 5 **Exam Practice**

This section of the book will take you through the type of tasks that you will be asked to complete for formal assessment, to offer you a realistic rehearsal of the skills you have learnt under examination conditions.

When using these practice assessments, it is important that you complete them with an eye to the timings required to complete a whole examination.

For example, the most sensible way to write a summary is to use the marks allocated for each task to work out what proportion of the total marks available this represents. You can divide the time available by these proportions to work out how much time to spend on each task.

Sample assessments provide a valuable opportunity to assess your own strengths and weaknesses. You can then adjust your revision plans and possible examination timings accordingly. For example, if you realise as a result of completing this chapter that you need further clarification of how to do a summary, you might revisit Chapter 4 to brush up your skills. You might also add another 5 minutes to your time allocation for the summary when doing your next practice assessment.

Approaching examinations is demanding because examination questions require exam technique – you need to apply the appropriate skills and knowledge to answer each question to your best ability. Use these practice assessments and the marking process to see precisely where you lose marks and focus on those key areas the next time. This should improve your exam technique.

Practice exam-style papers and advice

An Introduction to Practice Paper 1

The practice paper which follows on pages 302–307 is based on the model of the current Cambridge IGCSE examination.

Which skills should I be using?

Question 1 asks you to show only reading skills.
- You will need to use the key skills of **skimming**, **scanning** and **selecting** covered in Chapter 1 (pages 8–13). In addition, you will need to use your ability to understand **explicit** and **implicit meanings**, which are also covered in Chapter 1 (pages 16–27).
- You will need to use the skills of writing about **writers' effects** outlined in Chapter 5.

Question 2 asks you to show reading **and** writing skills.
- You will need to use the key skills of **skimming**, **scanning** and **selecting**, and your ability to understand **explicit** and **implicit meanings**.
- You will need to use the skills for **extended writing** outlined in Chapter 6.
- You will need to be able to use all the key writing skills, as outlined in Chapter 3.

Question 3 asks you to show reading and writing skills.
- You will need to use the key skills of **skimming**, **scanning** and **selecting**, and your ability to understand **explicit** and **implicit meanings**.
- You will need to use the **summary** writing skills outlined in Chapter 4.

Tips for success

- Manage your time well. Spend slightly longer on Question 1 as the marks suggest.
- Make sure that you **use your own words** if you are told to **explain** in Question 1.
- It is very important that you show detailed knowledge of the text in your answer to Question 2. This means that you must base your own ideas on **ideas and details from the text**, although using your own words to present these is usually best.
- For Question 3 you must write in continuous prose and **use your own words** wherever possible, basing your summary on your notes.

Reading Passages (Core)   **1 hour 45 minutes**

Answer **all** questions.

Dictionaries are **not** permitted.

The number of marks is given in brackets [   ] at the end of each question or part question.

Read Passage A carefully, and then answer Questions 1 and 2.

Answer all questions using your own words as far as possible.

Passage A

Brady Barr has a TV series on the Geographic Channel. Here is an article that he wrote for the channel's website about filming a particularly dangerous episode.

It was day three for our team in a snake cave on an island in Indonesia. On the previous two days we had seen many pythons, but all small, so we weren't expecting to see anything unexpected on day three. We were only going in to get some pick-up shots and move to the next filming location.   5

The cave was literally a chamber of horrors, probably the worst place I have worked in the ten years I have been at Geographic. The cave was filled with the usual customers (scorpions, roaches, maggots, spiders, millions of bats, lizards, and snakes), but it was the unbelievable amount of bat guano   10 that made it unbearable. There were places where you had to wade through chest-deep liquefied bat guano. The stuff was like quicksand, almost sucking you down and making progress very slow and cautious. This bat guano soup along with low oxygen levels eventually prevented our expedition from going deeper   15 into the cave.

On day three, about 200 feet (60 meters) into the cave, walking along the right-side wall where the fecal soup was the shallowest, I spied a large python partially exposed in a crack in the left wall, on the opposite side of the cave across the deepest   20 part of the fecal river.

[With cameras rolling] I frantically waded across the middle deepest portion of the fecal river (waist deep on me) and to the other side of the cave, where I was successful in grabbing the last few feet of the snake's tail before it escaped into the wall.   25

By this time Dr Mark Auliya, a python expert working with me on this project, arrived to assist me in pulling this large snake

out of the wall. I handed over the tail to Mark while I attempted
to free more of the large snake's body from the crevice as Mark
pulled.   30

After a brief power struggle, the python popped out of the
crack in a blur of coils and quickly started to wrap us up. In the
waist-deep fecal soup, the darkness of the cave and myriad of
coils, it was difficult to locate the head, which was our major
concern. With Mark still holding the tail, the big snake wrapped   35
its powerful coils around Mark's body once and around both
of my legs down low at least once, and maybe two coils. The
snake's head was horrifyingly all over the place, popping in and
out of the fecal soup and making securing it almost impossible.
Before we could formulate a plan to get out of the quicksand-   40
like fecal soup, where drowning was a serious issue while trying
to subdue a giant snake, it bit me.

I felt the snake attach to my leg right below my left buttock,
which sent me literally through the roof with pain. These guys
are armed with dozens of strongly recurved razor-sharp teeth.   45
After securing its hold, it threw the weight and power of its
muscular body into the bite and started ripping downward. The
power of these snakes is beyond comprehension … remember,
they are constrictors, and power is the name of their game.

Since the bite was occurring underwater, no one but me really   50
knew what was occurring, and I was in such indescribable pain I
couldn't convey much information, other than guttural screams.
I was so completely incapacitated by the pain I couldn't even
attempt to remove the snake from my leg. I was terrified that
the snake was going to pull me off my feet with its coils around 55
my legs and drag me underwater, yet after what seemed like an
eternity the snake released its bite yet continued to hold me
with its coils. It most likely needed to get a breath of air, since
the bite occurred under the water. After letting the team know
that it released its bite, we still could not locate the head after 60
frantic searching.

This was the time I was most concerned, and without doubt
one of the scariest moments I have ever been a part of, because
the horror of taking another bite was simply overwhelming.
I really did not think that I could remain conscious if I took   65
another bad bite, and I knew that another bite was coming for
someone if we didn't secure the head.

Prayers answered – the snake relinquished some of its coils,
and I finally spotted the head at the surface of the water a long
way away. Mark quickly dragged the snake to the opposite side   70
of the cave, the shallow side, and I threw a bag over its eyes
and quickly secured the head. We immediately placed the large
snake into a capture bag, and then Mark inspected my wounds.
They were bad; it was a horrific bite.

They have so many teeth that produce these deep ripping 75
wounds, it's excruciating if you are on the receiving end.
When the team discovered how severe the injuries were, we
immediately exited the cave and cleaned the wound. Infection
was really the biggest concern. Snake bites are always bad
because they have such unclean mouths, but to receive a bite 80
in a cave environment in a liquefied slurry of bat faeces simply
has to be the absolute worst of all septic situations. We were in
a very remote area, so I had to hike out many kilometers to our
truck.

The entire sequence was filmed. It is chilling footage to 85
watch. It was an epic snake capture, one to go down in the
history books.

Question 1

(a) Explain, **using your own words**, why the writer describes the cave as
a 'chamber of horrors' in paragraph 2. [2]

(b) Why do you think Brady described himself as 'frantically' wading after
the snake when he sees it in paragraph 4? [2]

(c) Why was it so important to get out of the quicksand in paragraph 6?

[1]

(d) (i) Re-read paragraph 6 ('After a brief…bit me'). Explain using your
own words, what the writer means by the words in italics in three
of the following phrases:
(a) the python popped out of the crack in *a blur* of coils
(lines 31–2)
(b) *wrapped its powerful coils* around Mark's body (line 35)
(c) The snake's head was horrifyingly *all over the place*, (line 38)
(d) *popping in and out* of the fecal soup (line 39)
(ii) The snake moves around a great deal in this section of the
account. Explain how the words and phrases in each of the
phrases help you to imagine its movement. [6]

Phrase selected a), b), c) or d)	The meaning of the words in italics	How the words and language in a), b), c) or d) the phrase help imagine the snake's movement

(e) Explain, **using your own words**, what the writer means by:
    (i) 'guttural screams'(line 52, paragraph 8)   [2]
    (ii) 'deep ripping wounds' (lines 75–76, paragraph 11)   [2]
    (iii) 'chilling footage' (line 85, paragraph 12)   [2]

(f) Which two-word phrase in paragraph 9 tells you that Brady could
    not bear the idea of being bitten again?   [1]

(g) Explain **using your own words** what Brady meant by 'an epic
    snake capture,
    one to go down in the history books' in paragraph 12.   [2]

                                                [Total: 20]

Question 2

Imagine that you are a Geographic Channel viewer. You have just watched
Brady's television series for the first time and were horrified by the scene
that he described in the extract when you saw it on screen. You have also
read his account on the web page.

Write a **letter of complaint** to the channel's website, trying to
persuade them not to make programmes that involve the 'hunting' of
dangerous animals for entertainment.

In your letter, you should include:

• what you disliked about the incident shown

• what you think in general about such television programmes.

Base your letter on what you have read in Passage A, but do not copy
from it.

Be careful to use your own words. Address each of the three bullets.

Begin your letter of complaint like this: 'As soon as I switched of the
Brady Barry TV episode featuring the python, I had to write...'

You should write about 200–300 words allowing for the size of your
handwriting.

**Up to 10 marks are available for the content of your answer and
up to 5 marks for the quality of your writing.**

                                                  [Total: 15]

Read carefully Passage B, a transcript of a blog posted on a forum for viewers of The Nature Channel, and then answer Question 3 (a) and (b).

Passage B

Just flick on the television on any given night of the week and you will be faced with a mind-boggling array of documentaries focusing on all manner of exotic beasts from every corner of the globe – and they're just the presenters! No, seriously, I now have access to virtually any creature, in any location from Pole to Pole. 5

Progress indeed, you may say. In my childhood we were lucky if we saw the occasional lemur peeling a grape on Animal Magic or a rogue elephant knocking down the set on Blue Peter. They were glamorous strangers imported for our viewing pleasure and usually accompanied by a zoo keeper in a smart uniform. How 10 we laughed at their strange features and 'aahed' at their cute habits when they were let out of their boxes for a few minutes of air-time...

After our bed-time our parents watched their once-a-week dose of some exceedingly dull programme with close-up film 15 of insects constructing elaborate dens and birds jumping off cliffs. The voice over was factual, often very knowledgeable, but awfully sensible ... frankly I didn't mind that I wasn't allowed to stay up.

Nowadays young and old can see anything, anywhere, doing 20 everything – including quite a few things that frankly put me off my dinner! We see animals in their natural environments, living, dying, just as nature intended. It can be tough to watch but it is reality. Modern nature programmes often tell a story. We get involved with a family or a character. Recently we had to delay 25 dinner just to check whether a little meerkat lived or died!

Of course the presenters are a bit more high profile than I'm used to. They seem to be as much on show as the animals but they really know what they're talking about and they certainly have a gift when it comes to making things interesting. I do 30 wish they wouldn't do stupid things though: putting your hand in something's mouth doesn't strike me as setting a great example! I think I preferred it when the presenter just kept a polite distance and whispered to the camera.

You know we ought to think ourselves lucky. From the comfort 35 of our sofa we can share the lives of all sorts of amazing creatures in a way that generations past could not even imagine. Perhaps soon we won't even need zoos at all – now that would be progress!

Question 3

Answer the questions in the order set.

(a) Notes

What do you learn about the changes in wildlife themed television shows according to Passage B?

Write your answers using short **notes**.

You do not need to use your own words.

Up to 10 marks are available for the content of your answer.

(b) Summary

Now use your notes to write a summary of what **Passage B** tells you about the changes in wildlife themed TV shows.

You must use **continuous writing** (not note form) and **use your own words** as far as possible.

Your summary should include all 10 of your points in **Question 3(a)** and must be 100 to 150 words.

Up to 5 marks are available for the quality of your writing.

An Introduction to Practice Paper 2

The practice paper which follows on pages 309–313 is based on the model of the current Cambridge IGCSE examination.

Which skills should I be using?

Question 1 requires you to show reading and writing skills.

- You will need to use the key skills of **skimming**, **scanning** and **selecting**, covered in Chapter 1 (pages 8–13). In addition, you will need to use your ability to understand **explicit** and **implicit meanings**, which are also covered in Chapter 1 (pages 16–27).
- You will need to use the skills contained in Chapter 6, which takes you through the process of responding to a **extended writing** task (pages 157–188).
- You will need to be able to use all the key writing skills, as outlined in Chapter 3.

Question 2 requires you to show only reading skills.

- You will need to use the key skills of **skimming**, **scanning** and **selecting**, covered in Chapter 1 (pages 8–13). You also need to show you understand **explicit** and **implicit meanings**, covered in Chapter 1 (pages 16–27).
- You will need to use the skills contained in Chapter 5, which takes you through the process of writing about **writers' effects**.

Question 3 requires you to show reading and writing skills.

- You will need to use the key skills of **skimming**, **scanning**, and **selecting** all covered in Chapter 1 (pages 8–13). In addition, you will need to use your ability to understand **explicit** and **implicit meanings**, which are also covered in Chapter 1.
- You will need to use the skills practised in Chapter 4 (which takes you through the process of writing a **summary**).
- You will need to be able to use all the key writing skills, as outlined in Chapter 2.

Tips for success

- Manage your time effectively. The mark allocation suggests that you should spend 80% of the time on Questions 1 and 3 (40 minutes on each).
- It is vital to show detailed knowledge of the text in your answer to Question 1. This means basing your own ideas on **ideas and details from the text**, although using your own words to present these is usually best.
- In Question 2, make sure that you **select words or phrases** from the text and that you **explain their effect** on the reader and how this is created. This means explaining the meaning of the words and the ideas that they put into your head or the senses/emotions that they stimulate.
- In Question 3 you must **use your own words** wherever possible and should never quote or explain or add your own ideas.

Reading Passages (Extended)   **2 hours**

Answer **all** questions.

Dictionaries are **not** permitted.

The number of marks is given in brackets [   ] at the end of each question or part question.

Part 1

Read Passage A carefully and then answer Questions 1 and 2.

Passage A

One minute I was asleep, strapped in snugly under my blanket, with three weeks of adventure drifting in front of my eyes in hazy flashes; a grin playing on my lips as I re-lived the dopey smile of a sloth hanging sideways whilst I zip-wired past high in the tree canopy. The next I was wrenched awake by the   5 scream of metal tearing from metal and a glimpse of stark white skeletal fingers of lightning reaching for the trembling wings of the plane.

It must have been hours later – my watch had broken on impact (which I'm told was at about 1:30 a.m.) and there were   10 now shadows being cast on the jungle floor from a distant, cloud-strangled sun. I shivered, irritably shrugging as water dripped warm, but not warm enough, onto my sodden clothes from the tendrils of my fringe hanging down over my face. I was upside down, still strapped in, suspended in the triangular   15 haven of my seat. Apart from the obvious tunnel of snapped branches and stretched creepers which signalled my arrival, there was nobody and nothing to be seen of the rest of my fellow passengers or our plane. There was a huge temptation to stay there, safe, almost warm, drifting in and out of consciousness.   20 If I had done so, I wouldn't be writing this now. They found my seat, still attached to two others, days from anywhere and largely hidden from sight by the high tree canopy which had opened to embrace me and then resealed itself with hardly an outward sign of intrusion. Luckily my dad's voice – loud and   25 jolly – rang in my mind: 'Up and at 'em. Slackers never get anywhere!'

It's best not to think too much if you're scared, I always find. It's got me through some nail-biting moments, though most of those were self-imposed: white water rafting through rapids,   30 kayaking down swollen rivers, climbing telegraph poles… But this time I was in the middle of nowhere, in the midst of a jungle that I knew to be full of all sorts of things that forest rangers tell you not to go near and I had no idea what to do next!   35

Except, actually, if I sorted through the junk in my mind, I probably did have some idea of what to do. Yes! Find water and follow it. My basic survival training – now a long time ago – slowly drifted back into my consciousness. Think! Think! I grumbled at myself. I'd been on so many guided walks of 40 jungles and National Parks. Surely I knew something useful! I unbuckled and fell to the ground, glad of the soft mulch below but still letting out a scream to rival the howler monkeys' calls around me.

Of course, moving in any direction proved to be less than 45 easy. My eyes were bloodshot (from the change in air pressure as the plane descended I was later told) and my head ached as if a hammer was clanging against an anvil lodged inside it. I was covered in cuts and scratches and I could see instantly that one deep wound looked dangerously open and was already 50 inhabited by maggots. (Later I was able to tip gasoline on it, an excruciating but effective trick I remembered from treating our dog when it had a tick.) I later found that I had various fractures and minor injuries – but miraculously nothing major. I ached, and any movement felt like the day after a workout 55 with a demon as my own personal trainer! I fought to block out the pain and the voice telling me to give up and take a rest. I had to get out of there. I had to!

It was easiest to float in the water, swimming when I had the energy, trying not to think about the crocodiles and turtles that 60 I had so joyously fed with bread only days before as we toured these very waters. I sang to myself, silly bits and pieces of pop songs I had on my iPod, and I pictured my mum and dad's faces, imagining the warm smell of shepherd's pie waiting for me at home. I conjured up rosy scenes of Christmas mornings 65 around the tree, of my – totally fictional – wedding day to come; anything to keep me going, anything to keep me focused on a happy ending. I found myself offering small bribes: you can rest for a few minutes if you get to that bit of sandy outcrop; if you see three heron you can stop and find some shade for an 70 hour. I would count steps, strokes, heliconia flowers – anything to mark the passing of time and distance. I took shelter on ledges parallel to the water, my back to the river bank, hopeful that nothing would clamber out and find me huddled in its favourite resting spot.   75

Question 1

Imagine that you are the author of Passage A. You have been asked to give a speech at the Graduation ceremony of a local High School.

Write your speech, in which you:

* explain what happened to you and how you coped with the challenges that you faced
* use your experience to inspire and motivate the audience to make the most of themselves.

Base your speech on what you have read in Passage A, but be careful to use your own words. Address each of the three bullets.

Begin your speech 'Imagine waking up strapped upside down in a plane seat, high up in the tree canopy after the most terrifying experience of your life... this was what happened to me ...'

You should write about 250 to 300 words allowing for the size of your handwriting.

Up to 15 marks will be available for the content of your answer and up to 5 marks for the quality of your writing.

[Total: 20]

Question 2

Reread the descriptions of:

(a) the plane journey and the crash in paragraph 1, beginning 'One minute I was asleep ...'

(b) waking up after the crash in the tree canopy in paragraph 2, beginning 'It must have been hours later ...'

Select **four** powerful words and phrases from each paragraph. Your choices should include imagery. Explain how each word or phrase selected is used effectively in the context.

Write about 200 to 300 words, allowing for the size of your handwriting.

Up to 10 marks are available for the content of your answer.

[Total: 10]

Passage B

'A very long shift': a day in the life of the trapped Chilean miners

The 33 men trapped nearly half a mile under Chile's Atacama Desert are suffering terrible privations – but they are also experienced miners who know that to survive, they must be organised. The Guardian's Jonathan Franklin reports.

Day in the San José mine begins at 7:30 a.m., when a makeshift lighting rig powered by truck batteries and a portable generator flickers into life, casting a weak light on the refuge where the men have now spent 44 days. In the hours after the shaft was sealed the miners used truck headlamps to light their way, but   5
in the following days electrician Edison Pena wired up a series of lamps which provide between eight and 12 hours of light to provide a semblance of day and night.

Breakfast begins to arrive at 8:30 a.m. via a delivery system known as the 'pigeons' – the 3-metre metal tubes that are   10
packed with food, medicine and letters and lowered 700 metres through a 8.8 cm communications shaft. The food takes over an hour to arrive, with deliveries every 20 to 30 minutes. At the bottom of the mine, three men are tasked with receiving the 'pigeons', unpacking bottled water, hot sandwiches and   15
morning medicines, then stuffing the latest letters and messages into the torpedo-shaped tube, which slowly rises out of sight.

After breakfast the men clean their living area. 'They know how to maintain their environment. They have a designated bathroom area and a garbage area, and are even recycling,' said   20
Dr André Llarena, an anaesthesiologist with the Chilean navy. 'They put plastic stuff away from biological [wastes], in different holes. They are taking care of their place.' Morning showers require the men to climb aboard a bulldozer-type mining vehicle that rumbles 300 metres up the tunnel to a natural waterfall   25
where they shower, shampoo and clean off the ubiquitous rust-coloured mud. Showers and breakfast are followed by morning chores, some under instruction from mining engineers above ground, others in obedience to common sense.

Nineteen-year-old Jimmy Sanchez, the youngest of the   30
group, is the 'environmental assistant', who roams the caverns with a handheld computerised device that measures oxygen, CO_2 levels and air temperature, which usually averages around 31°C. Every day Sanchez takes the reading from the gas detector

and sends his reports to the medical team outside the mine. 35
Another group of men reinforce the mine walls and divert
streams of water seeping into their refuge. Several of the drilling
and communications tubes connecting the men to the surface
use water as lubricant, meaning a constant stream of muddy
gunk trickles into their world. 40

> 'Dermatological infections, toothaches, constipation and
> withdrawal from tobacco addiction have caused problems.'

Throughout the morning, some of the men maintain regular
security patrols to scan the perimeter of their sleeping and living
quarters, alert for signs of another rockfall. Others spend hours 45
working with long-handled picks to lever loose large rocks that
threaten to fall from the ceiling. What the miners most fear is
that a small rockfall could suddenly trigger a full-scale collapse,
leaving them trapped in an even more confined space.

Food deliveries and meals take up much of the day. Lunch 50
delivery starts at noon and takes a full hour and a half to deliver
the hot meals.

Question 3

Answer the questions in the order set.

(a) Notes

What are the the hardships faced by the trapped miners in Passage B?

Write your answer using short notes.

You do not need to use your own words.

Up to 15 marks are available for the content of your answer. [15]

(b) Summary

Now use your notes to write a summary of what Passage B tells you
about the hardships faced by the trapped miners.

You must use continuous writing (not note form) and use your own
words as far as possible.

Your summary should include all 15 of your points in Question 3(a)
and must be 200 to 250 words.

Up to 5 marks are available for the quality of your writing. [5]

An Introduction to Practice Paper 3

The practice paper which follows on pages 315–317 is based on the model of the current Cambridge IGCSE examination.

Which skills should I be using?

Section 1 requires you to show both reading and writing skills.

- You will need to use the key skills of **skimming**, **scanning**, **selecting** and **synthesising** covered in Chapter 1 (pages 8–13, 34–35). In addition, you will need to use your ability to understand **explicit** and **implicit meanings**, which are also covered in Chapter 1 (pages 16–27).
- You will need to use the skills contained in Chapter 6, which takes you through the process of responding to a **Directed writing** task (pages 157–188).
- You will also need to be able to use the key writing skills covered in Chapter 3 and in particular those of writing to argue or explore an idea and writing in a letter or article form.

Section 2 requires you to show only writing skills.

- You will need to be able to use all the key writing skills as outlined in Chapter 3 and use the detailed advice given in Chapter 7 (pages 189–213) for the type of writing that you decide to do.

Tips for success

- It is vital that you manage your time effectively and do not spend too long on one part of the exam paper at the expense of the other.
- It is very important that you show detailed knowledge of the text in your answer in Section 1. This means that you must base your own ideas on **ideas and details from the text**, although using your own words to present these is usually best.
- **Planning is vital** for both tasks, but especially so for the Composition task.
- Remember to **select language** and **make structural choices consciously** to fit the task, considering your form, viewpoint and audience.

Practice Paper 3 Directed Writing and Composition

Directed Writing and Composition   **2 hours**

Answer **two** questions: **Question 1 (Section 1)** and **one** question from **Section 2**.

Dictionaries are **not** permitted.

All questions in this paper carry equal marks.

Section 1: Directed Writing

Question 1

Write a letter to your grandparents in which you should:

- evaluate the arguments for and against the purchase of a console
- explain the reasons behind your wish to have one.

Base your letter on the fact file and the article, but be careful to use your own words. Address each of the two bullets.

Begin your letter:
'Dear Nan and Grandad…'

You should write about 250 to 350 words, allowing for the size of your handwriting.

Up to 10 marks are available for the content of your answer, and up to 15 marks for the quality of your writing.

[Total: 25]

- Parents should take more responsibility. Use locks? Go shopping with kids?
- Violent games account for one in 2000 new games produced every year.
- Children know the difference between reality and fantasy. Think of the fairy tales they read!
- Too much violence on screen can make children less sensitive to it in real life.
- Games are rated as films, e.g. 18/12/PG etc.
- Adult content videos can be kept behind the counter.
- Laws regarding adult content apply to games?
- Do children copy what they see?

This article from *The Times*, was written as a reaction to a report, called The Byron Review, which proposed tighter controls on computer games and raised concerns about their effects.

Not all gaming is bad – it can be as engrossing as a novel or chess

Nigel Kendall

Times games reviewer

If there was a time when the market for video games in this country truly came of age, it was the run-up to last Christmas. Spurred on by the launch of three new home consoles in the space of 12 months, sales of video game titles hit £332.6 million in the final quarter of last year, up 19 per cent by volume and 36 per cent by revenue from the year before, according to figures released by the industry body ELSPA. Over the full year, 78 million video games were sold in Britain. So who is playing them all?

The Byron Review comes at a time when more families than ever are playing video games, thanks largely to the motion sensitive Nintendo Wii console, which allows players to mimic the movements of real sport. For the first time since Space Invaders arrived in arcades 30 years ago, gaming is becoming a social and sociable activity. The Wii excels at on-screen sports such as table tennis and golf, and the reason for its popularity with both parents and children is that it brings the fun back into playing. Playing it is enjoyable and watching someone else flailing around with a remote controller is hilarious.

Yet the Wii is technically a primitive machine compared with its competitors: the Microsoft Xbox 360 and Sony PlayStation 3 (PS3). These two consoles, dubbed 'next-generation' because they can display high definition images on modern flat-screen televisions, retain an undeniably masculine bias. These are the gorillas of gaming and many of the games are designed to get players beating their chests in an artificial world, to the exclusion of the real one.

Many of the early releases for these consoles were squarely aimed at young males, with a heavy emphasis on shooting, driving and sports. Both consoles are also capable of connecting to the internet, opening up the possibility of playing against hundreds of opponents online. It is this aspect of gaming, and the perceived target market, that has caused the most concern. If, as expected, the Byron Review comes out in favour of statutory certification, one option open to the makers of the consoles is to make the parental lock feature (currently installed as an option) the default setting. Adults would then need to key in a secret code to play the game of their choice.

But to label all gaming as 'bad' is to do the industry a disservice. As with novels, films and internet websites, there are good and bad games, and the process of becoming engrossed in a well-told story is similar, whether it unfolds digitally or on the pages of a book. Many games, notably the 77-million-selling Japanese *Final Fantasy* series, tap into the market for modern myth, marrying storylines and are as satisfying to play – and as demanding – as chess.

Faced with the success of the Wii, Sony and Microsoft have recently changed marketing tack to get themselves out of the spare room and into the living room, repositioning themselves as home entertainment hubs.

Both machines can play DVDs. The Sony PS3 also plays high-definition Blu-ray discs and comes with a built-in hard disc that can be used to store photos, videos, music or content downloaded from the internet via the built-in wi-fi capability.

Section 2: Composition

Questions 2 and 3

Write about 350 to 450 words, allowing for the size of your handwriting, on one of the following questions.

Up to 13 marks are available for the content and structure of your answer, and up to 12 marks for the style and accuracy of your writing.

Descriptive writing

2 (a) 'The Forgotten Corner'. Write a detailed description of this place, paying particular attention to the sights and sounds that can be experienced there.   [25]

OR

2 (b) 'The Threat'. Use this title to create a description of a person who creates a menacing atmosphere around them.   [25]

Narrative writing

3 (a) Write the dramatic moments of a story that involves the escape of an animal.   [25]

OR

3 (b) 'Abandoned'. Write the opening chapter of an account of being lost when you or a character that you can invent accidently get left behind.   [25]

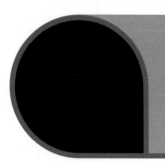

Glossary of key terms

Adjective: a word that describes a noun: *ugly, brown rat*

Adverb: a word that describes a verb or occasionally an adjective: *ran speedily; fairly good*

Anecdote: a brief account of an incident in your or someone else's life that makes your argument more believable

Climax: the most interesting or exciting point in a story

Cohesion: how a paragraph is knitted together and linked to other paragraphs around it. Topic sentences, connectives and linking phrases all help to make a text cohesive

Complex sentence: a sentence with a **main clause** and a subordinate clause (or clauses): *When the sun is shining, **I love to go to the beach**.*

Compound sentence: a sentence made of two simple sentences joined by *or, and* or *but*: *I like cats **but** you prefer dogs.*

Connective: a word or phrase used to link sentences or paragraphs together: *however, furthermore, on the other hand*

Connotations: the associations of a word or thing: for example, a flag can immediately make someone think 'my country'

Dialogue: a written conversation between two or more people

Explicit meaning: meaning that is literal or obvious

Fact: something known to be true: for example, the date a building was built

Idiom: typical phrases common to a language: for example, *dead funny* meaning 'really funny'; *a right laugh* meaning 'a lot of fun'

Imagery: words or comparisons that create a mental picture

Implicit meaning: meaning that is suggested or implied

Infer: to read between the lines to work out a viewpoint or implicit meaning from clues in the language used or information given

Metaphor: a powerful image in which two different things or ideas are compared without using 'like' or 'as': for example, *my fingers were tiny splinters of ice*

Minor sentence: a short sentence of one or two words that does not contain a verb

Monologue: a speech by one character without interruption

Noun: a word for a person, thing or idea: *table, animal, happiness, John*

Noun phrase: the combination of a noun and an adjective (or adjectives): for example, *coming-of-age movie*

Opinion: something the writer believes or feels: for example, whether he or she likes doing something

Pathetic fallacy: when a writer reflects human emotions in natural features or objects: for example, *the balloons swayed happily* or *the leaden clouds hung heavy above the figure on the moorland path*

Pattern of three: where three ideas are introduced together to enforce a point: for example, *we meet in fields and factories, in village markets and supermarkets, in living rooms and board rooms*

Preposition: a word or phrase that shows the relationship between objects: *the pot **beside** the sink; the car **in front of** the house*

Rhetorical question: a question that is used for effect to make the audience or reader think

Simile: a vivid comparison of two things or ideas using 'like' or 'as': for example, *the hoarse voice sounded out like a broken brick on sandpaper*

Simple sentence: a sentence with one subject and one verb: *We went fishing.*

Standard English: the most widely-used form of 'correct' English that is not specific to a particular location or region: for example, in standard English you would say *we **were** going* not *we **was** going* and you would use the word *argument* rather than *tiff* or *barney*

Style: the vocabulary, sentence structures and literary techniques used

Subordinate clause: a clause that does not make sense on its own but is dependent on the main clause: *When the sun is shining*, I love to go to the beach.

Synonym: a word or phrase that is very similar in meaning to another: for example, *angry* and *cross*

Synthesis: the process of bringing information together from a range of sources and making sure that it is clearly organised for its purpose

Tone: the way you vary your voice and/or language to suit your audience or convey meaning: for example, to express a certain emotion or create a particular mood

Verb: words that describe actions, states of mind or states of being: *he **is**; I **was going**; we run*

Viewpoint: the particular attitude, perspective or opinions of the narrator, character or writer

Voice: the specific persona or style of speech or writing used by a narrator or character

William Collins's dream of knowledge for all began with the publication of his first book in 1819. A self-educated mill worker, he not only enriched millions of lives, but also founded a flourishing publishing house. Today, staying true to this spirit, Collins books are packed with inspiration, innovation and practical expertise. They place you at the centre of a world of possibility and give you exactly what you need to explore it.

Collins. Freedom to teach.

Published by Collins Education
An imprint of HarperCollins*Publishers*
77–85 Fulham Palace Road
Hammersmith
London
W6 8JB

Browse the complete Collins Education catalogue at www.collinseducation.com

© HarperCollins Publishers Limited 2013
10 9 8 7 6 5 4 3 2 1

ISBN 978 0 00 751705 3

Keith Brindle, Julia Burchell, Geraldine Dunn, Steve Eddy and Mike Gould assert their moral rights to be identified as the authors of this work.

British Library Cataloguing in Publication Data.
A Catalogue record for this publication is available from the British Library.

About the authors
Keith Brindle is a senior examiner who was a Head of English for many years. He has written over fifty books on English and spends much of his time supporting skills development in secondary schools. Geraldine Dunn was a secondary school English teacher for over twenty years and she has extensive experience as a senior examiner and trainer. Steve Eddy is an experienced English teacher and examiner. He also lectures in English at the University of Wales, Newport and is the author of numerous educational textbooks and study guides. Mike Gould is a former Head of English and a university lecturer in English and education, who has written over 150 books for students and teachers in the UK and overseas.

Commissioned by Catherine Martin
Edited and project-managed by Lucy Hobbs
Design by JPD
Page design by G. Brasnett, Cambridge
Cover design by Paul Manning
Picture research by Caroline Green and Grace Glendinning

With thanks to our reviewers: Mrs Rachel Hitchcock, South Africa; Mrs Naghma Shaikh, VIBGYOR High, Mumbai, India; Mr Chris Green, The Perse School, Cambridge, UK; Ms Catherine Franklin, The British School of Rio, Rio de Janeiro, Brazil; Ms Chris Riley, The British International School of Cracow, Kraków, Poland; Ms Claire Houliston and Dr Heather Mayer, ACG Senior College, Auckland, New Zealand; Christine Cayley.

Acknowledgements
The publishers gratefully acknowledge the permission granted to reproduce the copyright material in this book. While every effort has been made to trace and contact copyright holders, where this has not been possible the publishers will be pleased to make the necessary arrangements at the first opportunity.

The publishers would like to thank the following for permission to reproduce pictures in these pages:

p7 George Doyle/Getty Images, p8 HBO/Everett/Rex Features, p9 JI de Wet/Shutterstock, p11t Sergieiev/Shutterstock, pp11b, 12 & 13 CHI-Photo/Nick Cunard/Rex Features, p14 Christopher Elwell/Shutterstock, p15 BortN66/Shutterstock, p17 Lynne Carpenter/Shutterstock, p19 Pier Photography/Alamy, p21t Robert Crum/Shutterstock, p21b MikLav/Shutterstock, p22 The Granger Collection/TopFoto, p25t Radius Images/Alamy, pp25 main & 26 loriklaszlo/Shutterstock, p25 inset & 27 Bruce Rolff/Shutterstock, p28 Stuart Monk/Shutterstock, p29 Andrjuss/Shutterstock, p30 George Blonsky/Alamy, p33 Nataliia Antonova/Shutterstock, p34 Larina Natalia/Shutterstock, p35 EmiliaU/Shutterstock, p37 Pixsooz/Shutterstock, p39l Elena Elisseeva/Shutterstock, p39r Piotr Marcinski/Shutterstock, p39b Evgeny Murtola/Shutterstock, p40 Dan Breckwoldt/Shutterstock, p41 Suzanne Porter/Alamy, p43 enciktat/Shutterstock, p44t Adam Fraise/Shutterstock, p44b Anton Gvozdikov/Shutterstock, p47 monticello/Shutterstock, p48t Netfalls/Shutterstock, p48b James Thew/Shutterstock, p50 Chema Moya/epa/Corbis, p52t kbrowne41/Shutterstock, p52b Paul Vinten/Shutterstock, p53 20thC.Fox/Everett/Rex Features, p54 Mogens Trolle/Shutterstock, p54 Mogens Trolle/Shutterstock, p56l ansar80/Shutterstock, p56r Gamut Stock Images PVT Ltd/Alamy, p57l Yuri Arcurs/Shutterstock, p57r photobank.ch/Shutterstock, p58 Jeff Greenberg/Alamy, p59 Raisman/Shutterstock, p61 Diego Cervo/Shutterstock, p62 Chris Schmidt/iStockphoto, p63 Dana Nalbandian/Shutterstock, p65 Image Source/Alamy, p66 karamysh/Shutterstock, p67 ndrpggr/Shutterstock, p68 Eric Isselée/iStockphoto, p69 Cindy Haggerty/Shutterstock, p70 Monkey Business Images/Shutterstock, p71 Chris Fourie/Shutterstock, p73 courtesy of Oxfam, p74 Jozsef Szasz-Fabian/Shutterstock, p75 2009fotofriends/Shutterstock, p77 Dudarev Mikhail/Shutterstock, p79 mangostock/Shutterstock, p81 Deklofenak/Shutterstock, p83 Supri Suharjoto/Shutterstock, p84 Adrian Sherratt/Alamy, p85 yvoko/Shutterstock, p86 Robert Johns / Alamy, p87 FoodIngredients/Alamy, p88 Graham Monro/gm photographics/Getty Images, p91 PicturesofLondon/Alamy, p92 outdoorsman/Shutterstock, p94 Jeremy Smith/Shutterstock, p98 Louie Schoeman/Shutterstock, p99 Dr. Morley Read/Shutterstock, p100 Images & Stories/Alamy, p101 Lykovata/Shutterstock, p102 Oliver Sved/Shutterstock, p105 wavebreakmedia/Shutterstock, p107 B. O'Kane/Alamy, p109 wavebreakmedia/Shutterstock, p110 Caroline Green, p114 Mark Eveleigh/Alamy, p117 Nina B/Shutterstock, p119 Marc van Vuren/Shutterstock, pp120–121 Khaled Kassem/Alamy, pp122–123 Katarzyna Mazurowska/Shutterstock, p124 Jan Martin Will/Shutterstock, p125 Vladimir Chernyanskiy/Shutterstock, p131 gpointstudio/Shutterstock, p132 Stock Connection/SuperStock, p134 Alan Fishleder, p136 Nikonaft/Shutterstock, p139 Andrew Buckin/Shutterstock, p140 Aubrey Laughlin/Shutterstock, p142 Vicki France/Shutterstock, p143 stephanie connell/Shutterstock, p144 2009 fotofriends/Shutterstock, p147 Fireflash/Alamy, p152 fstockfoto/Shutterstock, p157 Robert Kneschke/Shutterstock, pp159 & 173 SNEHIT/Shutterstock, p160 courtesy of the crew of An-Tiki - Atlantic Raft Crossing 2010–2011, p163 Aflo/Rex Features, p165 tipograffias/Shutterstock, p166 Purestock/Alamy, p167 Monkey Business Images/Shutterstock, p168 Luminis/Shutterstock, p171 Alexander Raths/Shutterstock, pp159 & 173 Olivier Le Queinec/Shutterstock, p174 Rex Features, p179 Jim Barber/Shutterstock, pp180–181 Robert Elias/Shutterstock, p184 wavebreakmedia/Shutterstock, p189 Blend Images / SuperStock, p191 l i g h t p o e t/Shutterstock, p192 Ace Stock Limited/Alamy, p195 Limpopo/Shutterstock, p196 S.Dashkevych/Shutterstock, p199 Sergey Peterman/Shutterstock, p202 Ned White/iStockphoto, p205 DEKANARYAS/Shutterstock, p209 Mark Herreid/Shutterstock, pp215 & 229 Christo/Shutterstock, p216 Sipa Press/Rex Features, p219 Maria Dryfhout/Shutterstock, p220 Audrey Snider-Bell/Shutterstock, p223 CaterineXia Ontario Canada Collection/Alamy, p224 Karen Givens/Shutterstock, p225 AF archive/Alamy, pp215 & 229 Christo/Shutterstock, pp230–231 Caroline Green, p232 Khoroshunova Olga/Shutterstock, p233 David Rose/Rex Features, p234 Hung Chung Chih/Shutterstock, p237 Courtesy of the WWF, p239 IvicaNS/Shutterstock, p240 Klaas Lingbeek- van Kranen/iStockphoto, p243 Natursports/Shutterstock, p254 Eric Isselée/Shutterstock, pp257 & 273 Chris Schmidt/iStockphoto, p258 Tiplyashin Anatoly/Shutterstock, p259 Chris Schmidt/iStockphoto, p260 JHershPhoto/Shutterstock, p261 Johannes Burges/iStockphoto, pp262–263 Racheal Grazias/Shutterstock, p264 AF archive/Alamy, p265 YanLev/Shutterstock, p266 Tyler Olson/Shutterstock, p267 clu/iStockphoto, p268 Geraint Lewis/Rex Features, pp257 & 273 Chris Schmidt/iStockphoto, p274 Tiplyashin Anatoly/Shutterstock, p276 Regien Paassen/Shutterstock, pp276–277 Pete Niesen/Shutterstock, p278 Robert Kneschke/Shutterstock, p280 Josef Mohyla/Shutterstock, p285 sportgraphic/Shutterstock, p287 Graeme Shannon/Shutterstock, p289 Jim West/Alamy, p290 Photri Images/Alamy, p293 Arthur R./Shutterstock, p294 Ian Shaw/Alamy, p298 Indiapicture/Alamy.

The publishers would like to thank the following for permission to reproduce text in these pages:

p8: from The No. 1 Ladies Detective Agency, by Alexander McCall Smith, published by Little Brown. Reprinted with permission of David Higham Associates Ltd; p14: Short extract from P-Leisure Magazine Autumn/Winter 10. Reprinted with; p17: from THE SALT ROAD by Jane Johnson (Viking 2010, Penguin Books 2011). Copyright © Jane Johnson 2010. Reprinted with permission of Penguin Books UK, Baror International, and Random House, Canada; pp25–26 & 142: from SET IN STONE by Linda Newbery copyright © 2006 by Linda Newbery. Used by permission of David Flickling Books, an imprint of Random House Children's Books, a division of Random House Inc, Any third party use of this material, outside of this publication, is prohibited. Interested parties must apply directly to Random House Inc, for permission. and with permission of The Random House Group Limited UK; p31: Extract from a campaign leaflet belonging to www.animalaid.org.uk. Reprinted with kind permission; p54: from 'Birth of an Asian elephant is trumpeted by zoo' The Times, 29th July, 2009. Reprinted with permission of NI Syndication; p71: from www.wildernessdiary.com. Reprinted with kind permission; p75: from 'Mountain Goat Kills Hikers' by Alex Robinson, Outdoor Life; p76: from 'Why do men love dangerous dogs?' by Robert Crampton, The Times, July 5th 2008. Reprinted with permission of NI Syndication ; pp112–113: from A GAME OF POLO WITH A HEADLESS GOAT by Emma Levin, Andre Deutsch. Reprinted with permission of MBA Literary Agency; pp114–115: from 'The Darien Gap: Travels in the Rainforest of Panama' by Martin Mitchinson, Harbour Publishing, 2008. Reprinted with permission of Harbour Publishing; pp118–119: from 'Something approaching enlightenment' by Rolf Potts, from BEST OF LONELY PLANET TRAVEL WRITING, 1st edition, © 2009 Lonely Planet. Reprinted with permission; p120: from 'Egg Child' by Sarah Levine, from BEST OF LONELY PLANET TRAVEL WRITING, 1st edition, © 2009 Lonely Planet. Reprinted with permission; pp122–123: from IN PATAGONIA by Bruce Chatwin. Copyright © 1977 by Bruce Chatwin. All rights reserved. Reprinted with permission of Simon & Schuster Inc and The Random House Group Limited; p126: from A WALK IN THE WOODS by Bill Bryson, copyright © 1997 by Bill Bryson. Used by permission of Broadway Books, a division of Random House Inc. Any third party use of this material, outside of this publication is prohibited. Interested parties must apply directly to Random House, Inc for permission; pp138, 139 & 141 from 'Q & A by Vikas Swarup. Copyright © 2005 by Vikas Swarup. Reprinted with the permission of Scribner, a Division of Simon & Schuster Inc and Random House Group UK. All rights reserved (one word cut for textbook purposes with the kind permission of the author and his agent); p144: From HEART SONGS AND OTHER STORIES by Annie Proulx. Copyright © 1988, 1995 by E. Annie Proulx. Reprinted with the permission of Scribner, a Division of Simon & Schuster, Inc. All rights reserved; p146: from GREETINGS FROM BURY PARK by Sarfraz Manzoor, copyright © 2007 by Sarfraz Manzoor. Used by permission of Bloomsbury UK and Vintage Books, a division of Random House Inc. Any Third party use of this material, outside of this publication, is prohibited. Interested parties must apply directly to Random House Inc, for permission; pp152–153: from Honeymoon by Charlotte Wood, from Best Australian Short Stories, Black Inc Books, 2005. Reprinted with permission of Jenny Darling & Associates; p160: From 'Fantastic Voyage' by James Delingpole, Saga Magazine, pp47–49, November 2010. Reprinted with kind permission of SAGA Magazine; pp162–163: from The Old Patagonian Express by Paul Theroux, Penguin Books. Reprinted with permission of The Wylie Agency; p217: from LOSING MY VIRGINITY by Richard Branson. Copyright © 1998, 2002, 2005, 2007 by Richard Branson. Used by permission of Crown Business, a division of Random House Inc. Any third party use of this material, outside of this publication is prohibited. Interested parties to apply directly to Random House Inc, and The Random House Group Limited; p220: from 'The Snake' by D. H. Lawrence, 1921; pp222–223: from 'Confessions of a high rise window cleaner' by Carolyn Morris, Metro Toronto, 7th February, 2011. Reprinted with kind permission of the author; pp232–233: Is the giant panda really worth saving? Yes, says Chris Packham' by Leo Benedictus, The Guardian, 23 September, 2009. © Guardian News and Media 2009. Used with permission; pp302–304: From 'Brady's Bad Bite: in his own words' by Brady Barr, from http://channel.nationalgeographic.com/series/dangerous-encounters#tab-python-encounter Reprinted with permission of National Geographic; pp312–313: From 'Chilean miners: A typical day in the life of a subterranean miner' by Jonathan Franklin, The Guardian, 10 September, 2010. ©Guardian News and Media Ltd 2010. Reprinted with permission; p316: from 'Not all gaming is bad - it can be as engrossing as a novel or chess' by Nigel Kendall, Times game reviewer, The Times, 27 March, 2008. Reprinted with permission of NI Syndication.